Tennis

and the

Meaning

of Life

EDITED BY

Jay Jennings

With a Foreword by
George Vecsey

Tennis

A LITERARY

and the

ANTHOLOGY

Meaning

OF THE GAME

of Life

A Harvest Book

Harcourt Brace & Company

San Diego *New York* *London*

Requests for permission to make copies of
any part of the work should be mailed to:
Permissions Department, Harcourt Brace & Company,
6277 Sea Harbor Drive, Orlando, Florida 32887-6777.

Permissions acknowledgments appear on pages 391–94,
which constitute a continuation of the copyright page.

Library of Congress Cataloging-in-Publication Data
Tennis and the meaning of life:
a literary anthology of the game/
[edited by Jay Jennings].—1st Harvest ed.
        p.   cm.—(A Harvest book)
          ISBN 0-15-600407-0
      1. Tennis—Literary collections.
        2. American literature.
          3. English literature.
            I. Jennings, Jay.
        PS509.T39T46   1996
      810.8'0355—dc20   96-2013

Text set in Bulmer
Designed by Michael Farmer
Printed in the United States of America
First Harvest edition ·
A B C D E

Acknowledgements

Thanks to my colleague Peter Bodo for pointing me toward the excerpt from *Lolita*. Thanks to Garth Battista for the opportunity to make this long-simmering idea a reality. Thanks to my father, former Country Club of Little Rock men's champion, for teaching me tennis, and to my mother for enduring our matches in father-son tournaments. Finally, thanks beyond words to my wife, Jessica, who is everything.

—JAY JENNINGS

A note on spelling and punctuation

I have retained the British spellings in the stories and poems by British writers in order to maintain the integrity and flavor—or flavour—of the works. In quotations, however, I have chosen to use the American convention of double quotation marks instead of the British single marks on the justification that mixing the two in one book would be too jarring to the eyes. The spelling variations "racquet" and "racket" each appear on both sides of the Atlantic, and have been kept as originally found in each piece.   —J. J.

Contents

Contents

Poems

Contents

Contents

Foreword

GEORGE VECSEY

There is a place I go at Wimbledon whenever I get the chance. For some bizarre anachronistic reason, the nabobs of the All England Lawn Tennis and Croquet Club have reserved a front row at Court No. 1, right next to Centre Court, for reporters and photographers. If you get there early and beat out the crowd of your own colleagues, you can munch on your cheddar-and-pickle sandwich and sip fruit juice from a cardboard container and watch the greatest tennis players in the world from about two feet away.

With a five-hour time difference in my favor, I have spent entire afternoons hunkered down in this delightful corner of the world, watching McEnroe and Connors, Evert and Navratilova, and lesser warriors of the tour, play early-round matches, working on their strokes, trying to get into the rhythm of the tournament.

It is fantastic to sit this close and watch athletic immortals deal with the absurdities of a bad bounce on crushed grass, or an opponent playing way above form, or a backhand that isn't working that day. As a journalist, theoretically committed to the facts and the quotes of the day, I am often left wondering what was the real story behind something I just witnessed.

It's fine if McEnroe tells you the world would be a perfect place if only he could line up all the myopic line officials and the clicking photographers against a brick wall and have them executed by firing squad. And I'm sure he would. Or Navratilova might tell you that a patron's Batman T-shirt made her daydream about all the great movies she's seen in her life. And I'm sure this most intelligent and curious of athletes did just that. This makes for charming journalistic copy—but what was really, secretly going on in players' minds in that grassy rectangle in the southwest corner of London?

Sometimes we'll have glimpses or suspicions: the player who frittered away a match on a side court with her new lover sitting prominently in the front row; we all know love can make you swing wildly from your heels. Or the player with deep creases in his face, old before his time, trying to hang on for another round because he needs the money, after a decade of excess. It's all up close in tennis, unhampered by helmets or dugouts or bulky uniforms. You can see the faces, you can make educated guesses about the people.

Tennis fans understand their sport has it all—love, power, sex, money, violence, aggression, manipulation—the whole spectrum of human behavior, even the occasional sporting gesture or humane touch. Tennis sublimates it a bit, puts people on opposite sides of the net, and lets you watch them, even if you have to invent the internal dialogues.

This, of course, is where the imagination of the novelist or the poet takes over for the diligence of the journalist. As a journalist and as a reader, I say thank goodness for that. This anthology goes where journalists like myself are not licensed to travel: within the hearts of people who wield a tennis racket for money or for love, for hatred and revenge, for exercise and challenge. This anthology confirms my belief that tennis is the perfect sporting metaphor for life. Wherever the game is played—at Wimbledon, in the playground, on a private court—it matches the complexities of life in the boardroom or the bedroom or around the kitchen table.

Talk about the inner game of tennis. James Jones presents a solitary boy skulking around his yard, feverishly imagining—and acting out—a bitter international match. Ellen Gilchrist writes about a snobbish socialite who must face a humiliating loss on the court to a striving outsider. Irwin Shaw describes a wife who comes to realize that her husband's squandering his advantage on the tennis court is merely an extension of his failures in business and marriage. In several stories, fathers play their sons, with all the Freudian weirdness you can imagine. And Humbert Humbert rhapsodizes ecstatically about Lolita's tennis game.

There is very little in this collection to bring us up to date with the hard-bitten world of sponsors and agents and bodyguards and trainers and the grim isolated professionals who go out into the screaming arena. Most of the stories and poems smack of another time and place, the country-club era when tennis was for a certain, privileged type, as depicted in John Betjeman's "A Subaltern's Love-song," an ode from a vanquished male to the victorious female:

Miss J. Hunter Dunn, Miss J. Hunter Dunn,
Furnish'd and burish'd by Aldershot sun,
What strenuous singles we played after tea,
We in the tournament—you against me!

The focus on the old days, or on amateurs far from the crowds, makes the most sense to me because most tennis fans and players bring a romantic, personal, classical notion to the game. We watch tennis at ticky-tacky metallic Flushing Meadows, but we still sense the ivy and the grass and the manners of the old West Side Tennis Club, where the American championship used to be held. We know that of all the sports in the world, tennis works best at every level of confrontation—center-court competition as well as country-club gamesmanship and family vacation ritual. Not to mention the occasional subtle courtship across the net, as in Betjeman's poem: "But my shock-headed victor, she loves me no less."

Nobody ever said *that* about an opponent in the interview room at Wimbledon. Just as well, I guess; although the Rottweilers of Fleet Street would surely love it. More to the point, people who play tennis, and people who watch tennis, know that behind the professionalism there is also something soft and sweet, hopeful and transcendent about the sport. We can always use the reminders, from our novelists and our poets, of why this game has such a hold on us.

Introduction

These are the words of tennis: love, fault, serve, return.

With that kind of language built into it, is it any wonder writers fall in love with this sport?

Tennis may not have the extensive contemporary bibliography of baseball as a subject of fiction and poetry, but its literary history is much longer and, dare I say, more prestigious. We have little knowledge of Shakespeare's forehand (though some graduate student is doubtless researching it at this moment), but he did on several occasions use references to the game in key points of his plays. In *Henry V,* when the dauphin mocks the young king's claims to French territory by sending him a gift of tennis balls, Henry replies, "When we have matched our rackets to these balls, / We will in France, by God's grace, play a set / Shall strike his father's crown into the hazard." Or as John McEnroe might have put it to the dauphin, "You cannot be serious! You are the pits of the world!" McEnroe, however, never won in France, while Henry walked the walk with a resounding victory at Agincourt.

In his play *The Duchess of Malfi,* John Webster, Shakespeare's contemporary (and doubles partner?), invoked tennis as a metaphor for no less than the meaning of life. One of his characters, after a spate of Jacobean carnage, declares, "We are merely the stars' tennis-balls, struck and bandied / Which way may please them." That assumes, of course, that unlike many of us who play the game, the "stars" have steady ground strokes.

Some of the best writers of our own age have fleshed out the metaphor, using tennis not just in passing, but as a foundation for their stories and poems. The game seems beautifully suited for this kind of task: no other sport brings with it such a rich cargo of meaning. It is as elemental as boxing, in which an individual faces a single opponent, but tennis rewards delicacy as well as brutality. It is as geometrically elegant as baseball, but that sport's raptures are almost solely those of the spectator. Football lacks subtlety, basketball lacks cerebration, and golf has too much of both. Tennis is the only sport in which men and women can compete together on the same court. How's that for cargo?

Something in tennis moved the writers whose works appear here, and something in these stories and poems moved me—to laughter, to sadness, to get up off my butt and go hit some balls. That's what happened when I came upon Robert Pinsky's poem, "Tennis," which mixes traditional tennis instruction lingo with an exploration of the mysterious workings of our minds. You could learn to play tennis from worse sources than his poem. Some advice from the section called "Backhand":

Here panic may be a problem; in the clench
From back to jaw in manic you may come
Too close and struggling strike out with your arm,

Trying to make the arm do everything,
And failing as the legs and trunk resist.

Other works moved me in different ways. Anyone who has played tennis—or even competed in any sport—against a parent will feel the strong emotion of Roger Angell's "Tennis" and even the surreal dislocation of Jonathan Baumbach's "The Return of Service." After reading Jim Hall's "Tennis Elbow," I'll never think about that twinge in my arm the same way again. The collection's title, *Tennis and the Meaning of Life,* is admittedly exaggerated and ironic, but it is also to signal the reader that these writers found in tennis something more than just the game. But then good stories and poems are always about more than what they're about.

This is not to say that those simply looking for a good read will not be satisfied here. Take Ring Lardner's "Tennis by Cable," for example, which is about competition and the athletic ego and taking an idea to an illogical extreme, but it is mostly about laughing out loud. "The Blacktop Champion of Ickey Honey," by Robert T. Sorrells, speaks volumes about our capacity for greed and deception, but it is mostly just a damn good story in the tradition of Southern tall tales. Paul Theroux's "The Tennis Court" examines knee-jerk racism, but it does it in a nicely plotted package.

The stories and poems I chose here had to meet two criteria, best expressed by Humbert Humbert in the excerpt from *Lolita:* "Her tennis was the highest point to which I can imagine a young creature bringing the art of make-believe, although I daresay, for her it was the very geometry of basic reality." I tried to make sure that these works would satisfy both Humbert and Lolita; they had to combine imaginative art with good writing about tennis. In the course of my research, I found good stories and poems in which the tennis didn't seem true, and I found great tennis writing in bad stories and poems.

I avoided tennis novels, partly because there have been no great ones (nothing to compare to Bernard Malamud's *The Natural* for baseball, or Don DeLillo's *End Zone* for football) and partly because there were so many good stories and poems. Tennis novels worth reading—those by writers, and not by former players capitalizing on their names—are Lars Gustafsson's *The Tennis Players* and Michael Mewshaw's *Blackballed*.

The arrangement here is alphabetical, with the stories and poems each grouped in kind. The order is deliberate rather than simply convenient. I liked the way the English and American stories were mixed together and the way the section led off with Roger Angell and ended with the charming period piece by Bill Tilden and the melancholy evocation of England in the 1930s by William Trevor, for my money the best short story writer in the English language. Most of all, I liked ending the book with E. B. White's lovely poem, "The Tennis," in which he describes an end-of-summer tennis match and asks the question, "What is the power of this bland American scene / To claim, as it does, the heart? What is this sudden / Access of love for the rich overcast of fall?"

It is the question of how tennis relates to the meaning of life, and one I hope is answered here, with the words in this book.

Stories

Tennis

ROGER ANGELL

The thing you ought to know about my father is that he plays a lovely game of tennis. Or rather, he used to, up to last year, when all of a sudden he had to give the game up for good. But even last summer, when he was fifty-five years of age, his game was something to see. He wasn't playing any of your middle-aged tennis, even then. None of that cute stuff, with lots of cuts and drop shots and getting everything back, that most older men play when they're beginning to carry a little fat and don't like to run so much. That wasn't for him. He still played all or nothing—the big game with a hard serve and coming right in behind it to the net. Lots of running in that kind of game, but he could still do it. Of course, he'd begun to make more errors in the last few years and that would annoy the hell out of him. But still he wouldn't change—not him. At that, his game was something to see when he was on. Everybody talked about it. There was always quite a little crowd around his court on the weekends, and when he and the other men would come off the court after a set of doubles, the wives would see their husbands all red and puffing. And then they'd look at my old man and see him grinning and not even breathing hard after *he'd* been doing all the running back after the lobs and putting away those overheads, and they'd say to him, "Honestly, Hugh, I just don't see how you do it, not at your age. It's *amaz*ing! I'm going to take my Steve [or Bill or Tom] off cigarettes and put him on a diet. He's ten years younger and just look at him." Then my old man would light up a cigarette and smile and shake his head and say, "Well, you know how it is. I just play a lot." And then a minute later he'd look around at everybody lying on the lawn there in the sun and pick out me or one of the other younger fellows and say, "Feel like a set of singles?"

If you know north Jersey at all, chances are you know my father. He's Hugh Minot—the Montclair one, not the fellow out in New Brunswick. Just about the biggest realty man in the whole section, I guess. He and my mother have this place in Montclair, thirty-five acres, with a swimming pool and a big vegetable garden and this En-Tout-Cas court. A lovely home. My father got a little name for himself playing football at Rutgers, and that helped him when he went into business, I guess. He never played tennis in college, but after getting out he wanted something to sort of fill in for the football—something he could do well, or do better than the next man. You know how people are. So he took the game up. Of course, I was too little to remember his tennis game when he was still young, but friends of his have told me that it was really hot. He picked the game up like nothing at all, and a couple of pros told him if he'd only started earlier he might have gotten up there in the big time—maybe even with a national ranking, like No. 18 or so. Anyhow, he kept playing and I guess in the last twenty years there hasn't been a season where he missed more than a couple of weekends of tennis in the summertime. A few years back, he even joined one of these fancy clubs in New York with indoor courts, and he'd take a couple of days off from work and go in there just so that he could play in the wintertime. Once, I remember, he played doubles in there with Alice Marble and I think Sidney Wood. He told my mother about that game lots of times, but it didn't mean much to her. She used to play tennis years ago, just for fun, but she wasn't too good and gave it up. Now the garden is the big thing with her, and she hardly ever comes out to their court, even to watch.

I play a game of tennis just like my father's. Oh, not as good. Not nearly as good, because I haven't had the experience. But it's the same game, really. I've had people tell me that when they saw us playing together—that we both made the same shot the same way. Maybe my backhand was a little better (when it was on), and I used to think that my old man didn't get down low enough on a soft return to his forehand. But mostly we played the same game. Which isn't surprising, seeing that he taught me the game. He started way back when I was about nine or ten. He used to spend whole mornings with me, teaching me a single shot. I guess it was good for me and he did teach me a good, all-round game, but even now I can remember that those morning lessons would somehow discourage both of us. I couldn't seem to learn fast enough to suit him, and he'd get upset and shout across at me, "Straight arm! Straight arm!" and then *I'd* get jumpy and do the shot even worse. We'd both be glad when the lesson ended.

I don't mean to say that he was so *much* better than I was. We got so we played pretty close a lot of the time. I can still remember the day I first beat him at singles. It was in June of 1937. I'd been playing quite a lot at school and this was my first weekend home after school ended. We went out in the morning, no one else there, and, as usual, he walked right through me the first set—about 6-1 or so. I played much worse than my regular game then, just like I always did against him for some reason. But the next set I aced him in the second game and that set me up and I went on and took him, 7-5. It was a wonderful set of tennis and I was right on top of the world when it ended. I remember running all the way back to the house to tell Mother about it. The old man came in and sort of smiled at her and said something like, "Well, I guess I'm old now, Amy."

But don't get the idea I started beating him then. That was the whole trouble. There I was, fifteen, sixteen years old and getting my size, and I began to think, Well, it's about time you took him. He wasn't a young man any more. But he went right on beating me. Somehow I never played well against him and I knew it, and I'd start pressing and getting sore and of course my game would go blooey.

I remember one weekend when I was in college, a whole bunch of us drove down to Montclair in May for a weekend— my two roommates and three girls we knew. It was going to be a lot of fun. But then we went out for some tennis and of course my father was there. We all played some mixed doubles, just fooling around, and then he asked me if I wanted some singles. In that casual way of his. And of course it was 6-2, 6-3, or some such thing. The second set we were really hitting out against each other and the kids watching got real quiet, just as if it was Forest Hills. And then when we came off, Alice, my date, said something to me. About him, I mean. "I think your father is a remarkable man," she said. "Simply remarkable. Don't you think so?" Maybe she wanted to make me feel better about losing, but it was a dumb question. What could I say except yes?

It was while I was in college that I began to play golf a little. I liked the game and I even bought clubs and took a couple of lessons. I broke ninety one day and wrote home to my father about it. He'd never played golf and he wrote back with some little gag about its being an old man's game. Just kidding, you know, and I guess I should have expected it, but I was embarrassed to talk about golf at home after that. I wasn't really very good at it, anyway.

I played some squash in college, too, and even made the B team, but I didn't try out for the tennis team. That disappointed my father, I think, because I wasn't any good at football, and I think he wanted to see me make some team. So he could come and see me play and tell his friends about it, I guess. Still, we did play squash a few times and I could beat him, though I saw that with time he probably would have caught up with me.

I don't want you to get the idea from this that I didn't have a good time playing tennis with him. I can remember the good days very well—lots of days where we'd played some doubles with friends or even a set of singles where my game was holding up or maybe even where I'd taken one set. Afterward we'd walk back together through the orchard, with my father knocking the green apples off the path with his racket the way he always did and the two of us hot and sweaty while we smoked cigarettes and talked about lots of things. Then we'd sit on the veranda and drink a can of beer before taking a dip in the pool. We'd be very close then, I felt.

And I keep remembering a funny thing that happened years ago—oh, away back when I was thirteen or fourteen. We'd gone away, the three of us, for a month in New Hampshire in the summer. We played a lot of tennis that month and my game was coming along pretty fast, but of course my father would beat me every single time we played. Then he and I both entered the little town championship there the last week in August. Of course, I was put out in the first round (I was only a kid), but my old man went on into the finals. There was quite a big crowd that came to watch that day, and they had a referee and everything. My father was playing a young fellow—about twenty or twenty-one, I guess he was. I remember that I sat by myself, right down beside the court, to watch, and while they were warming up I looked at this man playing my father and whispered to myself, but almost out loud, "Take him! Take him!" I don't know why, but I just wanted him to beat my father in those finals, and it sort of scared me when I found that out. I wanted him to give him a real shellacking. Then they began to play and it was a very close match for a few games. But this young fellow was good, really good. He played a very controlled game, waiting for errors and only hitting out for winners when it was a sure thing. And he went on and won the first set, and in the next my father began to hit into the net and it was pretty plain that it wasn't even going to be close in the second set. I kept watching and pretty soon I felt very funny sitting there. Then the man won a love game off my father and I began to shake. I jumped up and ran all the way up the road to our cabin and into my room and lay down on my bed and cried hard. I kept thinking how I'd wanted to have the man win, and I knew it was about the first time I'd ever seen my father lose a love game. I never felt so ashamed. Of course, that was years and years ago.

I don't think any of this would have bothered me except for one thing—I've always *liked* my father. Except for this game, we've always gotten along fine. He's never wanted a junior-partner son, either in his office or at home. No Judge Hardy stuff or "Let me light your cigar, sir." And no backslapping, either. There have been times where I didn't see much of him for a year or so, but when we got together (at a ball game, say, or during a long trip in a car), we've always found we could talk and argue and have a lot of laughs, too. When I came back on my last furlough before I went overseas during the war, I found that he'd chartered a sloop. The two of us went off for a week's cruise along the Maine coast, and it was swell. Early-morning swims and trying to cook over charcoal and the wonderful quiet that comes over those little coves after you've anchored for the night and the wind has dropped and perhaps you're getting ready to shake up some cocktails. One night there, when we were sitting on deck and smoking cigarettes in the dark, he told me something that he never even told my mother—that he'd tried to get into the Army and had been turned down. He just said it and we let it drop, but I've always been glad he told me. Somehow it made me feel better about going overseas.

Naturally, during the war I didn't play any tennis at all. And when I came back I got married and all, and I was older, so of course the game didn't mean as much to me. But still, the first weekend we played at my father's—the very first time I'd played him in four years—it was the same as ever. And I'd have sworn I had outgrown the damn thing. But Janet, my wife, had never seen me play the old man before and she spotted something. She came up to our room when I was changing afterward. "What's the matter with you?" she asked me. "Why does it mean so much to you? It's just a game, isn't it? I can see that it's a big thing for your father. That's why he plays so much and that's why he's so good at it. But why you?" She was half kidding, but I could see that it upset her. "This isn't a contest," she said. "We're not voting for Best Athlete in the County, are we?" I took her up on that and tried to explain the thing a little, but she wouldn't try to understand. "I just don't like a sorehead," she told me as she went out of the room.

I guess that brings me down to last summer and what happened. It was late in September, one of those wonderful weekends where it begins to get a little cool and the air is so bright. Father had played maybe six or seven sets of doubles Saturday, and then Sunday I came out with Janet, and he had his regular tennis gang there—Eddie Earnshaw and Mark O'Connor and that Mr. Lacy. I guess we men had played three sets of doubles, changing around, and we were sitting there catching our breath. I was waiting for Father to ask me for our singles.

But he'd told me earlier that he hadn't been able to get much sleep the night before, so I'd decided that he was too tired for singles. Of course, I didn't even mention that out loud in front of the others—it would have embarrassed him. Then I looked around and noticed that my father was sitting in one of those canvas chairs instead of standing up, the way he usually did between sets. He looked awfully pale, even under his tan, and while I was looking at him he suddenly leaned over and grabbed his stomach and was sick on the grass. We all knew it was pretty bad, and we laid him down and put his cap over his eyes, and I ran back to the house to tell Mother and phone up the doctor. Father didn't say a word when we carried him into the house in the chair, and then Dr. Stockton came and said it was a heart attack and that Father had played his last game of tennis.

You would have thought after that and after all those months in bed that my father would just give up his tennis court—have it plowed over or let it go to grass. But Janet and I went out there for the weekend just last month and I was surprised to find that the court was in good shape, and Father said that he had asked the gang to come over, just so I could have some good men's doubles. He'd even had a chair set up in the orchard, halfway out to the court, so he could walk out there by himself. He walked out slow, the way he has to, and then sat down in the chair and rested for a couple of minutes, and then made it the rest of the way.

I haven't been playing much tennis this year, but I was really on my game there that day at my father's. I don't think

I've ever played better on that court. I hardly made an error and I was relaxed and I felt good about my game. The others even spoke about how well I played.

But somehow it wasn't much fun. It just didn't seem like a real contest to me, and I didn't really care that I was holding my serve right along and winning my sets no matter who my partner was. Maybe for the first time in my life, I guess, I found out that it was only a game we were playing—only that and no more. And I began to realize what my old man and I had done to that game. All that time, all those years, I had only been trying to grow up and he had been trying to keep young, and we'd both done it on the tennis court. And now our struggle was over. I found that out that day, and when I did I suddenly wanted to tell my father about it. But then I looked over at him, sitting in a chair with a straw hat on his head, and I decided not to. I noticed that he didn't seem to be watching us at all. I had the feeling, instead, that he was *listening* to us play tennis and perhaps imagining a game to himself or remembering how he would play the point—the big, high-bouncing serve and the rush to the net for the volley, and then going back for the lob and looking up at it and the wonderful feeling as you uncoil on the smash and put the ball away.

Beggars Would Ride

BERYL BAINBRIDGE

On 22 December 1605, two men on horseback, cloaks billowing, hoofs striking sparks from the frozen ground, rode ferociously from the Guildhall to a hill near the village of Hampstead. Dismounting some yards from the summit and a little to the east, they kicked a shallow depression in the earth. Several villagers, knowing in advance the precise and evil properties of the talisman they carried, gawped from a safe distance. Dropping to their knees, the horsemen buried a small round object wrapped in a piece of cloth. Upon rising, the taller of the two men was heard to observe that he wished he was in front of a warm hearth; at which moment the earth erupted and belched fire. For an instant the men stood transfixed and then, cloaks peeled by dancing flame, they whirled upwards, two lumps of burning rag spinning in a blazing arc against the sky.

On the Friday before Christmas, Ben Lewis and Frobisher met as usual in the car park behind the post office. Ben Lewis arrived a quarter of an hour late and, grimacing through the windscreen of his estate car, proceeded to take off his shoes. It annoyed Frobisher, still left waiting in the cold. When the wind stirred the dead leaves on the concrete ground, there was a sound like rats scampering.

"Bloody parky," shouted Frobisher, but the man in the car was now out of sight, slumped between seat and clutch as he struggled to remove his trousers.

Frobisher, chilled to the bone, jogged to the boundaries of the car park and back again, passing two women seated inside a green Mini, one reading a newspaper, the other noticeably crying.

Ben Lewis emerged wearing shorts and a pair of white sneakers with blue toecaps.

"There's two women back there," Frobisher told him. "By the wire netting. One's blubbing into a handkerchief."

"Really," said Ben Lewis.

"The other's reading," said Frobisher. He looked down at Ben Lewis's sneakers and smiled insincerely.

"They're new," he said. Privately he thought them ridiculous; his own plimsolls, though stained and short on laces, were otherwise all that they should be.

Ben Lewis unlocked the boot of his car and took out a long canvas bag. "Let's go into the bushes," he shouted, and ducking through a gap in the fence shouldered his way into a dense undergrowth of alder and old privet.

The ground was liberally strewn with broken glass and beer cans. "Funny," remarked Ben Lewis, "how few whatsits one sees these days."

"Don't follow you," said Frobisher.

"Contraceptives," said Ben Lewis, whose mind was often on such things.

Labouring over the rusted frame of a child's pushchair, Frobisher stubbed his toe on a small, round object half buried beneath decaying leaves. "I wish," he panted, "we could get the hang of the game. Just for an hour or so."

Twice a week, during the lunch hour, they played tennis together. Frobisher worked just across the road in the National Westminster Bank, and Ben Lewis drove from Hampstead where he was a partner in a firm of estate agents.

"Whose turn is it to pay?" asked Frobisher, when, out of breath, they reached the entrance to the tennis courts.

He always asked that. He knew perfectly well that he had paid on Wednesday. He had a horror of being thought mean.

"Yours," said Ben Lewis, who had no such fears.

The attendant marked them down for Court 14, which was listing slowly and surrounded on three sides by trees. Though the court itself was full of pot-holes and the net invariably wound too high, it did have the advantage of privacy. Neither Frobisher nor Ben Lewis cared to be watched. When they had first started to play together, having chummed up in a pub in Belsize Park and mutually complained of being unfit, they had imagined it would be a matter of weeks before their game improved. Both had last played, slackly, at school. A year had passed and improvement had not come. Ben Lewis's service was quite good but he gained little advantage from it because it was too good for Frobisher to return. Frobisher had a nice forehand of a sort, the sort that lobbed the ball high into the air. Ben Lewis couldn't see the ball unless it came low over the net. They comforted themselves with the thought of the benefit they obviously derived from bending down and trotting about in the open air.

Of the two, Ben Lewis was the more outwardly narcissistic. He used aftershave and he hinted that he'd once had a sauna. He worried about his hair, which was now sparse, and the way his cheeks were falling in. He felt it was all right for Frobisher to sport a weathered crown—his particular height and porky-boy belly put him into a defined category—but he himself was on the short side and slender. He didn't want to degenerate into an elderly whippet with emaciated flanks, running like hell after the rabbit in the Waterloo Cup, and balding into the bargain.

"People are awfully callous these days, aren't they?" said Frobisher.

"What?" said Ben Lewis.

"The way they read while other people cry."

"I shouldn't care for it," said Ben Lewis. "Not outdoors. Not in this weather." He pushed open the rusted gate to Court 14 and began to unzip his bag.

"How's Margaret?" asked Frobisher.

"Fine, fine," said Ben Lewis. He didn't inquire after Frobisher's wife. Not any more. Frobisher's wife was called Beth, and Ben Lewis, who some years ago had directed *Little Women* for his local Amateur Dramatic Society, had once referred to her, jokingly of course, as "Keep Death Off the Road." Frobisher, not having seen the play, hadn't seen the joke. Far from it. He'd made some pretty silly remarks about it sounding disrespectful to his wife. Ben Lewis thought it was hypocritical of him, seeing that Frobisher had admitted to having a woman on the side. The previous summer, when excessive heat had forced Frobisher to remove his shirt, he had positively boasted about the two scratch marks Ben Lewis had noticed on his back. At the time, Ben Lewis had thought of rubbing his own back against a rose bush in his front garden, only he forgot.

Frobisher removed his overcoat and scarf and was discovered to be wearing a dark-blue tracksuit with white stripes on each shoulder.

"That's new," said Ben Lewis, smiling insincerely. He had the strangest notion, when he strolled into position on the court, that his new shoes had springs in the heel.

Without warning, Frobisher hit a very good ball down the line. Ben Lewis returned it, though he was dazzled as usual by the horizontal of the grimy net and the glittering rectangles of the tower block built lower down the hill. For perhaps half a remarkable minute they successfully kept the ball in play until Ben Lewis, misjudging his own strength, sent it flying into the wire netting with such force that it lodged there like some unlikely fruit. "You won't believe it," he told Frobisher. "But I thought the net was higher or you were lower."

"Optical illusion," said Frobisher kindly, scrambling up the grass bank to pluck the ball from the wire. "It's that jetstream." And he indicated with his racket two white and wobbling lines stretched across the sky. He felt unusually light on his feet and remarked confidently that it was all a question of rhythm. He could feel, he asserted, a definite sense of rhythm creeping into his stroke. They were both exhilarated at this sudden improvement in form. Secretly, Ben Lewis thought it had something to do with his shoes. Frobisher openly expressed the belief that his tracksuit had contributed to his new-found skill.

"A fellow in the office," said Ben Lewis, "started to get into trendy trousers last summer. His wife egged him on. He pulled off a fairly complicated land deal in South Woodford."

"Direct result, you mean?" said Frobisher.

"Nothing was ever proved," replied Ben Lewis, and he bounced on his toes and served with quite extraordinary speed and verve.

After a quarter of an hour an awed Ben Lewis said that in his opinion they were Wimbledon standard and possibly better than that bad-tempered fellow on the box who was always arguing with the man up the ladder. "And you're right about the rhythm," he said. He kept to himself the fanciful idea that they were dancing a slow fox-trot, championship standard, not a foot wrong, every move correctly timed, sweeping backwards and forwards across the court to the beat of an invisible orchestra.

Frobisher would have given anything for his wife Beth to have been watching him. She was always telling the children that he had no sense of co-ordination. It struck him as absurd that only last week he and Ben Lewis, trailing towards the bushes to return to the car park, had openly sneered at the dedicated players on Court 12. The tall man with the sweatband round his head, who was generally there on Wednesday and Friday, had caused them particular amusement—"that ass with the hair ribbon," as Ben had called him. Frobisher wondered if it would be going too far to have a band round his own forehead.

It came to Ben Lewis, fleetingly, sadly, as he arched his back in preparation for a particularly deadly service, how different things might have been if he had always played like this. Only once in his life had he experienced applause, at the curtain call of *Little Women* in East Finchley. In imagination he multiplied the volume of that first, last and giddy applause, and flinging his racket to the linesman leaped, gazelle-like, over the net.

After a further twenty inspired minutes, Frobisher suggested that perhaps they should rest. Though perspiring, neither of them was the least tired.

"I do feel," said Ben Lewis, with a touch of hysteria, "that we might be hospital cases tomorrow." Weak with laughter they flopped down on the sodden bench at the side of the court and lolled against each other.

"Doing anything for Christmas?" asked Frobisher at last. It was better to behave as if everything was normal.

"Usual thing," said Ben Lewis. "Margaret's mother, Margaret's mother's sister . . . that sort of thing. What about you?"

"Nothing special," said Frobisher. "Just me and Death." From beyond the trees came the fragmented screams of children running in the playground of the Catholic school.

"Do you think," said Frobisher, unable to contain himself, "that it's the same thing as riding a bike?"

"A knack, you mean," said Ben Lewis. "Once learnt, never lost?"

"Yes," said Frobisher.

"Maybe," said Ben Lewis. But he didn't think it was. They both fell silent, reliving the last three-quarters of an hour, until Frobisher remarked generously that Ben Lewis might have won the last set if the ground hadn't been so full of pot-holes. "Not your fault," he added. "It was jolly bad luck."

Ben Lewis found that he was gripping the edge of the bench so tightly that a splinter of wood pierced his finger. He knew that if he relaxed his hold he would spring upward and in one bound rip from the rusted fence a length of wire to tie round Frobisher's neck. He said as calmly as he was able, "I don't believe in luck, bad or otherwise."

From the playground came the blast of a whistle. The chattering voices receded as the children flocked indoors. Frobisher stood up, and, adjusting the top half of his tracksuit, strode purposefully back to his previous position on the court. "My service," he called curtly.

His first ball bounced low on the ground. Ben Lewis, gripping his racket in both hands as if running in an egg-and-spoon race, stumbled forward and scooped it skywards. It flew over his head, over the wire, and vanished into the trees.

"My God," said Frobisher. He stood with one hand on his hip and gazed irritably at Ben Lewis. "You'd better retrieve it," he ordered, as though Ben Lewis were a dog. He watched his opponent lumber through the gate and heard him squelch down the muddy path in the direction of the attendant's hut. Frobisher took a running jump at the net and hurdled it with ease.

Ben Lewis, passing Court 12, saw that the man with the sweat-band round his head had a new opponent. A woman. She was crouching down, racket held in both hands, head swinging from side to side like a bull about to charge.

Having skirted the attendant's hut and entered the bushes, Ben Lewis tried to visualise the flight path of the erratic ball. He was probably not far enough back. He tried to clamber up the bank to see if Court 14 was visible, but the bushes grew too thickly. He scuffed with his shoes at the broken glass and refuse, thinking his search was hopeless, and almost at once uncovered the missing ball. He bent down and picked it up. He was now sweating and the muscles in his legs were trembling. He found he held not only the ball but something round and small clinging to a scrap of rotting cloth. Shivering with revulsion, he flung both ball and rag away from him and wiped his hands on his shorts.

He wished he was in a nice hot bath . . .

Frobisher, fretting on Court 14, was startled by the noise of steam escaping from some large funnel. He supposed it came from the ventilation system of the tower block further down the hill. When he looked in the direction of the car park he observed a large white cloud drifting above the trees. He went in pursuit of his opponent. Struggling through the bushes calling Ben Lewis's name, he was astonished to see that the ground had been swept clear of rubbish. Ben Lewis's car was still parked near the fence. The woman at the steering-wheel of the green Mini said she hadn't seen anybody, she'd been too busy reading.

"Didn't you hear that noise?" asked Frobisher severely. "Like a train stopping. A puffer train."

The woman stared at him. "Perhaps he's just gone home," she suggested.

"He's not wearing trousers," said Frobisher. He retraced his steps to Court 14 and found it deserted.

Frobisher told his colleagues in the bank that his friend Ben Lewis had in some mysterious way disappeared. They weren't interested. Most of them thought Frobisher a bit of a slouch.

Before it grew dark, Frobisher slipped over the road to see if Ben Lewis's car was still near the gap in the fence. It was. Frobisher went into the bushes again and this time found the tennis ball and a smooth round object lying side by side on the ground.

He wished he knew where Ben Lewis had gone . . .

The Return of Service

JONATHAN BAUMBACH

I am in a tennis match against my father. He is also the umpire and comes to my side of the court to advise me of the rules. "You have only one serve," he says. "My advice is not to miss." I thank him—we have always been a polite family—and wait for his return to the opposing side. Waiting for him to take his place in the sun, I grow to resent the limitation imposed on my game. (Why should he have two serves, twice as many chances, more margin for error?) I bounce the ball, waiting for him— he takes his sweet time, always has—and plan to strike my first service deep to his forehand. And what if I miss, what if ambition overreaches skill? The ordinary decencies of a second chance have been denied me.

"Play is in," says the umpire.

The irreversibility of error gives me pause. It may be the height of folly to attempt the corner of his service box—my shoulder a bit stiff from the delay—and risk losing the point without a contest. The moral imperative in a challenge match is to keep the ball in play. If I aim the service for the optical center of his box, margin for error will move it right or left, shallow or deep, some small or remarkable distance from its failed intention. Easily enough done. Yet there is a crowd watching and an unimaginative, riskless service will lower their regard for me. My opponent's contempt, as the night the day, would follow.

I can feel the restiveness of the crowd. The umpire holds his pocket watch to his ear. "Play is in," he says again. "Play is in, but alas it is not in."

It is my father, the umpire, a man with a long-standing commitment to paradox.

Paradox will only take a man so far. How can my father be in the judge's chair and on the other side of the net at the same time? One of the men resembling my father is an imposter. Imposture is an old game with him. No matter the role he takes, he has the trick of showing the same face.

I rush my first serve and fault, a victim of disorientation, the ball landing two perhaps three inches deep. I plan to take a second serve as a form of protest—a near miss rates a second chance in my view—and ready myself for the toss.

The umpire blows his whistle. "Over and done," he says. "Next point."

This one seems much too laconic to be my father, a man who tends to carry his case beyond a listener's capacity to suffer his words. (Sometimes it is hard to recognize people outside the context in which you generally experience them.) I indicate confusion, a failed sense of direction, showing my irony to the few sophisticates in the audience, disguising it from the rest.

My latest intuition is that neither man is my father, but that both, either by circumstance or design, are standing for him, conventional surrogates.

I protest to the umpire the injustice of only being allowed a single service.

"I'm sorry life isn't fair," he says.

I can tell he isn't sorry, or if he is, it is no great burden of sorrow.

The toss is a measure low and somewhat behind me. Concentrated to a fine degree, I slice the ball into the backhand corner of my father's box. The old man, coming out of his characteristic crouch, slides gracefully to his left and though the ball is by him, he somehow manages to get it back. A short lob, which I put away, smashing the overhead at an acute angle, leaving no possibility of accidental return.

A gratifying shot. I replay it in the imagination. The ball in the air, a lovely arc. The player, myself, stepping back to let it bounce, then racket back, waiting for the ball to rise again, uncharacteristically patient, feeling it lift off the ground, swelling, rising, feeling myself rise with the ball. My racket, that extension of myself, meets the ball at its penultimate height as if they had arranged in advance to meet at that moment and place, the racket delivering the message, the ball the message itself. I am the agent of their coming together, the orchestrator of their perfect conjunction.

I didn't want to leave that point to play another, hated to go on to what, at its best, would be something less. I offered to play the point again. There was some conversation about my request, a huddle of heads at the umpire's chair. The crowd, in traditional confusion, applauded.

The decision was to go on. My father advised, and I appreciated his belated concern, against living in the past.

What a strange man! I wondered if he thought the same about me, and if he did—strange men hold strange opinions—was there basis in fact for his view of my strangeness?

We were positioned to play the third point of the first game. It was getting dark and I expected that time would be called after this exchange or after the next. If I won the first of what I had reason to believe would be the last two points, I was assured of at least a draw. Not losing had always been my main objective. Winning was merely a more affirmative statement of the same principle. I took refuge in strategy, thought to tame the old man at his own game. (I kept forgetting that it wasn't really him, only somebody curiously like him.)

I took a practice toss which drew a reprimand from the umpire's chair. I said I was sorry, mumbled my excuses. It's not something, the toss of a ball, you have any hope of undoing when done. "This is for real," I said.

My credibility was not what it had been. I could feel the murmurs of disbelief whistling through the stands, an ill wind.

"Let's get the road on the show," said the umpire.

My service, impelled by anger, came in at him, the ball springing at his heart, requiring a strategic retreat.

I underestimated his capacity for survival. His return, surprising in itself, was forceful and deep, moving me to the backhand corner, against my intention to play there, with disadvantageous haste.

"Good shot," I wanted to say to him, though there wasn't time for that.

There's hardly ever time, I thought, to do the graceful thing. I was busy in pursuit of the ball (my failure perhaps was compliment enough), staving off defeat. Even if I managed the ball's return, and I would not have run this far without that intention, the stroke would not have enough arm behind it to matter. It would merely ask my opponent for an unforced error, a giving up of self-interest.

There were good reasons, then, not to make the exceptional effort necessary to put the ball in my father's court, and if I were a less stubborn man (or a more sensible one), I would not have driven myself in hopeless pursuit. My return was effected by a scooplike shot off the backhand, an improvised maneuver under crisis conditions. Wherever the ball would go, I had done the best I could.

My father tapped the ball into the open court for the point. His gentleness and restraint were a lesson to us all.

I was more dangerous—my experience about myself—coming from behind. Large advantages had always seemed to me intolerable burdens.

The strain of being frontrunner was beginning to tell on my father. His hair had turned white between points, was turning whiter by the moment, thinning and whitening. I perceived this erratic acceleration in the aging process as another one of his strategies. He was a past master in evoking guilt in an adversary.

The umpire was clearing his throat, a means of attracting attention to himself. "Defecate or desist from the pot," he said, winking at the crowd.

Such admonishments were intolerable. He had never let me do anything at my own time and pace. As if in speeded-up motion, I smashed the ball past my opponent—he seemed to be looking the wrong way—for the first service ace of the match.

There was no call from the umpire, the man humming to himself some private tune. We looked at each other a moment without verbal communication, a nod of understanding sufficient. I was readying the toss for the next serve when he called me back. "Let's see that again," he said.

Why again?

"Didn't see it. P'raps should. However didn't. 'Pologize." He wiped some dampness from the corner of his eye with a finger. I could see that he was trying to be fair, trying against predilection to control all events in his path, to perceive history as if it were the prophecy of his will.

I said I would play the point over, though under protest and with perceptible displeasure.

"I will not have this match made into a political spectacle," the umpire said. He gestured me back to the deuce court, world weary and disapproving, patient beyond human forbearance.

I would only accept the point, I said, if it were awarded to me in the proper spirit. I had already agreed to play it again and would not retract that agreement.

The umpire, my father, crossed his arms in front of him, an implacable figure. "Are we here to argue or play tennis?" he asked no one in particular.

I started to protest, then said, "Oh forget it," and returned to the court he had gestured me to, embarrassed at getting my way. I was about to toss the ball for the serve when I noticed that my opponent was sitting cross-legged just inside his own service box.

I asked the umpire if time had been called and he said, "Time calls though is almost never called to account," which made little sense in my present mood. My father, I remembered, tended to treat words as if they were playthings.

"Are you ready?" I shouted across the net. "I'm going to serve."

My opponent cocked his head as if trying to make out where the voice was coming from.

"I'm going to count to five," I said, "and then put the ball into play. One . . ."

There was no point in counting—the old man had no intention of rousing himself—though I was of the mind that one ought to complete what one started. I wasn't going to be the one to break a promise.

I finished counting in a businesslike way and served the ball.

"Indeed," said my father as it skittered off his shoe. The point was credited to my account.

My father stood in the center of the court, arms out, eyes toward the heavens, asking God what he had done to deserve ingratitude.

I would not let him shame me this time, not give him that false advantage.

The umpire coughed while my father got himself ready, dusting off the seat of his shorts, combing his hair.

I hit the next serve into the net cord, the ball catapulting back at me. I caught it with a leap, attracting the crowd's applause.

"Deuce," said the umpire with his characteristic ambiguity.

I had lost count, thought I was either ahead or behind, felt nostalgic for an earlier time when issues tended to have decisive resolutions.

I suspected the umpire not of bias, not so much that, no more than anyone's, but of attempting to prolong the match beyond its natural consequence.

The umpire spoke briefly, and not without eloquence, on the need to set our houses in order. "Sometimes wounds have to be healed in the process." He spoke as if the healing of wounds was at best a necessary evil.

My opponent said the present dispute was a family matter and would be decided at home if his prodigal son returned to the fold.

What prodigal son? I was too old, too grown up, to live with my parents. I had in fact a family of my own somewhere which, in the hurly-burly of getting on, I had somehow misplaced. "Why not stop play at this point," I said, "and continue the match at a later date under more convivial circumstances. Or . . ."

"What alternative, sir, are you proposing?" said my father from the umpire's chair, a hint of derision in the query.

I had planned to say that I would accept a draw, though thought it best to let the suggestion emerge elsewhere.

"I will not be the first one to cry *enough*," said my father. "Don't look to me for concessions. On the other hand . . ."

The umpire interrupted him. "The match will continue until one of the contestants demonstrates a clear superiority."

His message was announced over the loudspeaker and drew polite applause from the gallery.

My plan was to alternate winning and losing points. There was nothing to be gained, I thought, in beating him decisively and no need to take the burden of a loss on myself.

If I won the deuce point, I could afford to give away the advantage. I could afford to give it away so long as I created the illusion that it was being taken from me.

"Can't win for losing," I quipped after the second deuce.

"Deuces are wild," I said after the fourth tie.

These remarks seemed to anger my adversary. He spat into the wind, sending some of it my way, swore to teach me a lesson in manners. When he lost the next point after an extended rally he flung his racket and threw himself to the ground, lamenting his limitations and the blind malignity of chance.

I turned my back, embarrassed for him, kicked a few balls to show that I was not without passion myself.

I had served the last ad point into the net and assumed a repetition of that tactic would invite inordinate suspicion among an ordinarily wary and overbred audience. My inclination was to hit the serve wide to the backhand, an expression of overreaching ambition, beyond reproach.

A poor toss—the ball thrown too close—defeated immediate intention. I swung inside out (as they say in baseball when a batter hits an inside pitch to the opposite field), a desperation stroke whose only design was to go through the motions of design. (Perhaps this is rationalization after the fact. The deed of course manifests the intention.) The ball, which had no business clearing the net, found the shallow corner of his box, ticking the line. As if anticipating my accidental shot, he came up quickly. He seemed to have a way of knowing what I was going to do—perhaps it was in the blood—even before I knew myself. He was coming up, his thin knotted legs pushing against the artificial surface as he drove himself forward. There was a small chance that he might reach the ball on its first bounce, the smallest of chances.

His moment arrived and was gone.

My father swung majestically and connected with space, with platonic delusion, the ball moving in its own cycle, disconnected from his intention.

Game and match to the challenger. My father came to the net on the run as is the fashion, hand outstretched. We never did get to shake hands, our arms passing like ships in the night. "I was lucky," I said. "That serve had no business going where it did."

He looked through me, said in the iciest of voices, "I'm grateful for your lesson," and walked off.

Murmurs went through the gallery, an ominous buzzing sound. I asked one of the linesmen, a sleepy old man with thick glasses, what the murmurs signified.

"Well, sir," he wheezed, "this may be out of line, my saying this, but there's some feeling among the old heads that your final service was not in the best traditions of fair play."

I was perfectly willing to concede the point, I said, an unintentional ambiguity. "Why don't we call the match a stalemate."

The old linesman said that it was not within his authority

to grant such dispensation. He suggested that I talk directly to my father.

"If I could talk directly to my father, if either of us could talk to the other, we would never have gotten into this match." (That wasn't wholly true. Sometimes you said things because they had a pleasant turn to them.)

"Sir," said the linesman, "a broken heart is not easily repaired."

I walk up and down the now deserted corridors of the stadium, looking for the old man. He is, as always, deceptively difficult to find.

Someone comes up to me in the dark and asks if I'd be interested in a match against an aggressive and skillful opponent.

I say that I am looking for my father, perhaps another time.

"Hold on," he says, holding me by the shoulder. "What's this father of yours look like? An old dude passed here maybe ten minutes ago, tears running down his ancient face."

"The old man was crying?"

"Crying! Jesus, the falls of Niagara were nothing to those tears. I mean, it was not a good scene."

I try to get by, but my companion, a younger man with a vise-like grip, holds fast. "Excuse me," I say.

"After we play, we'll talk," says my companion. "I want to show you my new serve."

I am in no mood to look at serves and say so in a kind way, not wanting to hurt his feelings or not wanting to hurt them to excess.

"I may be your last chance, pal," the kid says in his brash

way. "To count on chances beyond the second is to live a life of unreproved illusion."

His remark, like most nonsense, has a ring of truth.

I return to the playing area alongside my insinuating companion. We take our places on opposing sides of center court, though I have not at any time, by word or sign, agreed to play him.

My father, or someone like him, is again in the umpire's chair and announces, after a few preliminary hits, that the match is begun.

It is the moment I've been waiting for. "I have not agreed to play this young man a match," I say. "This is not a contest for which I feel the slightest necessity."

My refusal to play either comes too late or goes unheard. My opponent has already tossed the ball for his service, a brilliant toss rising like a sun to the highest point of his extension. The meeting of racket and ball resounds through the stadium like the crash of cymbals. The ball is arriving. Before I can ready myself, before I can coordinate arm and racket, before I can coordinate mind and arm, the ball will be here and gone, a dream object, receding into the distance like a ghost of the imagination. The first point is lost. And so the game. And so the match. Waiting for the ball's arrival—it is on the way, it has not yet reached me—I concede nothing.

Rackets and Riches at Wimbledon

J. P. DONLEAVY

In June in a thick green summer valley. The sun pours down and they pop the fluffy white ball back and forth. The little grass arenas where they say deuce and love and first service and fault and quiet please. And I go bathe myself in the intolerable sadness all sport brings to my soul.

These tasty days of The Lawn Tennis Championships upon the lawns of The All England Club. Wimbledon fortnight of golden female legs. On court and off. And I came on my own white ones which I used lightly walking down a country lane past houses with lanterns polished and gleaming outside their freshly painted doors. Where grey haired ladies take tea on their terraces and children's voices come through the air of the quiet afternoon. And by the roadside a man sits benignly playing I Know That My Redeemer Liveth on his portable organ, an upturned hat on the grass for clinking silver.

The stadium looms dark green and ivy clad, holding rich hearts, eager hearts and my own grey one shortly arriving. Into the long concrete covered tunnel to pay five shillings. Through the turnstyle where the money is piling up in mountains and suddenly one stands terribly interested in a corridor thick with the tinted tender tempting smell of women. The perfume is musk and mad. Prices of the various smells pass me by at about thirty guineas an ounce. The flowered dresses, the bronze and freckled faces. Pearls and gracious beads. Hats straw and gay and striped and strange. A blond star of stage, a famous fair lady floating by, as heads turn and my mind mentions, please, may I touch you. But she's gone with smiles only for close friends, mostly ticket holders in the shade with cushions for bottoms and backs. And her beauty goes to sit a flower among the tan masks. I squeeze bereft into the free standing room. A sardine in the sun.

Two o'clock. I'm crushed by school girls reading programmes over each other's shoulders. All in uniforms. They shove and push me with absolutely no regard for my age. I'm confused by their early interest in tennis. Perhaps parents steering them away from men. The judges come out. Wearing red and some, yellow carnations, exuding rectitude in all directions. A grassy law court. Litigants wear white. The referee takes his measuring rod to the net. Photographers preparing cameras. Ball boys in their purple and green shirts, splay footed, hands folded behind backs. They've been trained to notice a player's whim, his nod, wink and wish. And I fear, to absorb growls at the odd time when his ill nature rears.

And then suddenly there's clapping. From under the Royal awninged box come the players. Traversing silently, snugly on their soft soles. Some lilt, some bounce. There is very little waddling due to the speed of this sport. But players come in all types and sizes, or all sorts of caprice and demeanours. There are the grass beaters, who fluff the return of a lob and hold the grass down with one hand and batter it with a racket with the other. Then the kneelers. They get down on knees, putting racket gently aside to slowly hold their heads in their hands. I rather prefer this sort. They don't damage the court and it's moving to watch supplication proffered to the open sky.

But let us play tennis. There is no eagerness to start the game. At this stage they cavort with some real snazzy shots, wearing indifference on the face. Until the umpire aloft on his high chair, score sheet on his lap, whispers into the mike, are you ready. The ball boys lift the lid of the refrigerator. The balls come out, cool to the touch, bouncing with perfection. Just ripe for players who come from all corners of the globe to play with these fuzzy spheres at a universal temperature. The idea is hypnotizing. And for two weeks I waited for someone to object to a warm ball.

The call for silence please. Lights lit in the scoreboard. All eyes on this sacred carpet of green. Ball boys on one knee at the net, ready to rush and scoop up on the run. Server casually to base line to carefully place a foot, and takes that instant of aim. I feel a message go to his opponent, I say chap, if you see this one at all, don't be foolish enough to stick your cat gut out because it will go right through. The player receiving the message crouches, a little flex of calf muscles and a bounce. Stares back, an eye on each side of his bat and sends back, my dear fellow I hope when my return lob passes from a ray of sunshine through your own cat gut you will be good enough to help them dig it out of your court. Needless to say not many in the crowd catch these wordless exchanges, which frankly are shockingly unspeakable between women competitors.

But there is sportsmanship. The backslap is there. For the loser at the net. The steel handshake of a winner. The arm around the shoulder walking off court. And in the heat of the match the acknowledging hand at the beauty of a drop shot. At this latter the crowd roars and claps, the executor of such a shot drops head and with humility humming, wipes face of all expression. This tells the crowd you've seen nothing yet. Which makes me long for those full women who brazenly and breast-fully hammer the ball in all directions and helplessly lose.

Day after day the eliminations go on. The angled cross court passing shot much favoured by the crowds. More and more the folks gravitate to centre and number one courts. Outside in the grounds now deserted by famous names, the people thin out. The first opening week seems far away when the crowds returned fresh, gay, packed on the underground train with their cocktail chatter of voices, the lean unmuscled arms of carefree women hanging everywhere. When I heard con-versation about the wine champagne and trunks for travelling and the good old days when people knew their place. And when I listened for a word of tennis and heard that an aunt Mirabelle had to let her second gardener go. I was alas, also amazed by the absolute indifference shown to my presence on the train.

And the evenings of these last days is a terrible time of sad-ness. Sun setting beyond the stands and further in the tips of trees. I suppose it's because Wimbledon will go on without me. I stand leaning against a fence watching the players leave.

Hair neat, faces shower fresh as they wait for their chauffeured cars. All this youth beauty and bounce. On the verge of a tear I heard a cry go up from behind me near the water tower on an outside court. I tripped down steps and along a deserted back lane between the evergreens. Reaching the water tower, a sentinel over this sadness, I come upon a doubles match. I was amazed as well as revitalized. Two short footed intense Russians playing two stringbean Americans from the Deep South.

A crowd collected. The Russian chunky bodies leaping around the court. They seemed awkward but friendly types and I wondered how it was that this naughty race had caused so much heartbreak. Then I heard the magnolia scented accents crackling out the dialogue. They were devastating these two from the East. Somehow I could bear tennis no longer. I went back through the evergreens. Past the members' lawn where they took sherry under colored umbrellas. I spied some players packed to go. I approached to ask don't you want to cry, absolutely break down and shed tears on the torn tickets in the road. And sidling near to make my heartfelt remark, I am taken aback by their flinty business man's eyes. They were soon to go to Barcelona all expenses paid.

More clapping and I know that inside centre court they're handing out the silver cups and plates. To those, who when it was match point and needed, got securely behind the cat gut and laid that chilled ball neatly at speed along the base line, out of reach. Over the tea lawn the casual labour pick up the paper cups. In the competitors' buffet, arrangements for championships elsewhere in the world are made and school girls collect autographs at the bottom of the steps. Out on the grounds the blue and the green canvas covers lie over the turf. The water tower like a lonely mausoleum standing over the empty courts. The grass worn and brown. And I make a last visit to the gents which was a day ago like a train station.

The Tennis Court

DOUGLAS DUNN

Polish officers freewheeled down that long hill in the early evenings. High-spirited men arrived first, whooping and shouting and waving their racquets. There were often two to a bicycle. More mournful, more conservative individuals followed them with judicious pressure on their brakes, as if they had not mastered the exhilarations of downhill bicycle-riding. Half an hour later those who preferred to walk would stroll through the village with their polite "Good evenings" and little bows. Our parents told us it was wonderful how these Poles could be pleasant to strangers when they had so much on their minds. Like the others, those who came on foot were dressed in as many bits and pieces of tennis clothes as they could lay their hands on. Some wore white slacks or white shorts and military shirts or sweaters. Others wore military shorts or drill trousers and white shirts or white sweaters. Only one or two possessed a complete white ensemble. Members of the Tennis Club presented them with what discarded whites they could, rather as head waiters keep a tie or two for those gentlemen thoughtless enough to arrive without one.

For two or three hours, on one or two evenings a week, the court seemed possessed by Polish players. Their excitable Polish language was shouted around while the sedate but tolerant members of the Club looked on or chatted with non-playing senior officers, who behaved as if they had made a point of being there to keep an eye on the younger officers of the regiment. Ladies of the Club chirruped as their hands were kissed, a gallant custom which, alas, has fallen into disuse on these islands. I distinctly remember a young woman protesting. "But he's so dashing, Daddy! And he's been through so much!" She was petulant, but her father was extremely cross. "He may be as dashing as fifty VCs put together," he said, with that dismissive but carefully controlled rage of which only the male parent is capable, "and for all I care, he can have been through Hell. But you will not see him again!"

Men found themselves stuck for words when these Polish officers presented them with "little presents" or brought flowers for their wives. One of them gave me a posy of wild flowers he had gathered on his way to the court. "A l'le girl," he said to my father, "shud hiv flo'rs. Blue flo'rs far blue ess. No? Yis, yis, *such* blue ess." "This little girl," said my mother, "is about ready for beddy-byes." I could have thrown a tantrum. I wanted to stay, and pose, with my wild bouquet, for I did not think of myself as little as all that and neither, I suspect, did my mother.

At dusk, the Polish officers pedalled back up that long hill to the commandeered mansion in which they were billeted. I saw them from my bedroom window. Sweaters, racquets, phrase-books, and other impedimenta, were balanced on the handlebars of their bicycles. Snatches of Polish conversation could be heard faintly from the pedestrian soldiers. I was fourteen at the time, but I still remember one last half-white figure disappearing into the darkening rhododendrons of Sir George Maclean's garden, one evening, when, as I heard from my father the following morning, that distinguished old soldier sent an invitation down to the court for the Poles to stop by his house for a drink.

British, Canadian and American fliers from the naval air base, sometimes from aircraft carriers anchored on the Clyde, came and played on our court. They arrived in an impressive miscellany of transport. Parked on the grass verge by the side of the road, there would be navy-blue cars driven by Wrens, jeeps, a truck or two, and sometimes a rakish sports car for our brothers to admire. Those dark blues were dappled in the evening sunlight as it filtered through the trees and penetrated the shadow cast by the high stone wall that masks the court from the road. That summer light on the vehicles made a colour that was memorable, which one would want to preserve. These airmen were high-spirited, too. They arrived in perfect attire. The Poles went first, in 1944. A year and a half later the court was ours again.

More tennis was played on our court in these last two summers of the war than at any time before or since. There was a tennis wedding in All Hallows in 1945. Arm-in-arm, under a salute of raised racquets, the American groom and his local bride smile on the fading newsprint in these bound volumes of the *Press & Advertiser* which anyone can leaf through in the Public Library in town. If they come from here, and do not feel like making the trip, then they can consult them in Mr. Ferrier's attic, for he has the best part of a complete set.

That, then, was Miss Devorgilla Cunningham, made Mrs. DeLancey O'Hara, of Boston, Mass. I was at the wedding. They return here from time to time, for Devorgilla's sister still lives in the family house of Craigenmun. Bella Cunningham is, I suppose, my one and only close friend. She is two years older then me, so I play against her, and, on those rare occasions when we can make up the numbers for a game of doubles, I play with her. As a combination, we are unbeatable locally. We are both spinsters. I do not like that word, but I am stuck with it. Bella is fifty-two, and I am fifty although you would not think it to look at me. For us both, tennis, and the Tennis Club, are large occupations and not to be taken lightly. I am the daughter of a Professor of Gynaecology, one of those earnestly amiable Scottish physicians of which the world, perhaps, has known too many. His vigorous but incompetent exertions on our tennis court fell into the category of once witnessed, never forgotten. He would justify his disastrous drives, his ungainly balletics and hopeless leaps and bounds, by saying, "It's all exercise anyway. What, after all, is tennis, if not a form of exercise?" He did not play tennis so much as keep fit. As a consequence of his reputation, no one—and they should have known better—took my tennis seriously until I had made it my business to win the Junior Ladies County Championship. Bella

Cunningham lifted that same trophy the year before. Two years younger than she on that moment of triumph, I can be said to be one up on her where it matters. In our games against each other, the score, I regret to confess, stands at 354 matches to Bella, and 76 to me. To set against this shameful statistic, I must point out that we have been keeping this tally for only the past ten years. It is a lot of tennis, but we did not keep a record until we were past our best. Bella has a black notebook in which she records each game, each set, each match. Yes, it would have to be black.

Why, at my age, you may ask, do I continue to play such a competitive game of tennis? In reply, I contend that Bella does not beat me by all *that* much. She beats me regularly, indeed, but the scores are *close.* This, I cannot help but observe, puts Bella in a better light than it places me. Or so it will look to those who do not know the facts. Bella, after all, is fifty-two. Yes, you are right, should you consider our heroic duels absurd. It is rather worse for her at fifty-two. Isn't it? My birthday falls gratifyingly in the midst of our summer contests, on the 9th of July. "Bella," I said this year, and I was far from breathless, "I think I'll call it a day."

"Have you had enough, my dear?" She is not the sort of person who remembers her own birthday let alone that of her oldest friend.

"At my age," I said, "this is all quite ridiculous. I'm fifty, you know."

"You are forty-seven," she said. "And don't you forget it. I know, because I am forty-nine and you are two years younger."

This confused me. I am easily contradicted. Silently, I counted back to the year of my birth. "No," I said, "my birthday is today, and I'm fifty."

"Congratulations!" She left me at the net and took up position to resume her service. She shot a venomous ball at me that bounced accurately just inside the line and left me completely adrift. "Happy birthday, my dear!" Another of her militaristic wallops came at me.

"That was *out!*" It wasn't, but there is never any harm in trying.

If I may say so, I have kept my neck in a state far closer to a swanlike and sporting ideal than has Bella Cunningham. Mrs. O'Hara's neck is the better for regular tennis, too, but I understand it is common practice in Boston, Mass., for expensive surgery to be performed upon perished skin, or sagging jaws. Apparently, a moment is reached when former beauties are forced to concede that the glassy information of their mirrors is the truth, after all, and that they must realize they have reached a matronly status. Or so I have heard.

As for my arms, then, these, I assure you, show no signs of deteriorating into that flabby, non-youthful condition which is common to ladies of my age. Bella Cunningham's arms are vulgarly muscular. I have a sneaking suspicion she indulges in weightlifting. It is not that I have ever come across her heaving heavy metal about in whatever room in Craigenmun she uses as her secret gymnasium. I am going by that other evidence of my eyes, her sheer bulk. Manly exercises of that sort would certainly explain why it is that Bella Cunningham has a moustache.

And now, my legs. I am justifiably proud of my legs. At one time I considered them to be far and away my best feature. Indeed, I was for ever showing them off when young men were in the vicinity. Exercise has not made them too muscular. They are, I dare say, conspicuous for their beauty, as much as for the extent to which they portray me as a woman in excellent physical condition. Bella Cunningham shaves hers. I have deduced this from her hirsute armpits, the dark hair on her arms, and the five o'clock shadow beneath her nose. "Why, Bella," I have asked her, "must you insist on wearing such awfully young tennis outfits?"

"What? I thought this one was rather becoming."

I do not wish for one moment to be unfair to Bella, but I think I succeeded in afflicting her with some of that consternation and self-perusal of which she stood in serious need this summer, although my charitable nature did not permit me to be as candid towards her as I should have been. That has always been my predicament in my long friendship with Bella Cunningham. Shall I tell her what I really think of her? Shall I come clean, and speak to her, as one friend to another? It has always been like that. But in the past few years it has weighed on me like a responsibility. We are all to some extent responsible for our friends' behaviour. It is up to us to prevent them from looking ridiculous in the eyes of those who do not love us. "It's those frilly pants," I said. "All very well for Miss Wade, or Miss Navratilova, but I fear they do not quite suit Miss Cunningham."

"I do hope you are not suggesting," she said, and a negative, on the lips of Bella, when she's feeling haughty, is like a threat, "you are not suggesting that I have reached the age of *slacks?*"

"Not for one moment. But look at you. There is," I reminded her, "a kind of, well, a sort of 'bend' in your legs."

"Bend?" she looked down at her legs. "I am *not* bandy-legged!"

"Your knees," I pointed out, "do not touch when you stand to attention. Now do they?"

She drew her feet together and looked down. "They *don't.*" I could not quite decide if her tone of voice was one of plaint, or one of defiance.

"What if someone should see you?"

"Who," she asked, "is likely to?"

Her answer had the effect of perplexing me. It was true, the Club is usually unpopulated. In a sense it is no longer a Tennis Club at all. The Macleans' gardeners keep it in good order, but this generosity on their part has come to took more like a special favour to us than to the Tennis Club. Twenty-two members we may have, on paper, but we hardly ever see them. The Club House is not what it was, but we keep it as clean and as adequate as we can. Fortunately, we can afford it. From time to time we have seen evidence of tennis having been played before our arrival at the court. Here and there, the odd soft-drinks can, trampled grass, a ball that is certainly not one of ours, a rolled Kleenex, give the show away. We cannot help but notice an uncouthly rolled net, flung any-old-how in a corner of the Club House. Enquiries made of the Macleans' gardeners inform us that so-and-so was there, young persons, taking advantage of their parents' memberships. Keys are needed, one to unlock the gate in the wall, another to open the gate into the court itself, and a third for the Club House door. "Someone," I said, "may be walking his dog. And children often play in these woods. *Anyone* could see you."

"It's hardly changed. It seems just the same, doesn't it, DeLancey?" Thus the former Devorgilla Cunningham to her husband, when they visited last year. It was an enchanting tennis reunion. The evening began with a gentle game between that couple from Boston, Mass. They looked like bride and groom again, setting off on the first waltz of married life. That court must mean so much to them. We all applauded with soft pats of the hand, although the standard of tennis was disgraceful. Several club members managed to drag themselves from their houses to be present. Friends of Devorgilla's, living elsewhere, turned up for the occasion. We had mixed doubles after the O'Haras finished their intimate, significant game. "Bella, for Heaven's sake, *must* you?" That was not me, for I am well used to Bella's barbaric serve, and that deeply breathed, fiercesome squaring of her shoulders which precedes it, she of the barbers and calisthenics. Mrs. O'Hara did her best, but gave up, claiming she was no longer a match for Bella's vindictive interpretation of the game. Nor was Mr. O'Hara who, by the end of the evening, was, undoubtedly, in that "bad shape" to which he confessed. He was also in need of a recuperative liedown, of which he promptly availed himself on our return to Craigenmun.

"I rather think," I said quietly to Bella, on the court that evening as the O'Haras played, "that you are suffering from envy."

"How odd," she said. "That's *exactly* what I thought I read on your face."

When our tennis season is over, we go on holiday together. For some years we have frequented Aix-en-Provence where tennis in September is rather fun. We were sitting, after dinner, having played a taxing game of doubles against two French ladies that afternoon. "I could hardly hold back the giggles when they said they were here for the Spa," I said.

"But surprisingly good players," said Bella.

"You played rather well," I said. Bella was suspicious of this compliment. "Such a pity they couldn't join us for dinner. It would be nice to play them again."

"They could never beat us," Bella said, which was satisfying.

"I do miss our own court when we're away," I said. "Don't you?"

"Yes, I do," she said, in that cold manner of hers whenever anything personal is brought up.

"Especially at this time of year, when the first leaves of autumn fall, and blow across it."

"You can be so sentimental about that court." Bella consulted the menu. People with appetites as hearty as Bella's like to reread the menu, after dinner, already looking forward to what they will have tomorrow. "No, you're right. I miss it at this time of year, too. I think of it as resting, as hibernating. And I don't know what there is to gloat over," she said, crossly, "just because I admit to an affection for our tennis court."

"I think these French ladies rather disliked us, by the end."
It had been a hard-fought match. Bella chortled through her
nose.

"My dear, I should think they detested us. I don't think
they're used to being beaten."

I shared in this for a moment, then said, "I was not gloat-
ing, you know. I simply felt pleased that you should feel the
same way as I do." My assurances did not seem to satisfy her.
For years I had been wondering if I might go a little further in
my exploration of our mutual fondness for our tennis court.
Of course, I always knew what Bella felt, but she is not the sort
of person who speaks her feelings. Allowances have to be made
for her. I decided to press on. She was in a good mood, with a
notable victory under her belt, not to mention an excellent
dinner and several glasses of *Côtes d'Aix* vin rosé, which is to
be recommended. "I have this wonderful memory of the Poles,"
I said. "Such unhappy, courteous and charming men. And of
the Americans and the Canadians. Remember?"

"I think you are so very like me," I said, "only you will never
bring yourself to admit it." I thought she might bray at me
with disbelief. Instead, she did not say anything; she merely
shrugged. On such shoulders, broad shoulders, a shrug is ex-
pressive and very noticeable. We were ten days away from our
own court—on which the grass was lengthening, leaves were
browning—and I thought Bella would be in the mood to let
me say what I wanted without chastisingly tut-tutting at every
turn. "We want so much to go back to that time, don't we?"

"No one," she said, "ever goes back."

"No, I suppose not. But we would like to. That's the point,

you see. Sometimes," I said, "it's crossed my mind that we're two ageing girls, hanging around that tennis court, in the hope of another war. Isn't that awful?" To my surprise, Bella was still listening, her head tilted slightly away from me. I expected her to tell me to shut up and not talk such rubbish. "And then the Poles would come down on their bicycles. There would be the Fleet Air Arm, the United States Navy, and the DeLancey O'Haras of this world. "Anyway," I said, "I know it's silly of me, but that's what I feel. Sometimes," I added, because I did not want her to think that I felt like that very often. There is such a thing as discretion, even between very old friends. She bit her lower lip and managed to smile at the same time, with a little laugh. "And you?" I asked. That was the difficult question.

I thought she might cry, but I do not believe Bella could ever cry in a public restaurant. "Not often," she said. "Not often. But I sometimes feel like that too."

There. I had said it. And I was right. I don't know what people thought of us, if they saw me reach across the table, to hold Bella's hand, which, I saw, was posed above the white linen, waiting.

In the Land of Dreamy Dreams

ELLEN GILCHRIST

On the third of May, 1977, LaGrande McGruder drove out
onto the Huey P. Long Bridge, dropped two Davis Classics
and a gut-strung PDP tournament racket into the Mississippi
River, and quit playing tennis forever.

"That was it," she said. "That was the last goddamn straw."
She heaved a sigh, thinking this must be what it feels like to
die, to be through with something that was more trouble than
it was worth.

As long as she could remember LaGrande had been playing tennis four or five hours a day whenever it wasn't raining
or she didn't have a funeral to attend. In her father's law office
was a whole cabinet full of her trophies.

After the rackets sank LaGrande dumped a can of brand-
new Slazenger tennis balls into the river and stood for a long
time watching the cheerful, little, yellow constellation form
and re-form in the muddy current.

"Jesus Fucking A Christ," she said to herself. "Oh, well,"
she added, "maybe now I can get my arms to be the same size
for the first time in my life."

LaGrande leaned into the bridge railing, staring past the white circles on her wrists, souvenirs of twenty years of wearing sweatbands in the fierce New Orleans sunlight, and on down to the river where the little yellow constellation was overtaking a barge.

"That goddamn little new-rich Yankee bitch," she said, kicking the bridge with her leather Tretorns.

There was no denying it. There was no undoing it. At ten o'clock that morning LaGrande McGruder, whose grandfather had been president of the United States Lawn Tennis Association, had cheated a crippled girl out of a tennis match, had deliberately and without hesitation made a bad call in the last point of a crucial game, had defended the call against loud protests, taken a big drink of her Gatorade, and proceeded to win the next twelve games while her opponent reeled with disbelief at being done out of her victory.

At exactly three minutes after ten that morning she had looked across the net at the impassive face of the interloper who was about to humiliate her at her own tennis club and she had changed her mind about honor quicker than the speed of light. "Out," she had said, not giving a damn whether the serve was in or out. "Nice try."

"It couldn't be out," the crippled girl said. "Are you sure?"

"Of course I'm sure," LaGrande said. "I wouldn't have called it unless I was sure."

"Are you positive?" the crippled girl said.

"For God's sake," LaGrande said, "look, if you don't mind, let's hurry up and get this over with. I have to be at the country club for lunch." That ought to get her, LaGrande thought.

At least they don't let Jews into the country club yet. At least that's still sacred.

"Serving," the crippled girl said, trying to control her rage.

LaGrande took her position at the back of the court, reached up to adjust her visor, and caught the eye of old Claiborne Redding, who was sitting on the second-floor balcony watching the match. He smiled and waved. How long has he been standing there, LaGrande wondered. How long has that old fart been watching me? But she was too busy to worry about Claiborne now. She had a tennis match to save, and she was going to save it if it was the last thing she ever did in her life.

The crippled girl set her mouth into a tight line and prepared to serve into the forehand court. Her name was Roxanne Miller, and she had traveled a long way to this morning's fury. She had spent thousands of dollars on private tennis lessons, hundreds of dollars on equipment, and untold time and energy giving cocktail parties and dinner parties for the entrenched players who one by one she had courted and blackmailed and finagled into giving her matches and return matches until finally one day she would catch them at a weak moment and defeat them. She kept a mental list of such victories. Sometimes when she went to bed at night she would pull the pillows over her head and lie there imagining herself as a sort of Greek figure of justice, sitting on a marble chair in the clouds, holding a scroll, a little parable of conquest and revenge.

It had taken Roxanne five years to fight and claw and worm her way into the ranks of respected Lawn Tennis Club Ladies. For five years she had dragged her bad foot around the carefully manicured courts of the oldest and snottiest tennis club in the United States of America.

For months now her ambitions had centered around La-Grande. A victory over LaGrande would mean she had arrived in the top echelons of the Lawn Tennis Club Ladies.

A victory over LaGrande would surely be followed by invitations to play in the top doubles games, perhaps even in the famous Thursday foursome that played on Rena Clark's private tennis court. Who knows, Roxanne dreamed, LaGrande might even ask her to be her doubles partner. LaGrande's old doubles partners were always retiring to have babies. At any moment she might need a new one. Roxanne would be there waiting, the indefatigable handicapped wonder of the New Orleans tennis world.

She had envisioned this morning's victory a thousand times, had seen herself walking up to the net to shake LaGrande's hand, had planned her little speech of condolence, after which the two of them would go into the snack bar for lunch and have a heart-to-heart talk about rackets and balls and backhands and forehands and volleys and lobs.

Roxanne basked in her dreams. It did not bother her that LaGrande never returned her phone calls, avoided her at the club, made vacant replies to her requests for matches. Roxanne had plenty of time. She could wait. Sooner or later she would catch LaGrande in a weak moment.

That moment came at the club's 100th Anniversary Celebration. Everyone was drunk and full of camaraderie. The old members were all on their best behavior, trying to be extra nice to the new members and pretend like the new members were just as good as they were even if they didn't belong to the Boston Club or the Southern Yacht Club or Comus or Momus or Proteus.

Roxanne cornered LaGrande while she was talking to a famous psychiatrist-player from Washington, a bachelor who was much adored in tennis circles for his wit and political connections.

LaGrande was trying to impress him with how sane she was and hated to let him see her irritation when Roxanne moved in on them.

"When are you going to give me that match you promised me?" Roxanne asked, looking wistful, as if this were something the two of them had been discussing for years.

"I don't know," LaGrande said. "I guess I just stay so busy. This is Semmes Talbot, from Washington. This is Roxanne, Semmes. I'm sorry. I can't remember your last name. You'll have to help me."

"Miller," Roxanne said. "My name is Miller. Really now, when will you play with me?"

"Well, how about Monday?" LaGrande heard herself saying. "I guess I could do it Monday. My doubles game was canceled." She looked up at the doctor to see if he appreciated how charming she was to everyone, no matter who they were.

"Fine," Roxanne said. "Monday's fine. I'll be here at nine. I'll be counting on it so don't let me down." She laughed. "I thought you'd never say yes. I was beginning to think you were afraid I'd beat you."

"Oh, my goodness," LaGrande said, "anyone can beat me, I don't take tennis very seriously anymore, you know. I just play enough to keep my hand in."

"Who was that?" Semmes asked when Roxanne left them. "She certainly has her nerve!"

"She's one of the new members," LaGrande said. "I really try so hard not to be snotty about them. I really do believe that every human being is just as valuable as everyone else, don't you? And it doesn't matter a bit to me what anyone's background is, but some of the new people are sort of hard to take. They're so, oh, well, so *eager*."

Semmes looked down the front of her silk blouse and laughed happily into her aristocratic eyes. "Well, watch out for that one," he said. "There's no reason for anyone as pretty as you to let people make you uncomfortable."

Across the room Roxanne collected Willie and got ready to leave the party. She was on her way home to begin training for the match.

Willie was glad to leave. He didn't like hanging around places where he wasn't wanted. He couldn't imagine why Roxanne wanted to spend all her time playing tennis with a bunch of snotty people.

Roxanne and Willie were new members. Willie's brand-new 15 million dollars and the New Orleans Lawn Tennis Club's brand-new $700,000 dollar mortgage had met at a point in history, and Willie's application for membership had been approved by the board and railroaded past the watchful noses of old Claiborne Redding and his buddies. Until then the only Jewish member of the club had been a globetrotting Jewish bachelor who knew his wines, entertained lavishly at Antoine's, and had the courtesy to stay in Europe most of the time.

Willie and Roxanne were something else again. "What in the hell are we going to do with a guy who sells ties and a crippled woman who runs around Audubon Park all day in a pair of tennis shorts," Claiborne said, pulling on a pair of the thick white Australian wool socks he wore to play in. The committee had cornered him in the locker room.

"The membership's not for him," they said. "He doesn't even play. You'll never see him. And she really isn't a cripple. One leg is a little bit shorter than the other one, that's all."

"I don't know," Claiborne said. "Not just Jews, for God's sake, but Yankee Jews to boot."

"The company's listed on the American Stock Exchange, Claiborne. It was selling at 16fi this morning, up from 5. And he buys his insurance from me. Come on, you'll never see them. All she's going to do is play a little tennis with the ladies."

Old Claiborne rued the day he had let himself be talked into Roxanne and Willie. The club had been forced to take in thirty new families to pay for its new building and some of them were Jews, but, as Claiborne was fond of saying, at least the rest of them tried to act like white people.

Roxanne was something else. It seemed to him that she lived at the club. The only person who hung around the club more than Roxanne was old Claiborne himself. Pretty soon she was running the place. She wrote *The Lawn Tennis Newsletter*. She circulated petitions to change the all-white dress rule. She campaigned for more court privileges for women. She dashed in and out of the bar and the dining room making plans with the waiters and chefs for Mixed Doubles Nights, Round Robin Galas, Benefit Children's jamborees, Saturday Night Luaus.

Claiborne felt like his club was being turned into a cruise ship.

On top of everything else Roxanne was always trying to get in good with Claiborne. Every time he settled down on the balcony to watch a match she came around trying to talk to him, talking while the match was going on, remembering the names of his grandchildren, complimenting him on their serves and backhands and footwork, taking every conceivable liberty, as if at any moment she might start showing up at their weddings and debuts.

Claiborne thought about Roxanne a lot. He was thinking about her this morning when he arrived at the club and saw her cream-colored Rolls-Royce blocking his view of the Garth Humphries Memorial Plaque. He was thinking about her as he got a cup of coffee from a stand the ladies had taken to setting up by the sign-in board. This was some more of her meddling, he thought, percolated coffee in Styrofoam cups with plastic spoons and some kind of powder instead of cream.

At the old clubhouse waiters had brought steaming cups of thick chicory-flavored café au lait out onto the balcony with cream and sugar in silver servers.

Claiborne heaved a sigh, pulled his pants out of his crotch, and went up to the balcony to see what the morning would bring.

He had hardly reached the top of the stairs when he saw Roxanne leading LaGrande to a deserted court at the end of the property. My God in Heaven, he thought, how did she pull that off? How in the name of God did she get hold of Leland's daughter?

Leland McGruder had been Claiborne's doubles partner in their youth. Together they had known victory and defeat in New Orleans and Jackson and Monroe and Shreveport and Mobile and Atlanta and as far away as Forest Hills during one never to be forgotten year when they had thrown their rackets into a red Ford and gone off together on the tour.

Down on the court LaGrande was so aggravated she could barely be civil. How did I end up here, she thought, playing second-class tennis against anyone who corners me at a party.

LaGrande was in a bad mood all around. The psychiatrist had squired her around all weekend, fucked her dispassionately in someone's *garçonnierre,* and gone back to Washington without making further plans to see her.

She bounced a ball up and down a few times with her racket, thinking about a line of poetry that kept occurring to her lately whenever she played tennis. "Their only monument the asphalt road, and a thousand lost golf balls."

"Are you coming to Ladies Day on Wednesday?" Roxanne was saying, "We're going to have a great time. You really ought to come. We've got a real clown coming to give out helium balloons, and we're going to photograph the winners sitting on his lap for the newsletter. Isn't that a cute idea?"

"I'm afraid I'm busy Wednesday," LaGrande said, imagining balloons flying all over the courts when the serious players arrived for their noon games. "Look," she said, "let's go on and get started. I can't stay too long."

They set down their pitchers of Gatorade, put on their visors and sweatbands, sprayed a little powdered resin on their hands, and walked out to their respective sides of the court.

Before they hit the ball four times LaGrande knew something was wrong. The woman wasn't going to warm her up! LaGrande had hit her three nice long smooth balls and each time Roxanne moved up to the net and put the ball away on the sidelines.

"How about hitting me some forehands," LaGrande said. "I haven't played in a week. I need to warm up."

"I'll try," Roxanne said, "I have to play most of my game at the net, you know, because of my leg."

"Well, stay back there and hit me some to warm up with," LaGrande said, but Roxanne went right on putting her shots away with an assortment of tricks that looked more like a circus act than a tennis game.

"Are you ready to play yet?" she asked. "I'd like to get started before I get too tired."

"Sure," LaGrande said. "Go ahead, you serve first. There's no reason to spin a racket over a fun match." Oh, well, she thought, I'll just go ahead and slaughter her. Of course, I won't lob over her head, I don't suppose anyone does that to her.

Roxanne pulled the first ball out of her pants. She had a disconcerting habit of sticking the extra ball up the leg of her tights instead of keeping it in a pocket. She pulled the ball out of her pants, tossed it expertly up into the air, and served an ace to LaGrande's extreme backhand service corner.

"Nice serve," LaGrande said. Oh, well, she thought, everyone gets one off occasionally. Let her go on and get overconfident. Then I can get this over in a hurry.

They changed courts for the second serve. Roxanne hit short into the backhand court. LaGrande raced up and hit a forehand right into Roxanne's waiting racket. The ball dropped neatly into a corner and the score was 30-love.

How in the shit did she get to the net so fast, LaGrande thought. Well, I'll have to watch out for that. I thought she was supposed to be crippled.

Roxanne served again, winning the point with a short spinning forehand. Before LaGrande could gather her wits about her she had lost the first game.

Things went badly with her serve and she lost the second game. While she was still recovering from that she lost the third game. Calm down, she told herself. Get hold of yourself. Keep your eye on the ball. Anticipate her moves. It's only because I didn't have a chance to warm up. I'll get going in a minute.

Old Claiborne stood watching the match from a secluded spot near the door to the dining room, watching it with his heart in his throat, not daring to move any farther out onto the balcony for fear he might distract LaGrande and make things worse.

Why doesn't she lob, Claiborne thought. Why in the name of God doesn't she lob? Maybe she thinks she shouldn't do it just because one of that woman's legs is a little bit shorter than the other.

He stood squeezing the Styrofoam cup in his hand. A small hole had developed in the side, and drops of coffee were making a little track down the side of his Fred Perry flannels, but he was oblivious to everything but the action on the court.

He didn't even notice when Nailor came up behind him. Nailor was a haughty old black man who had been with the club since he was a young boy and now was the chief grounds-keeper and arbiter of manners among the hired help.

Nailor had spent his life tending Rubico tennis courts without once having the desire to pick up a racket. But he had watched thousands of tennis matches and he knew more about tennis than most players did.

He knew how the little fields of energy that surround men and women move and coalesce and strike and fend off and re-treat and attack and conquer. That was what he looked for when he watched tennis. He wasn't interested in the details.

If it was up to Nailor no one but a few select players would ever be allowed to set foot on his Rubico courts. The only time of day when he was really at peace was the half hour from when he finished the courts around 7:15 each morning until they opened the iron gates at 7:45 and the members started arriving.

Nailor had known LaGrande since she came to her father's matches in a perambulator. He had lusted after her ass ever since she got her first white tennis skirt and her first Wilson autograph racket. He had been the first black man to wax her first baby-blue convertible, and he had been taking care of her cars ever since.

Nailor moonlighted at the club polishing cars with a spe-cial wax he had invented.

Nailor hated the new members worse than Claiborne did.

Ever since the club had moved to its new quarters and they had come crowding in bringing their children and leaving their paper cups all over the courts he had been thinking of retiring.

Now he was watching one of them taking his favorite little missy to the cleaners. She's getting her little booty whipped for sure this morning, he thought. She can't find a place to turn and make a stand. She don't know where to start to stop it. She's got hind teat today whether she likes it or not and I'm glad her daddy's not here to watch it.

Claiborne was oblivious to Nailor. He was trying to decide who would benefit most if he made a show of walking out to the balcony and taking a seat.

He took a chance. He waited until LaGrande's back was to him, then walked out just as Roxanne was receiving serve.

LaGrande made a small rally and won her service, but Roxanne took the next three games for the set. "I don't need to rest between sets unless you do," she said, walking up to the net. "We really haven't been playing that long. I really don't know why I'm playing so well. I guess I'm just lucky today."

"I just guess you are," LaGrande said. "Sure, let's go right on. I've got a date for lunch." Now I'll take her, she thought. Now I'm tired of being polite. Now I'm going to beat the shit out of her.

Roxanne picked up a ball, tossed it into the air, and served another ace into the backhand corner of the forehand court.

Jesus Fucking A Christ, LaGrande thought. She did it again. Where in the name of God did that little Jewish housewife learn that shot?

LaGrande returned the next serve with a lob. Roxanne ran back, caught it on the edge of her racket and dribbled it over the net.

Now LaGrande lost all powers of reason. She began trying to kill the ball on every shot. Before she could get hold of herself she had lost three games, then four, then five, then she was only one game away from losing the match, then only one point.

This is it, LaGrande thought. Armageddon.

Roxanne picked up the balls and served the first one out. She slowed herself down, took a deep breath, tossed up the second ball and shot a clean forehand into the service box.

"Out," LaGrande said. "Nice try."

"It couldn't be out," Roxanne said, "are you sure?"

"Of course I'm sure," LaGrande said. *"I wouldn't have called it unless I was sure."*

Up on the balcony Old Claiborne's heart was opening and closing like a geisha's fan. He caught LaGrande's eye, smiled and waved, and, turning around, realized that Nailor was standing behind him.

"Morning, Mr. Claiborne," Nailor said, leaning politely across him to pick up the cup. "Looks like Mr. Leland's baby's having herself a hard time this morning. Let me bring you something nice to drink while you watch."

Claiborne sent him for coffee and settled back in the chair to watch LaGrande finish her off, thinking, as he often did lately, that he had outlived his time and his place. "I'm not suited for a holding action," he told himself, imagining the entire culture of the white Christian world to be stretched out on some sort of endless Maginot Line besieged by the children of the poor carrying portable radios and boxes of fried chicken.

Here Claiborne sat, on a beautiful spring morning, in good spirits, still breathing normally, his blood coursing through his veins on its admirable and accustomed journeys, and only a few minutes before he had been party to a violation of a code he had lived by all his life.

He sat there, sipping his tasteless coffee, listening to the Saturday lawn mowers starting up on the lawn of the Poydras Retirement Home, which took up the other half of the square block of prime New Orleans real estate on which the new clubhouse was built. It was a very exclusive old folks' home, with real antiques and Persian rugs and a board of directors made up of members of the New Orleans Junior League. Some of the nicest old people in New Orleans went there to die.

Claiborne had suffered through a series of terrible luncheons at the Poydras Home in an effort to get them to allow the tennis club to unlock one of the gates that separated the two properties. But no matter how the board of directors of the Lawn Tennis Club pleaded and bargained and implored, the board of directors of the Poydras Home stoutly refused to allow the tennis-club members to set foot on their lawn to retrieve the balls that flew over the fence. A ball lost to the Poydras Home was a ball gone forever.

The old-fashioned steel girders of the Huey P. Long Bridge hung languidly in the moist air. The sun beat down on the river. The low-hanging clouds pushed against each other in fat cosmic orgasms.

LaGrande stood on the bridge until the constellation of yellow balls was out of sight around a bend in the river. Then she drove to her house on Philip Street, changed clothes, got in the car, and began to drive aimlessly up and down Saint Charles Avenue, thinking of things to do with the rest of her life.

She decided to cheer herself up. She turned onto Carrollton Avenue and drove down to Gus Mayer.

She went in, found a saleslady, took up a large dressing room, and bought some cocktail dresses and some sun dresses and some summer skirts and blouses and some pink linen pants and a beige silk Calvin Klein evening jacket.

Then she went downstairs and bought some hose and some makeup and some perfume and some brassieres and some panties and a blue satin Christian Dior gown and robe.

She went into the shoe department and bought some Capezio sandals and some Bass loafers and some handmade espadrilles. She bought a red umbrella and a navy blue canvas handbag.

When she had bought one each of every single thing she could possibly imagine needing she felt better and went on out to the Country Club to see if anyone she liked to fuck was hanging around the pool.

Mother Coakley's Reform

BRENDAN GILL

Even in old age, Mother Coakley was as round and smooth-skinned as a ripe chestnut. In her billowing black habit, she had always the air of being about to be caught up in a gust of mountain wind and carried aloft to the sunny, well-scrubbed corner awaiting her in heaven. Despite the mother superior's hints of disapproval, hints which by anyone else would have been taken as commands, Mother Coakley enjoyed playing tennis with the younger convent girls. The tennis court was on the crest of a hill behind the ramshackle wooden buildings which made up the convent chapel and school; and what seemed in the North Carolina town below an agreeable summer breeze approached—on that dusty oblong of root-ribbed and rocky court—the force and temperature of a winter's gale. Luckily, Mother Coakley paid no attention to temperatures, hot or cold. Gathering the full skirts of her habit into her left hand, she scampered about the court like an energetic chipmunk, letting her veil float out behind her in ghostly disarray, and only just showing the tops of her high black shoes. She had learned to play tennis as a novice at the mother house in France, no one knew how many years ago, and she played it unexpectedly well. Like most people who learned the game in the nineteenth century, she felt no real interest in volleying. She was willing to lose point after point in order to attempt a smashing forehand drive, or to drop an occasional cut shot over the net; and when she had succeeded in doing so, the ball being unreturnable, Mother Coakley would drop her racquet and clap her hands in unaffected delight.

She had no use, in fact, for any of the effete mannerisms of latter-day tennis. If she failed to return an opponent's serve, she never called, "Good shot," but, screwing up her face into an expression of self-contempt, would announce sharply, "I should have had it! I should have had it!" As she played, her cheeks grew more and more deeply suffused with blood. Though she looked as if she might be about to suffer a stroke, she never heeded suggestions that it would be sensible to rest for a few minutes between sets. "I always get to look like this," she would say, panting heartily. The French neatness of speech taught her at the mother house in Dijon would then slur away to a soft Irish brogue. "Sure, I got to look like this when I was six." Also, as she continued to play, her rosary, carelessly stuffed inside her heavy black belt, would work itself loose and flail about her waist until finally, with tears of excitement streaming down her cheeks and wisps of clipped gray hair showing at the sides of her wimple, she would be forced to stop playing. "If I didn't stop now, I'd strangle myself on my own beads," she would say. "But for them, I'd be playing till dark."

She usually contrived, however, to retire from the game while she was still winning. This mild vanity was one of the two or three enormous sins with which she wrestled all but visibly from year to year. It was noted by the other nuns in the convent that Mother Coakley spent more than twice as much time in the confessional during the height of the tennis season as she did during the rest of the year. They never commented on this directly, but sometimes they would tease her, out of love and curiosity, as she left the chapel. "Goodness, you took a long time saying your penance," they would whisper, climbing the steep, worn stairs to their cells. "Father Nailer must have been in a dreadful temper by the time you reached him." Mother Coakley, who, after Mother Bonnet, was the oldest nun in age and point of service in the convent, would flush and answer, in a pretext of anger, "*Attendez!* What kind of talk is that? *Vous savez les règles!*"

Mother Bonnet preferred to remain at the convent, except when, as mother superior, she had official business to transact, and it was Mother Coakley's duty and joy to shepherd the girls of the school on their occasional visits to town. She was well acquainted in all the shops around the square. She helped the girls to choose gloves and girdles, and chaste perfumes, which she always referred to as "toilet water." The mother superior frowned on the use of perfumes and girdles, but Mother Coakley answered her objections by saying mildly, "God love them, we'll be lucky if that's all the harm they do with their money." During every such visit to town it was customary to drop in at Mr. Feinman's little combination cigar and sports shop on the square and pick up tennis or ping-pong balls, and to cap the afternoon by drinking chocolate frosteds at Fater's corner drugstore. Mother Coakley never ate or drank anything while in town, but she liked to purchase from Mrs. Fater, as unobtrusively as possible, a ten-cent Hershey bar, which she would slip into one of her capacious interior pockets. "Energy food," she would say, making her eyes round and bright. "When you get to be my age . . ."

Mother Coakley's age was one of the few secrets which she had been able to carry over from her girlhood outside the convent, but she must have been past seventy when the mother superior attempted to take a stand on the subject of her playing tennis. Mother Bonnet, who was as lean and slow moving as Mother Coakley was plump and bouncing, had never approved of the latter's athletic activities, and as the years went by it seemed to her less and less appropriate for one of Mother Coakley's age and position to be making of herself, as mother superior said, "a gross spectacle truly." She had been looking for an excuse to put an end to the display and the incident in Mr. Feinman's shop was more than enough, she felt, to justify speaking soberly to her.

One winter day, while Mother Bonnet was engaged in her annual skirmish with the tax collector in his office beside the courthouse, Mother Coakley and five or six of the girls spent a strenuous two hours shopping and walking about the town. The girls bought writing paper, cotton stockings, and some sensible, oversize sweaters, and enjoyed the usual chocolate frosteds at Fater's while Mother Coakley bought, and concealed on her person, the usual ten-cent Hershey bar. Having a few minutes to spare before rejoining Mother Bonnet, they decided to stop off at Mr. Feinman's. Though it was February, the midday sun was always bright and the tennis court was in no worse condition than it would be in June; Mother Coakley and the girls played nearly every afternoon, glorying in their indifference to the calendar. One of the girls had been planning for some time to buy a new racquet, but Mother Coakley and Mr. Feinman had yet to come to terms.

Today, welcoming them, Mr. Feinman swore that he had just what the doctor ordered. He brought out from the dusty shelves at the back of the store, where he kept piled in indiscriminate confusion cases of cigars and baseball mitts, a racquet called the Bluebird Special. "Sweetest little racquet I ever had in the place," Mr. Feinman said, blowing off the dust and hefting the racquet with professional care. Mr. Feinman had never played any game more taxing than pinochle, but he knew how to sell merchandise. He stroked the gut with his fingers. "Like music," he said. "With this racquet is easy wictory. Is steady wictory."

Mother Coakley enjoyed shopping. She particularly enjoyed haggling with her old friend Mr. Feinman. The girls formed an interested half circle about her as she took up the challenge, and a few of the inevitable courthouse loungers gathered at the open door of the shop. Mother Coakley swept this familiar audience with a glance, then, turning to Mr. Feinman, she asked simply, "How much?"

Mr. Feinman held up his hands as if to ward off the wounding mention of money. "For such a racquet? For workmanship like this?"

"How much?" Mother Coakley repeated.

Mr. Feinman consented, with a shrug, to discuss the sordid question. "Ten dollars."

Mother Coakley tapped her broad black belt, making the

wooden rosary beads rattle as if in reproach. "Nonsense," she said. When she bargained, she seemed purely French; even her voice took on the accents of Dijon in place of those of Dublin. "It isn't worth five."

Mr. Feinman appealed to the girls behind Mother Coakley and, by extension, to the crowd outside the door. "Five dollars! A work of art for five dollars!" He raised his eyes to the stamped tin ceiling over his head. "May God strike me dead if I didn't pay six dollars for it wholesale. I can—"

"Leave God out of this," Mother Coakley interrupted promptly. "What kind of pagan chatter is that?" She took the racquet from Mr. Feinman's hands and began to execute a few tentative strokes, cutting at and lobbing an imaginary ball. What happened next no one was able afterward to decide. Some people thought that Mr. Feinman had caught sight of the mother superior nearing the entrance to his store and had leaned forward to welcome her. Others thought that he had detected a price tag dangling from the end of the racquet and, being uncertain of what it said, had bent down to retrieve it. In any event, he lowered his head in time to receive, on his left temple, the full force of one of Mother Coakley's savage forehand drives. He dropped in his tracks like a sack of meal, without so much as a moan.

The girl who had intended to buy the racquet began to cry hysterically, "He did it! God did it! God did it!" Mother Coakley knelt beside the motionless figure of Mr. Feinman, her round cheeks looking oddly drawn and pale. "He's not dead," she said sharply, "he can't be. He's breathing. You can see he's breathing." She drew the Hershey bar from her pocket and, breaking off a piece, attempted to force it between Mr. Feinman's lips. At that moment he opened his eyes. In another moment he was on his knees. Slowly, painfully, he pulled himself up. "Is nothing," he said faintly. "Is just a tap."

Mother Coakley had barely begun her apology when another, deeper voice reached her over the heads of the crowd. "*Tais-toi,*" said the mother superior. "I am in charge here." She worked her way through the crowd, her habit rustling with authority. She stared first at Mr. Feinman, half crumpled against the counter, and then at Mother Coakley, still armed with the Bluebird Special. "The racquet," she said to Mr. Feinman. "One of the girls is buying this racquet?"

Mr. Feinman nodded.

"How much?"

With the air of a man who knows that it is useless to fight against the power of God, Mr. Feinman said brokenly, "Seven fifty. For a work of art, I will take seven fifty."

The mother superior, fresh from her annual triumph over the tax collector, said, "Very well." She set seven dollars and fifty cents on the counter. Then, turning to the girls, she made a gesture with her hands like that of a farmer's wife scattering hens. "Now, then, *dépêchons.*"

The little group was halfway across the square before the mother superior spoke to Mother Coakley. "You and your wretched tennis!" she said bluntly.

Mother Coakley nodded. "I have been thinking it over. I have come to feel that perhaps you are right." She pursed her lips. "Perhaps I am getting old."

"I have wanted you to make your own decision," said the

mother superior. She was always glad to be able to temper sternness with magnanimity. Besides, she and Mother Coakley were old friends, and it would be cruel to make her humble herself too far. "It is not that I am angry about this merely. Accidents can happen to anybody."

"No, it was my fault," Mother Coakley said, her voice softening to the brogue. She slipped a piece of the Hershey bar into her mouth. "I shall have to give up my forehand drive. You were right in thinking that I should have done so long ago." Then, despite her best efforts at self-control, her feet began to skip along the asphalt sidewalk. "From now on," she said penitently, "I shall play as badly as I can."

Return to Return

BARRY HANNAH

They used to call French Edward the happiest man on the court, and the prettiest. The crowds hated to see him beaten. Women anguished to conceive of his departure from a tournament. Once, when Edward lost a dreadfully long match at Forest Hills, an old man in the audience roared with sobs, then female voices joined his. It was like seeing the death of Mercutio or Hamlet going down with a resigned smile.

Dr. Levaster drove the Lincoln. It was rusty and the valves stuck. On the rear floorboard two rain pools sloshed, disturbing the mosquitoes that rode the beer cans. The other day Dr. Levaster became forty. His hair was thin, his eyes swollen beneath the sunglasses, his ears small and red. Yet he was not monstrous. He seemed, though, to have just retreated from conflict. The man with him was two years younger, curly passionate hair, face dashed with sun. His name was French Edward, the tennis pro.

A mosquito flew from one of the beer cans and bit French Edward before it was taken out by the draft. Edward became remarkably angry, slapping his neck, turning around in the seat, rising and peering down on the cans in the back, reaching over and smacking at them. Then he fell over the seat head-down into the puddles and clawed in the water. Dr. Levaster slowed the Lincoln and drove into the grass off the highway.

"Here now, here now! Moan, moan!" Dr. Levaster had given up profanity when he turned forty, formerly having been known as the filthiest-mouthed citizen of Louisiana or Mississippi. He opened the back door and dragged Edward out into the sedge. "You mule." He slapped Edward overvigorously, continuing beyond the therapeutic moment.

"He got me again . . . I thought. He. Doctor Word," said Edward.

"A bug. Mule, who do you think would be riding in the back of my car? How much do you have left, anything?"

"It's clear. A bug. It felt just like what he was doing."

"He's dead. Drowned."

"They never found him."

"He can't walk on water."

"I did."

"You just think you did." Dr. Levaster looked in the back seat. "One of your rackets is in the water, got wet. The strings are ruined."

"I'm all right," French Edward said.

"You'd better be. I'm not taking you one mile more if we don't get some clarity. Where are we?"

"Outside New York City."

"Where, more exactly?"

"New Jersey. The Garden State."

At his three-room place over the spaghetti store on Eighty-ninth, Baby Levaster, M.D., discovered teenagers living. He knew two of them. They had broken in the door but had otherwise respected his quarters, washed the dishes, swept, even revived his house plants. They were diligent little street people. They claimed they knew by intuition he was coming back to the city and wanted to clean up for him. Two of them thought they might have gonorrhea. Dr. Levaster got his bag and jabbed ten million units of penicillin in them. Then French Edward came up the stairs with the baggage and rackets and went to the back.

"Dear God! He's, oh. Oh, he looks like *love!*" said Carina. She wore steep-heeled sandals and clocked about nineteen on the age scale. The others hung back, her friends. Levaster knew her well. She had shared his sheets, and, in nightmares of remorse, he had shared her body, waking with drastic regret, feeling as soiled and soilsome as the city itself.

"Are you still the mind, him the body?" Carina asked.

"Now more than ever. I'd say he now has about an eighth of the head he was given," Levaster said.

"What happened?"

"He drowned. And then he lived," Levaster said.

"Well, he looks happy."

"I am happy," said French Edward, coming back to the room. "Whose thing is this? You children break in Baby's apartment and, not only that, you carry firearms. I don't like any kind of gun. Who are these hoodlums you're talking to, Baby?" Edward was carrying a double-barreled .410 shotgun/

pistol; the handle was of cherrywood and silver vines embossed the length of the barrels.

"I'll take that," said Dr. Levaster, since it was his. It was his Central Park nighttime gun. The shells that went with it were loaded with popcorn. He ran the teenagers out of his apartment, and when he returned, Edward was asleep on the couch, the sweet peace of the athlete beaming through his twisted curls.

"I've never slept like that," Levaster said to Carina, who had remained. "Nor will I ever."

"I saw him on TV once. It was a match in Boston, I think. I didn't care a rat's prick about tennis. But when I saw him, that face and in his shorts, wow. I told everybody to come here and watch this man."

"He won that one," Dr. Levaster said.

Levaster and Carina took a cab to Central Park. It was raining, which gave a congruous fashion to Levaster's raincoat, wherein, at the left breast pocket, the shotgun/pistol hung in a cunning leather holster. Levaster swooned in the close nostalgia of the city. Everything was so exquisitely true and forthright. Not only was the vicious city there, but he, a meddlesome worthless loud failure from Vicksburg, was jammed amok in the viciousness himself, a willing lout in a nightmare. He stroked Carina's thigh, rather enjoying her distaste.

They entered the park under a light broken by vandals. She came close to him near the dark hedges. What with the inconsequential introversion of his youth, in which he had not honed any skill but only squatted in derision of everything in Vicksburg, Levaster had missed the Southern hunting experience. This was more sporting, bait for muggers. They might have their own pistols, etc. He signaled Carina to lie on the grass and make with her act.

"Oh, I'm coming, I'm coming! And I'm so rich, rich, rich! Only money could make me come like this!"

The rain had stopped and a moon was pouring through the leaves. Two stout bums, one with a beer can opened in his hand, circled out of the bush and edged in on Carina. The armed bum made a threatening jab. In a small tenor voice, Levaster protested.

"Please! We're only visitors here! Don't take our money! Don't tell my wife!" They came toward Levaster, who was speaking. "Do you fellows know Jesus? The Prince of Peace?" When they were six feet away, he shot them both in the thigh, whimpering, "Glory be! Sorry! Goodness. Oh, wasn't that *loud!*"

After the accosters had stumbled away, astounded at being alive, Levaster sank into the usual fit of contrition. He removed his sunglasses. He seemed racked by the advantage of new vision. It was the first natural light he had seen since leaving French Edward's house in Covington, across the bridge from New Orleans.

They took a cab back and passed by French Edward, asleep again. He had taken off his trousers and shirt, appeared to have shucked them off in the wild impatience of his sleep, like an infant, and the lithe clusters of his muscles rose and fell with his breathing. Carina sat on the bed with Levaster.

He removed his raincoat and everything else. Over his spreadcollar shirt was printed a sort of Confederate flag as drawn by a three-year-old with a sludge brush. Levaster wore it to Elaine's to provoke fights but was ignored and never even got to buy a writer or actor a drink. Undressed, it was seen how oversized his head was and how foolishly outsized his sex, hanging large and purple, a slain ogre. Undressed, Levaster seemed more like a mutinous gland than a whole male figure. He jumped up and down on his bed, using it for a trampoline. Carina was appalled.

"I'm the worst, the awfulest!" he said. Carina gathered her bag and edged to the door. She said she was leaving. As he bounced on the bed, he saw her kneeling next to the couch with her hand on Edward's wrist. "Hands off!" Levaster screamed. "No body without the mind! Besides, he's married. A New Orleans woman wears his ring!" Jump, jump! "She makes you look like a chimney sweep. You chimney sweep!" Levaster bounced as Carina left.

He fell on the bed and moiled two minutes before going into black sleep. He dreamed. He dreamed about his own estranged wife, a crazy in Arizona who sent him photographs of herself with her hair cut shorter in every picture. She had a crew cut and was riding a horse out front of a cactus field in the last one. She thought hair interfered with rationality. Now she was happy, having become ugly as a rock. Levaster did not dream about himself and French Edward, although the dream lay on him like the bricks of an hysterical mansion.

In high school, Baby Levaster was the best tennis player. He was small but devious and could run and get the ball like a terrier. Dr. Word coached the college team. Dr. Word was a professor of botany and was suspected as the town queer. Word drew up close to the boys, holding them to show them the full backhand and forehand of tennis, snuggled up to their bodies and worked them like puppets as large as he was.

Rumorers said Dr. Word got a thrill from the rear closeness to his players. But his team won the regional championship.

Dr. Word tried to coach Baby Levaster, but Levaster resisted being touched and handled like a big puppet and had heard Word was a queer. What he had heard was true—until a few months before French Edward came onto the courts.

Dr. Word first saw French Edward in a junior-high football game; the boy moved like a genius, finding all the openings, sprinting away from all the other boys on the field. French was the quarterback. He ran for a touchdown nearly every time the ball was centered to him, whenever the play was busted. The only thing that held him back was passing and handing off. Otherwise, he scored, or almost did. An absurd clutter of bodies would be gnashing behind him on the field. It was then that Dr. Word saw French's mother, Olive, sitting in the bleachers, looking calm, auburn-haired and handsome. From then on Dr. Word was queer no more. Mrs. Edward was a secretary for the P. E. department, and Dr. Word was baldheaded and virile, suave with the grace of his Ph.D. from Michigan State, obtained years ago but still appropriating him some charm as an exotic scholar. Three weeks of tender words and French's mother was his, in any shadow of Word's choosing.

Curious and flaming like a pubescent, he caressed her on back roads and in the darkened basement of the gym, their trysts protected by his repute as a queer or, at the outside, an oyster. Her husband—a man turned lopsided and cycloptic by sports mania—never discovered them. It was her son, French Edward, who did, walking into his own home wearing sneakers and thus unheard—and unwitting—to discover them coiled infamously. Mr. Edward was away as an uninvited delegate to a rules-review board meeting of the Southeastern Conference in Mobile. French was not seen. He crawled under the bed of his room and slept so as to gather the episode into a dream that would vanish when he awoke. What he dreamed was exactly what he had just seen, with the addition that he was present in her room, practicing his strokes with ball and racket, using a great mirror as a backboard, while on the bed his mother and this man groaned in approval, a monstrous twin-headed nude spectator.

Because by that time Word had taken French Edward over and made him quite a tennis player. French could beat Baby Levaster and all the college aces. At eighteen, he was a large angel-bodied tyrant of the court, who drove tennis balls through, outside, beyond and over the reach of any challenger Dr. Word could dig up. The only one who could give French Edward a match was Word himself, who was sixty and could run and knew the few faults French had, such as disbelieving Dr. Word could keep racing after the balls and knocking them back, French then knocking the odd ball ten feet out of court in an expression of sheer wonder. Furthermore, French had a tendency to soft-serve players he disliked, perhaps an unthinking gesture of derision or perhaps a self-inflicted handicap, to punish himself for ill will. For French's love of the game was so intense he did not want it fouled by personal uglinesses. He had never liked Dr. Word, even as he learned from him. He had never liked Word's closeness, nor his manufactured British or Boston accent, nor the zeal of his interest in him, which French supposed surpassed that of mere coach. For instance, Dr. Word would every now and then give French Edward a *pinch,* a hard, affectionate little nip of the fingers.

And now French Edward was swollen with hatred of the man, the degree of which had no name. It was expelled on the second day of August, hottest day of the year. He called up Word for a match. Not practice, French said. A match. Dr. Word would have played with him in the rain. At the net, he pinched French as they took the balls out of the can. French knocked his hand away and lost games deliberately to keep the match going. Word glowed with a perilous self-congratulation for staying in there; French had fooled Word into thinking he was playing even with him. French pretended to fail in the heat, knocking slow balls from corner to corner, easing over a drop shot to watch the old man ramble up for it. French himself was tiring in the disguise of his ruse when the old devil keeled over, falling out in the alley with his racket clattering away. Dr. Word did not move, though the concrete must have been burning him. French had hoped for a heart attack. Word mumbled that he was cold and couldn't see anything. He asked French to get help.

"No. Buck up. Run it out. Nothing wrong with you," said French.

"Is that you, French, my son?"

"I ain't your son. You might treat my mother like I was, but I ain't. I saw you."

"A doctor. Out of the cold. I need medical help," Dr. Word said.

"I got another idea. Why don't you kick the bucket?"

"Help."

"Go on. Die. It's easy."

When French got home, he discovered his mother escaping the heat in a tub of cold water. Their house was an unprosperous and unlevel connection of boxes. No door of any room shut properly. He heard her sloshing the water on herself. His father was up at Dick Lee's grocery watching the Cardinals on the television. French walked in on her. Her body lay underwater up to her neck.

"Your romance has been terminated," he said.

"French?" She grabbed a towel off the rack and pulled it in the water over her.

"He's blind. He can't even find his way to the house anymore."

"This was a sin, you to look at me!" Mrs. Edward cried.

"Maybe so," French said, "but I've looked before, when you had company."

French left home for Baton Rouge, on the bounty of the scholarship Dr. Word had hustled for him through the athletic department at Louisiana State. French swore never to return. His father was a fool, his mother a lewd traitor, his mentor a snake from the blind side, the river a brown ditch of bile, his town a hill range of ashes and gloomy souvenirs of the Great Moment in Vicksburg. His days at college were numbered. Like that of most natural athletes, half French Edward's mind was taken over by a sort of tidal barbarous desert where men ran and struggled, grappling, hitting, cursing as some fell into the sands of defeat. The only professor he liked was one who spoke of "muscular thought." The professor said he was sick and tired of thought that sat on its ass and vapored around the room for the benefit of limp-wrists and their whiskey.

As for Dr. Word, he stumbled from clinic to clinic, guided by his brother Wilbur, veteran of Korea and colossal military boredoms all over the globe, before resettling in Vicksburg on the avant-garde of ennui.

Baby Levaster saw the pair in Charity Hospital when he was a med student at Tulane. Word's arm was still curled up with stroke and he had only a sort of quarter vision in one eye. His voice was frightful, like that of a man in a cave of wasps. Levaster was stunned by seeing Dr. Word in New Orleans. He hid in a closet, but Word had already recognized him. Brother Wilbur flung the door open, illuminating Levaster demurring under a bale of puke sheets.

"Our boy won the Southern!" shouted Word. "He's the real thing, more than I ever thought!"

"Who are you talking about?" said Baby Levaster. The volume of the man had blown Levaster's eyebrows out of order.

"Well, French! French Edward! He won the Southern tournament in Mobile!"

Levaster looked to Wilbur for some mediator in this loudness. Wilbur cut away to the water fountain. He acted deaf.

"And the Davis Cup!" Word screamed. "He held up America in the Davis Cup! Don't you read the papers? Then he went to Wimbledon!"

"French went to Wimbledon?"

"Yes! Made the quarterfinals!" A nurse and a man in white came up to crush the noise from Word. Levaster went back into the closet and shut the door. Then he peeped out, seeing Word and his brother small in the corridor, Word limping slightly to the left, proceeding with a roll and capitulation. The stroke had wrecked him from brain to ankles, had fouled the centers that prevent screaming. Levaster heard Word bleating a quarter mile down the corridor.

Baby Levaster read in the *Times-Picayune* that French was resident pro at the Metairie Club, that French was representing the club in a tournament. Levaster hated med school. He hated the sight of pain and blood, and by this time he had become a thin, weak, balding drunkard of a very disagreeable order, even to himself. He dragged himself from one peak of cowardice to the next and began wearing sunglasses, and when he saw French Edward fend off Aussie, Wop, Frog, Brit and Hun in defending the pride of the Metairie Club, Levaster's body left him and was gathered into the body of French. He had never seen anything so handsome as French Edward. He had never before witnessed a man as happy and winsome in his occupation. Edward moved as if certain animal secrets were known to him. He originated a new, dangerous tennis, taking the ball into his racket with a muscular patience; then one heard the sweet crack, heard the singing ball, and hung cold with a little terror at the speed and the smart violent arc it made into the green. French was by then wearing spectacles. His coiled hair, the color of a kind of charred gold, blazed with sweat. On his lips was the charmed smile of the seraphim. Something of the priest and the brute mingled, perhaps warred, in his expression. Baby Levaster, who had no culture, could not place the line of beauty that French Edward descended from, but finally remembered a photograph of the David statue he'd seen in an old encyclopedia. French Edward looked like that.

When French Edward won, Levaster heard a louder, baleful, unclublike bravo from the gallery. It was Dr. Word. Levaster watched Word fight through the crowd toward French. The man was crazed with partisanship. Levaster, wanting to get close to the person of French himself, three-quarters drunk on gin he'd poured into the iced Cokes from the stand, saw Word reach for French's buttock and give it a pinch. French turned, hate in his eye. He said something quick and corrosive to Word. All the smiles around them turned to straight mouths of concern. Dr. Word looked harmless, a tanned old fellow wearing a beige beret.

"You ought to be dead," said French.

"As graceful, powerful an exhibition of the grandest game as your old coach would ever hope to see! I saw some of the old tricks I taught you! Oh, son, son!" Dr. Word screamed.

Everyone knew he was ill then.

"Go home," said French, looking very soon sorry as he said it.

"You come home and see us!" Word bellowed, and left.

French's woman, Cecilia Emile, put her head on his chest. She was short, bosomy and pregnant, a Franco-Italian blessed with a fine large nose, the arrogance of which few men forgot. Next came her hair, a black field of delight. French had found her at LSU. They married almost on the spot. Her father was Fat Tim Emile, a low-key monopolist in pinball and wrestling concessions in New Orleans—filthy rich. Levaster did not know this. He stared at the strained hot eyes of French, having surrendered his body to the man, and French saw him.

"Baby Levaster? Is it you? From Vicksburg? You look terrible."

"But you, you . . ." Levaster tripped on a tape and fell into the green clay around Edward's sneakers. ". . . are beauty . . . my youth memory elegant, forever!"

The Edwards took Levaster home to Covington, across the bridge. The Edwards lived in a great glassy house with a pool in back and tall pines hanging over.

French was sad. He said, "She still carries it on with him. They meet out in the Civil War park at night and go to it in those marble houses. One of my old high-school sweethearts saw them and wrote me about it. She wrote it to hurt me, and it did hurt me."

"That old fart Word? Impossible. He's too goddamn loud to carry on any secret rendezvous, for one thing. You could hear the bastard sigh from a half mile off."

"My mother accepts him for what he is."

"That man is destroyed by stroke."

"I know. I gave it to him. She doesn't care. She takes the

limping and the bad arm and the hollering. He got under her skin."

"I remember her," Baby Levaster said. "Some handsome woman, auburn hair with a few gray ends. Forgive me, but I had teenage dreams about her myself. I always thought she was waiting for a romance, living on the hope of something out there, something...."

"Don't leave me, Baby. I need your mind with me. Somebody from the hometown. Somebody who knows."

"I used to whip your little ass at tennis," Levaster said.

"Yes." French smiled. "You barely moved and I was running all over the court. You just stood there and knocked them everywhere like I was hitting into a fan."

They became fast friends. Baby Levaster became an intern. He arrived sober at the funeral of the Edwards' newborn son and saw the tiny black grave its coffin went into behind the Catholic chapel. He looked over to mourners at the fringe. There were Dr. Word and his brother Wilbur under a mimosa, lingering off fifty feet from the rest. Word held his beret to his heart. Levaster was very glad that French never saw Word. They all heard a loud voice, but Word was on the other side of the hill by then, bellowing his sympathetic distress to Wilbur, and the Edwards could not see him.

"Whose voice was that?" asked French.

"Just a voice," said Levaster.

"Whose? Don't I know it? It makes me sick." French turned back to Cecilia, covered with a black veil, her handkerchief pressed to lips. Her child had been born with dysfunction of the involuntary muscles. Her eyes rose toward the hot null blue of the sky. French supported her. His gaze was angrier. It penetrated the careless heart of nature, right in there to its sullen root.

On the other side of the cemetery, Dr. Word closed the door of the car. Wilbur drove. Loyal to his brother to the end, almost deaf from the pitch of his voice, Wilbur wheeled the car with veteran patience. Dr. Word wiped his head and held the beret to his chest.

"Ah, Wilbur! They were so unlucky! Nowhere could there be a handsomer couple! They had every right to expect a little Odysseus! Ah, to see doubt and sorrow cloud the faces of those young lovers! Bereft of hope, philosophy!"

Wilbur reached under the seat for the pint of philosophy he had developed since his tour of Korea. It was cognac. The brotherly high music came, tasting of burnt plums, revealing the faces of old officer friends to him.

"James," he said. "I think after this . . . that this is the moment, now, to break it off with Olive—forever. Unless you want to see more doubt and sorrow cloud the face of your young friend."

Word's reply was curiously quiet.

"We cannot do what we cannot do. If she will not end it—and she will not—I cannot. Too deep a sense of joy, Wilbur. The whole quality of my life determined by it."

"Ah, Jimmy," Wilbur said, "you were just too long a queer. The first piece you found had to be permanent. She ain't Cleopatra. If you'd just've started early, nailing the odd twat like the rest of us . . ."

"I don't want old soldier's reason! No reason! I will not suffer that contamination! Though I love you!"

Dr. Word was hollering again. Wilbur drove them back to Vicksburg.

Cecilia was too frightened to have another child after she lost the first one. Her body would not carry one longer than a month. She was constantly pregnant for a while, and then she stopped conceiving. She began doing watercolors, the faintest violets and greens. French Edward took up the clarinet. Baby Levaster saw it: they were attempting to become art people. Cecilia was pitiful. French went beyond that into dreadfulness; ruesome honks poured from his horn. How wrong and unfortunate that they should have taken their grief into art, thought Levaster. It made them fools who were cut from glory's cloth, who were charmed darlings of the sun.

"What do you think?" asked French, after he'd hacked a little ditty from Mozart into a hundred froggish leavings.

"Yes," Dr. Levaster said. "I think I'll look through some of Cissy's pictures now."

"You didn't like it," French said, downcast, even angry.

"When are you going to get into another tournament? Why sit around here revealing your scabs to me and the neighbors? You need to get out and hit the ball."

French left, walked out, smoldering and spiteful. Baby Levaster remained there. He knocked on Cecilia's door. She was at her spattered art desk working over a watercolor, her bare back to Levaster, her hair lying thick to the small of it, and below, her naked heels. Her efforts were thumbtacked around from ceiling to molding, arresting one with their meek, awkward redundancies, things so demure they resisted making an image against the retina. They were not even clouds; rather, the pale ghosts of clouds: the advent of stains, hardly noticeable against paper.

"I can't turn around but hello," said Cecilia.

"What are all these about?"

"What do you think?"

"I don't know . . . smudges? The vagueness of all things?"

"They aren't things. They're emotions."

"You mean hate, fear, desire, envy?"

"Yes. And triumph and despair." She pointed.

"This is subtle. They look the same," Levaster said.

"I know. I'm a nihilist."

"You aren't any such thing."

"Oh? Why not?"

"Because you've combed your hair. You wanted me to come in here and discover that you're a nihilist," Levaster said.

"Nihilists can comb their hair." She bit her lip, pouting.

"I'd like to see your chest. That's art."

"You toilet. Leave us alone."

"Maybe if you *are* art, Cissy, you shouldn't try to *do* art."

"You want me to be just a decoration?"

"Yes," Levaster said. "A decoration of the air. Decoration is more important than art."

"Is that what you learned in med school? That's dumb."
She turned around. "A boob is a boob is a boob."

Dr. Levaster fainted.

At the River Oaks Club in Houston, French played again.
The old happiness came back to him, a delight that seemed to
feed off his grace. The sunburned Levaster held French's towel
for him, rosined French's racket handles, and coached him on
the weaknesses of the opponents, which is unsportsmanly, un-
tennislike, and all but illegal. A Spaniard Edward was cream-
ing complained, and they threw Levaster off the court and back
to the stands. He watched French work the court, roving back
and forth, touching the ball with a deft chip, knocking the
cooties off it, serving as if firing a curved musket across the
net, the Spaniard falling distraught. And throughout, French's
smile, widening and widening until it was just this side of
loony. Here was a man truly at play, thought Levaster, at one
with the pleasant rectangle of the court, at home, in his own
field, something *peaceful* in the violent sweep of his racket. A
certain slow anomalous serenity invested French Edward's
motion. The thought of this parched Levaster.

"Christ, for a drink!" he said out loud.

"Here, son. Cold brandy." The man Levaster sat next to
brought out a pint from the ice in a Styrofoam box. Levaster
chugged it— exquisite!—then almost spat up the boon as he
noticed the fellow on the far side of the brandy man. It was
Dr. Word. The man beside Levaster was Wilbur. Word's noble
cranium glinted under the sun. His voice had modulated.

"Ah, ah, my boy! An arc of genius," Word whispered as they saw French lay a disguised lob thirty feet from the Spaniard. "He's learned the lob, Wilbur! Our boy has it all now!" Word's voice went on in soft screaming. He seemed to be seeing keenly out of the left eye. The right was covered by eyelid, the muscles there having finally surrendered. So, Levaster thought, this is what the stroke finally left him.

"How's Vicksburg?" Levaster asked Wilbur.

"Nothing explosive, Doctor. Kudzu and the usual erosion."

"What say you try to keep Professor Word away from French until he does his bit in the tournament. A lot depends on his making the finals here."

"I'm afraid the professor's carrying a letter on him from Olive to French. That's why he's not hollering. He's got the letter. It's supposed to say everything."

"But don't let French see him till it's over. And could I hit the brandy again?" Levaster said.

"Of course," said Wilbur. "One man can't drink the amount I brought over. Tennis bores the shit out of me."

In the finals, Edward met Whitney Humble, a tall man from South Africa whose image and manner refuted the usual notion of the tennis star. He was pale, spindly, hairy, with the posture of a derelict. He spat phlegm on the court and picked his nose between serves. Humble appeared to be splitting the contest between one against his opponent and another against the excrescence of his own person. Some in the gallery suspected he served a wet ball. Playing as if with exasperated distaste for the next movement this game had dragged him to, Humble was nevertheless there when the ball came and knocked everything back with either speed or a snarling spin.

The voice of Dr. Word came cheering, bellowing for French. Humble identified the bald head in the audience that had hurrahed his error at the net. He served a fine drive into the gallery that hit Word square in his good eye.

"Fault!" cried the judge. The crowd was horrified.

Humble placed his high-crawling second serve to French.

Levaster saw little of the remaining match. Under the bleachers, where they had dragged Word, Levaster and Wilbur attended to the great black peach that was growing around Word's good eye. With ice and a handkerchief, they abated the swelling, and then all three men returned to their seats. Dr. Word could see out of a black slit of his optic cavity, see French win in a sequel of preposterous dives at the net. Levaster's body fled away from his bones and gathered on the muscles of French Edward. The crowd was screaming over the victory. Nowhere, nowhere, would they ever see again such a clear win of beauty over smut.

Fat Tim, Cecilia's father, would be happy and put five thousand in French's bank if French won this tournament, and Fat Tim would pay Levaster one thousand, as promised, for getting French back on the track of fame. Fat Tim Emile, thumbing those greasy accounts of his concessions, saw French as the family knight, a jouster among grandees, a champion in the whitest sport of all, a game Fat Tim viewed as a species of cunning highbrowism under glass. So he paid French simply for being himself, for wearing white, for symbolizing the pedigree Fat Tim was without, being himself a sweaty dago, a tubby with smudged shirt cuffs and phlebitis. "Get our boy back winning. I want to read his name in the paper," said Fat Tim.

"I will," said Levaster.

So I did, thought Levaster. French won.

Dr. Levaster saw Dr. Word crowding up, getting swarmed out to the side by all the little club bitches and fuzzchins with programs for autographing in hand. Word fought back in, however, approaching French from the back. Levaster saw Word pinch French and heard Word bellow something hearty. By the time Levaster reached the court, the altercation had spread through the crowd. A letter lay in the clay dust, and Word, holding up his hand to ameliorate, was backing out of sight, his good eye but a glint in a cracked bruise, the lid falling gruesome.

"Baby! Baby!" called French, the voice baffled. Levaster reached him. "He pinched me!" French screamed. "He got me right there, really hard!"

Levaster picked up the letter and collected the rackets, then led French straight to the car. No shower, no street clothes.

My Dearest French,

This is your mother Olive writing in case you have forgotten what my handwriting looks like. You have lost your baby son and I have thought of you these months. Now I ask you to think of me. I lost my grown son years ago. You know when, and you know the sin which is old history. I do not want to lose you, my darling. You are such a strange hand-somely made boy I would forget you were mine until I remembered you fed at my breast and I changed your diapers. When I saw you wearing new glasses at your wedding if I looked funny it was because I wanted to touch your eyes under them they changed you even more. But I knew you didn't want me anywhere near you. Your bride Cissy was charming as well as stunning and I'm deeply glad her father is well-off and you don't have to work for a living if you don't want to. Your father tried to play for a living or get near where there was athletics but it didn't work as smoothly for him. It drove him crazy, to be truthful. He was lost for a week in February until James Word, the bearer of this letter, found him at the college baseball field throwing an old wet football at home plate. He had been sleeping in the dugout and eating nothing but these dextrose and salt tablets. I didn't write you this before because you were being an expectant father and then the loss of your child. Maybe you get all your sports drive from your father. But you see how awfully difficult it was to live with him? Certain other things have happened before, I never told you about. He refereed a high-school football game between Natchez and Vicksburg and when it was tight at the end he threw a block on a Natchez player. We love him, French, but he has been away from us a long time.

So I fell in love with James Word. Don't worry,

your father still knows nothing. That is sort of proof where his mind is, in a way. Your father has not even wanted "relations" with me in years. He said he was saving himself up. He was in a poker game with some coaches at the college but they threw him out for cheating. James tried to arrange a tennis doubles game with me and your father against another couple, but your father tried to hit it so hard when it came to him that he knocked them over into the service station and etc. so we had no more balls.

The reason I sent this by James is because I thought if it was right from his hand you would see that it was not just a nasty slipping-around thing between us but a thing of the heart. His stroke has left him blind in one eye and without sure control of his voice. But he loves you. And he loves me. I believe God is with us too. Please take us all together and let's smile again. I am crying as I write this. But maybe that's not fair to mention that. James has mentioned taking us all, your father included, on a vacation to Padre Island in Texas, him paying all the expenses. Can't you please say yes and make everything happy?

Love,
Mother

"It was his fingers pinching me," whined French. "He pinched me all the time when he was coaching me."

Levaster said, "And if he hadn't coached you, you wouldn't be anything at all, would you? You'd be selling storm fencing in Vicksburg, wouldn't you? You'd never have pumped that snatch or had the swimming pool."

Back at his clinic, Levaster slept on a plastic couch in the waiting room. The nurse woke him up. He was so lonely and horny that he proposed to her, though he'd never had a clear picture of her face. Months ago he'd called her into his office. He'd had an erection for four days without rest.

"Can you make anything of this, Louise? Get the *Merck Manual.* Severe hardship even to walk." She had been charming. But when he moved to her leg, clasping on it like a spaniel on the hot, she denied him, and he had since considered her a woman of principle.

She accepted his proposal. They married. Her parents, strong Methodists living somewhere out in New Mexico, appeared at the wedding. They stood in a corner, leaning inward like a pair of sculling oars. Levaster's mother came too, talking about the weather and her new shoes. Someone mistook her for nothing in one of the chairs and sat on her lap. French was best man. Cecilia was there, a dress of lime sherbet and titties, black hair laid back with gemlike roses at the temples. She made Levaster's bride look like something dumped out of a ship, a swathed burial at sea. Cecilia's beauty was unfair to all women. Furthermore, Levaster himself, compared to French (nugget-cheeked in a tux), was no beau of the ball. He was balding, waxen, all sweat, a small man with bad posture to boot.

Levaster expected to lean on the tough inner goodness of his bride, Louise. He wanted his life bathed and rectified.

They resumed their life as doctor and nurse at the alley clinic, where Levaster undercharged the bums, winos, hustlers, hookers, artists and the occasional wayward debutante, becoming something of an expert on pneumonia, herpes, potassium famine and other diseases of the street. He leaned on the tough inner goodness of Louise, leaning and leaning, prone, supine, baby-opossum position. Levaster played tennis, he swam in the Edwards' pool, he stuck to beer and wine. In the last whole surge of his life, he won a set from French at the Metairie Club. This act caused Dr. Levaster a hernia and a frightful depletion of something untold in his cells, the rare *it* of life, the balm that washes and assures the brain happiness is around the corner. Levaster lost this sense for three months. He became a creature of the barbarous moment; he had lost patience. Now he cursed his patients and treated them as malingering clutter. He drank straight from a flask of rye laced with cocaine, swearing to the sick about the abominations they had wreaked on themselves. At nights Levaster wore an oversized black sombrero and forced Louise into awkward and nameless desecrations. And when they were over, he called her an idiot, a puppet. Then one morning the hopeful clarity of the mind returned to him. He believed again in sun and grass and the affable complicity of the human race. But where was his wife? He wanted to lean on her inner goodness some more. Her plain face, her fine muscular pale legs, where were they? Louise was gone. She had typed a note. "One more week of this and you'd have taken us to the bottom of hell. I used to be a weak but good person. Now I am strong and evil. I hope you're satisfied. Good-bye."

At the clinic, his patients were afraid of him. The freeloaders and gutter cowboys shuddered. What will it be, Doc? "French. It was French Edward who . . . took it away from me. It cost me. I suppose I wanted to defeat beauty, the outrage of the natural, the glibness of the God-favored. All in that one set of tennis. Ladies and gentlemen, the physician has been sick and he apologizes." He coughed, dry in the throat. "It cost me my wife, but I am open for business." They swarmed him with the astounded love of sinners for a fallen angel. Levaster was nursed by whores. A rummy with a crutch fetched him coffee. Something, someone, in a sputumcolored blanket, functioned as receptionist.

At last he was home. He lived in a room of the clinic. On his thirty-fourth birthday, they almost killed him with a party and congratulations. The Edwards came. Early in the morning French found Levaster gasping over his fifth Cuban cigar on the roof of the clinic. The sky over New Orleans was a glorious blank pink.

"We're getting older, Baby."

"You're still all right, French. You had all the moves at Forest Hills. Some bad luck, three bad calls. But still the crowd's darling. You could've beat Jesus at Wimbledon."

"I always liked to play better than to win," said French.

"I always liked to win better than to play," said Levaster.

"But, Baby, I never played. First it was my father, then Word. I don't know what kind of player I would be like if I truly *played* when I play."

"But you smile when you play."

"I love the game, on theory. And I admire myself."

"You fool a lot of people. We thought you were happy."

"I am. I feel like I'm doing something nearly as well as it could ever be done. But it's not play. It's slavery."

"A slave to your talent."

"And to the idea of tennis. But, Baby, when I die I don't want my last thought to be a tennis court. You've got people you've cured of disease to think about. They're down there giving you a party. Here I am, thirty-two."

"I'm thirty-four. So what?"

"I want you to tell me, give me something to think about. You've done it before, but I want something big." French pointed to the sky.

"I won't do that. Don't you understand that the main reason you're a star is the perfect mental desert you're able to maintain between your ears for hours and hours? You memorize the court and the memory sinks straight to your muscles, because there is nothing else in there to cloud the vision."

"Are you calling me stupid?"

"No. But a wild psychic desert. I'm sure it works for artists as well as jocks."

"You mean," said French, "I can't have a thought?"

"You could have one, but it wouldn't live for very long. Like most athletes, you'll go straight from glory to senility with no interlude of thought. I love you," Levaster said.

French said, "I love you, Baby."

Dr. Levaster could no longer bear the flood of respect and affection spilling from the growing horde at the clinic. The

Times-Picayune had an article about his work among the down-and-out. It was as if Levaster had to eat a tremendous barge of candy every day. The affection and esteem bore hard on a man convinced he was worthless. He had a hundred thousand in the bank. No longer could he resist. He bought a Lincoln demonstrator, shut the clinic, and drove to New York, carrying the double-barreled .410 shotgun/pistol with cherry-wood handle paid to him in lieu of fee. He sifted into Elaine's, drunk, Southern and insulting, but was ignored. By the time Levaster had been directed to a sullen playwright, some target frailer than he, on whom he could pour the black beaker of his hatred of art, the movement of the crowd would change and Levaster would be swept away to a group of new enemies. Idlers, armchairers, martini wags, curators of the great empty museums (themselves), he called them. Not one of them could hold a candle to Willum Faulkner, Levaster shouted, having never read a page of the man. He drove his Lincoln everywhere, reveling in the hate and avarice of the city, disappearing into it with a shout of ecstasy.

Then Dr. Levaster met V.T., the Yugoslav sensation, drinking a beer at Elaine's with a noted sportswriter. Forest Hills was to begin the next day. Levaster approved of V.T. Heroic bitterness informed V.T.'s face and he dressed in bad taste, a suit with padded shoulders, narrow tie, pointy shoes.

"Who did you draw first round?" asked Levaster.

"Freench Edwaird," V.T. said.

"Edward won't get around your serve if you're hitting it," said the sportswriter. V.T.'s serve had been clocked at 170 mph at Wimbledon.

"Ees always who find the beeg rhythm. You find the beeg rhythm or you play on luck."

"If you beat Edward tomorrow," Levaster said, "I will eat your suit."

But the two men had turned away and never heard.

He took the Lincoln out to the West Side Tennis Club and tore his sweater clambering over a fence. He slept in a blanket he had brought with him, out of the dew, under the bleachers. When morning came, Levaster found the right court. The grass was sparkling. It was a heavy minor classic in the realm of tennis. The crowd loved French Edward and V.T., the both of them. When Edward hit one from behind the back for a winner off an unseen overhead smash from V.T., the crowd screamed. V.T. was in his rhythm and knocking his serve in at 160 mph. The crowd adored this too. French, who had always had a big, very adequate serve, took up the velocity of it to match the great bullet of V.T. At the end, they were men fielding nothing but white blurs against each other. Edward won.

For a half second the crowd was quiet. They had never imagined the ball could be kept in play at such stupendous speed. Then they roared. French Edward leaped over the net. Levaster swooned. His head sailed and joined the head of French Edward, rolled and tossed in the ale-colored curls. Then Levaster saw Dr. Word run out onto the grass, his bellowing lost in the crowd's bellowing. The old man, whose beret had fallen off on the churned service court, put his hand on French's back. Word looked frail, liver spots on his forearms, his scalp speckled and lined. Levaster saw French turn in anger. Then the both of them were overrun by a whirlpool of well-groomed tennis children and mothers and men who rode trains to work, half of their mental life revolving around improvement of the backhand. Levaster wished for his elegant pistol. He left, picking fights with those who looked askance at his blanket.

A few years passed and Levaster was almost forty. He opened the clinic in New Orleans again. Then he closed it and returned to New York. Now Levaster admitted that he languished when French Edward was out of his vision. A hollow inconsequence filled his acts, good or evil, whenever Edward was not near. He flew with Edward to France, to Madrid, to Prague. He lay angry and mordant with hangover on hotel beds as French Edward worked out on the terrible physical schedule Levaster had prescribed—miles of running, sit-ups, swimming, shadow-boxing.

Edward was hardly ever beaten in an early round, but he was fading in the third and fourth day of tournaments now. He had become a spoiler against high seeds in early rounds, though never a winner. His style was greatly admired. A Portuguese writer called him "the New Orleans ace who will not surrender his youth." The Prague paper advocated him as "the dangerous happy cavalier"; Madrid said, "He fights windmills, but, viewing his style, we are convinced his contests matter." Yes, thought Levaster, this style must run its full lustrous route. It cannot throw in the towel until there is the last humiliation, something neither one of us can take.

Then it occurred to Levaster. French had never been humiliated in a match. He had lost, but he had never been humiliated. Not in a single match, not a single game. The handsome head had never bowed, the rusting gold of French Edward's curls stayed high in the sun. He remained the sage and brute that he was when he was nineteen. There was still the occasional winner off his racket that could never have been predicted by the scholars of the game. Levaster felt his soul rise in the applause for this. In Mexico City, there was a standing ovation for the most uncanny movement ever seen on the court. El Niño de Merida smacked down an overhead that bounced high and out of play over the backstop. But Edward had climbed the fence to field it, legs and one arm in the wire, racket hand free for the half second it took to strike the ball back, underhanded. The ball took a boomerang arc to the other side and notched the corner of the ad court. My Christ, thought Levaster, as the Mexicans screamed, he climbed the fence and never lost style.

When they returned from this trip, Levaster read in the paper about an open tournament at Vicksburg. Whitney Humble had already been signed up. The prize money was two thousand dollars, singles winner take all. They called it the Delta Open.

"I know Word has something to do with this. Nobody in Vicksburg ever gave a damn about tennis but him, you Baby, and me," French Edward said.

"You should let the home folks finally see you. Your image would do wonders for the place," said Levaster. "They've read about you. Now they want to see you. Why not? I've been wanting to go back and put a head-marker on my mother's grave, though it would be false to what she was. I've got all this money hanging around. I get sentimental, guilty. Don't you ever?"

"Yes," French Edward said.

They went back to Vicksburg. On the second day of the tournament, they got a call at the Holiday Inn. Fat Tim Emile had died. Nobody had known he was dying but him. He had written a short letter full of pride and appreciation to Cecilia and French, thanking French for his association with the family and for valiant contests in the tennis world. Fat Tim left them two hundred thousand and insisted on nobody giving any ceremony. He wanted his remaining body to go straight to the Tulane med school. "This body," he wrote, "it was fat maybe, but I was proud of it. Those young doctors-to-be, like Baby Levaster, might find something new in me. I was scared all my life and stayed honest. I never hurt another man or woman, that I know of. When I made money, I started eating well. Baby Levaster warned me. I guess I've died of success."

"My poor Cecilia," said French.

"Cissy is fine," said Levaster. "She said for you to finish the tournament."

So he did.

Levaster looked on in a delirium of sober nostalgia. Through the trees, in a slit of the bluffs, he could see the river. French's mother and father sat together and watched their son. Dr. Word, near eighty, was a linesman. They are old people, thought Levaster, looking at the Edwards. And him, Word, he's a goddamned *relic.* A spry relic. Younger brother Wilbur was not there because he was dead.

Whitney Humble and French Edward met in the finals. Humble had aged gruesomely too, Levaster saw, and knew it was from fighting it out in small tournaments for almost two decades, earning bus fare and tiny fame in newspapers from Alabama to Idaho. But Humble still wanted to play. The color of a dead perch, thinner in the calf, Humble smoked cigarettes between ad games. All his equipment was gray and dirty, even his racket. He could not run much anymore. Some teeth were busted out.

A wild crowd of Vicksburg people, greasers and their pregnant brides from the mobile homes included, met to cheer French. Humble did not have a fan. He was hacking up phlegm and coughing out lengths of it, catching it on his shirt, a tort even those for the underdog could not abide. The greasers felt lifted to some estate of taste by Humble.

It was a long and sparkling match. Humble won.

Humble took the check and the sterling platter, hurled the platter outside the fence and into the trees, then slumped off.

The image of tennis was ruined for years in Vicksburg.

Dr. Word and the Edwards met French on the court. Levaster saw Word lift an old crabby arm to French's shoulder, saw French wince. Mr. Edward said he had to hurry to his job. He wore a comical uniform and cap. His job was checking vegetable produce at the bridge house of the river so that boll weevils would not enter Mississippi from Louisiana. Levaster looked into the eyes of Mrs. Edward. Yes, he decided, she still loves Word; her eyes touch him like fingers, and perhaps he still cuts it, and perhaps they rendezvous out in the Civil War cemetery so he won't have far to fall when he explodes with fornication, the old infantryman of lust.

"Mother," said French, "let's all meet at the bridge house."

Levaster saw the desperate light in French's eye.

"Don't you, don't you!" said Levaster afterward, driving the Lincoln.

"I've got to. It'll clear the trash. I can't live in the world if Word's still in it."

"He's nothing but bones," said Levaster. "He's done for."

"She still loves him," said French.

They all gathered at the bridge house, and French told his father that his wife had been cheating on him for twenty years, and brought up his hands, and began crying, and pointed to Word. Mr. Edward looked at Word, then back to his son. He was terribly concerned. He asked Word to leave the little hut for a second, apologizing to Word. He asked Olive to come stand by him, and put his arm over his wife's shoulders.

"Son," he whispered, "Jimmy Word, friend to us and steady as a brick to us, is a homosexual. Look out there, what you've done to him. He's running."

Then they were all strung out on the walkway of the bridge, Levaster marveling at how swift old Word was, for Word was out there nearing the middle of the bridge, Mrs. Edward next, fifty yards behind, French passing his mother, gaining on Word. Levaster was running too. He, too, passed Olive, who had given out and was leaning on the rail. Levaster saw Word mount the rail and balance on it like a gymnast. He put on a burst of speed and caught up with French, who had stopped running and was walking toward Word cautiously, his hand on the rail.

"Just close your eyes, son, I'll be gone," Word said, looking negligible as a spirit in his smart tennis jacket and beret. He trembled on the rail. Below Word was the sheen of the river, the evening sun lying over it down there, low reds flashing on the brown water.

That's a hundred feet down there, Levaster thought. When he looked up, French had gotten up on the rail and was balancing himself, moving step by step toward Word.

"Don't," said Levaster and Word together.

French, the natural, was walking on the rail with the ease of an avenue hustler. He had found his purchase: this sport was nothing.

"Son! No closer!" bawled Word.

"I'm not your son. I'm bringing you back, old bastard."

They met. French seemed to be trying to pick up Word in an infant position, arm under legs. Word's beret fell off and floated, puffed out, into the deep hole over the river. French had him, had him wrestled into the shape of a fetus. Then Word gave a kick and Olive screamed, and the two men fell backward into the red air and down. Levaster watched them coil together in the drop.

There was a great deal of time until they hit. At the end, Edward flung the old suicide off and hit the river in a nice straight-legged jump. Word hit the water flat as a board. Levaster thought he heard the sound of Word's back breaking.

The river was shallow here, with strong devious currents.

Nothing came up. By the time the patrol got out, there was no hope. Then Levaster, standing in a boat, spotted French, sitting under a willow a half mile downriver from the bridge. French had drowned and broken one leg, but had crawled out of the river by instinct. His brain was already choked.

French Edward stared at the rescue boat as if it were a turtle with vermin gesturing toward him, Levaster and Olive making their cries of discovery.

Carina, Levaster's teenager, woke him up. She handed him a cold beer and a Dexedrine. At first Levaster did not understand. Then he knew that the sun had come up again, seeing the grainy abominable light on the alley through the window. This was New York. Who was this child? Why was he naked on the sheets?

Ah, Carina.

"Will you marry me, Carina?" Levaster said.

"Before I saw your friend, I might have," she said.

French Edward came into the room, fully dressed, hair wet from a shower.

"Where do I run, Baby?" he said.

Levaster told him to run around the block fifty times.

"He does everything you tell him?" said Carina.

"Of course he does. Fry me some eggs, you dumb twat."

As the eggs and bacon were sizzling, Levaster came into the kitchen in his Taiwan bathrobe, the huge black sombrero on his head. He had oiled and loaded the .410 shotgun/pistol.

"Put two more eggs on for French. He's really hungry after he runs."

Carina broke two more eggs.

"He's so magnificent, " she said. "How much of his brain does he really have left?"

"Enough," Levaster said.

Levaster drove them to New Hampshire, to Bretton Woods. He saw Laver and Ashe approach French Edward in the lobby of the inn. They wanted to shake hands with French, but he did not recognize them. French stood there with hands down, looking ahead into the wall.

The next day Levaster took French out on the court for his first match. He put the Japanese Huta into his hand. It was a funny manganese and fiberglass racket with a split throat. The Huta firm had paid French ten thousand to use it on the circuit just before he drowned in the river. French had never hit with it before.

French was looking dull. Levaster struck him a hard blow against the heart. French started and gave a sudden happy regard to the court.

"I'm here," said French.

"You're damned right. Don't let us down."

Edward played better than he had in years. He was going against an Indian twenty years his junior. The boy had a serve and a wicked deceptive blast off his backhand. The crowd loved the Indian. The boy was polite and beautiful. But then French Edward had him at match point on his serve.

Edward threw the ball up.

"Hit it, *hit.* My life, hit it," whispered Levaster.

The Tennis Game

JAMES JONES

Lying irritably and sweating between the rows of radishes in the hot humid air under the beating sun, he peered through the screen of tall grass and weeds that formed the boundary of the garden, at the man moving slowly under the shade trees beyond. A slow, warm, secretive pleasure crept over him replacing the irritation as he carefully got the man in his sights. He would never know what hit him. Slowly he cocked the hammer of his pistol and then squeezed the trigger, and the hammer fell upon the little red paper cap igniting it with a low splatting sound.

The man, who was colored and whose name was George and whom the boy's uncle had only recently brought up north from Florida to work for him, was too far away even to hear the sound and went on slowly pushing his lawn mower across the grass under the shade trees and the boy, whose name was John Slade and who was eleven years old, watched him secretively and with that wholly contained private pleasure that nobody else in the whole world knew about from between the rows of radishes in the garden he was supposed to be weeding for his mother. No, sir, he would never have known what hit him.

"Johnnn-y-y-y!" his mother's voice came from behind him, shrill, penetrating, nasal, demanding, insistent, rising in the air and going outward in all directions from the back porch of his house as if it were some kind of audible radio wave and himself the sole receiving set.

"I am!" he cried furiously. He holstered the gun, not really holstered, he didn't have a holster for this one, but jammed between his belly and the belt of his overall pants that he always had to wear when he worked in the garden to keep better clothes clean. He hated them. And he hated her. And that shrill ear-shivering, penetrating, insistent voice of hers. In his mind's eye he could see her standing there in the shade on the back porch looking out at him through the screen and drying and drying her hands over and over on a dish towel from the kitchen. Without even bothering to look around he began pulling out weeds again from between the dirty damn radishes, the gun barrel he could feel pressed against his belly just above his peepee, his only hope, his only friend. Like Daniel Boone in the forest.

He had tried making a game of it, playing he was the army and the weeds the enemy and watching his hands which were his troops capturing more and more and more clean ground from them and killing them by the hundreds, infiltrating around the heavier pockets of resistance until they had them completely surrounded by clean captured ground and then uprooting the whole big bunch that died to the last man. But there was too much garden and too many too-big weeds, and in the hot humid summer air under the suffocating sun the game had just run down of itself. He had been at it over an hour, John had, if you counted too all the little bits of time he managed to sneak away from pulling.

Across the back-yard fence and screen of cover the colored man George under the shade trees had stopped pushing his mower when he heard John's mother's voice and looked up and grinned, his teeth flashing white in his dark face even at that distance. Now he called sympathetically, "Hot work, ain't it Mister Johnny, on a day like this."

John preferred not to answer and, pretending he had not heard, ignored him and went on pulling weeds lethargically. He would never tell him how he had got him dead to rights so he never knew what hit him. He would never tell it to anybody. Nobody in the world. And it would be one more thing he would have that his mother wouldn't know about, or his father, or any of the other grownups in the world. Or kids either, for that matter. The very thought of it, of having that to add to all the others, the secret, made the pit of his stomach whirl round and round inside him with excitement and he stopped pulling and lay down full length between the rows on the captured clean dirt and wallowed himself on it, all that dirty dirt, rubbing his hands in it above his head and grinding the gun barrel in his pants hurtfully, against his pubis bone, filled with a consuming luxurious hatred for himself, and for her, and for the colored man George, and for his father, and everybody else in the whole world. He'd show them. Let them all see him, wallowing here in the dirt. And just wait till she saw how dirty he got, too, boy, would she be mad, he thought with pleasure. Weeding her old damned vegetable garden.

"Johnnn-y-y-y!" his mother's voice came. "I *am!*" he cried immediately.

"But what are you doing! Rolling around like that!"

"Working!" he cried with wild outrage, but frightened now, and guilty. "Pullin' weeds! I got to get hold of them, don't I?" Cautiously and slyly he raised himself partially onto his hands and knees and went back to pulling, pretending he had not stopped. After a moment she went back in. God, would she never leave him alone? Ever? Would he never be free of that shrill, insistent, constantly checking voice? Would it follow him around the world forever?

Right in front of him, but a couple of steps off to the left beyond the radish rows, and growing in and around and over the back-yard fence, was the big snowball bush his grandfather had planted long ago before he himself was even born, when grandfather lived in the house his uncle lived in now, the big house. The bush had grown until its branches had fallen back over and made a hidden cave inside it. He often hid in there when nobody knew it, or when he was playing Tarzan or just plain jungle explorers. It was even more secret and he liked it even better than his tree house he had built in the old hollow tree out behind the garage. He had sneaked out his father's pliers and cut away a large section of the wire fence beneath the bush so that he had a secret tunnel between his yard and his uncle's yard that nobody else knew about and could go from one yard to the other without being seen. And now for a moment, crouched on his hands and knees between the radishes, his heart still beating in his ears from her almost catching him, he debated making a run for there when she wasn't looking. The tickle of secrecy was still with him but now it was an angry tickle. He could sit in there where he could see out but nobody could see in and take down his pants and rub handfuls of the fresh dirt all over his peepee with his grubby hands. The thought of doing that excited him because he would be getting even with her. And she would never catch him provided he could get to the house and in the bathroom and wash himself first. And he thought he could. Because she'd never think to make him take his pants down. But he wisely decided against trying to make the run for it. She would surely be looking out again in a minute and see him gone, and anyway if he didn't get the weeding done he would be out here all day and not get to play at all. She would see to that. And after this, there was still the front half of the yard to mow. And of course he would have to go to the store for her too, for something she'd forgotten.

Furiously, in a violent if momentary burst of vigorous energy, he attacked the weeds because it was the only way out of this that he could find. And he had been wanting to play his tennis game today, ever since early morning.

Johnny Slade wasn't any damned fool. And he knew enough to know that he didn't have to weed the garden, or mow the yard. They didn't even have to have a damned old vegetable garden. His mother said it was to save money, and then would put a sad look on her face, but he knew better. He had watched his father shopping at the A&P store, and he knew the money they saved by putting out a garden was not enough even to count. He knew there was a Depression on, and had been for five years ever since the President had closed the banks when he was little; but he also knew the money his father made in his dentist's office downtown was enough that they could afford to hire a man to mow the yard, and weed the damned garden if they had to have one, just like his uncle who was a lawyer had hired the colored man George in Florida. But they were just too cheap to do it. That was the truth. That, and because his mother wanted something to hold over his father when he got drunk. And because, as she said when she got mad, her son was going to learn to work because it built character and was good for his soul—and he was going to learn it if it killed the both of them. But the real truth was she couldn't stand to see him outdoors playing and having fun while she herself had to clean house and cook. She just couldn't stand it, he could tell by the look on her face, and so the whole thing was no more than one damned big lie. One of those grownup lies, that grownups told each other and pretended to believe, and that children because they were little had to accept and pretend to believe too, because they could not argue back.

Thinking about it, and the whole entire huge conspiracy of it all, in which a kid as long as he was little had no chance at all, depressed him so his violent burst of energy dwindled away inside of him leaving him feeling only weary, and defeated, completely beaten, and lethargic. He had, in his burst of activity, cleared two feet of ground. There was at least twenty more to go. How would he ever get it done in time to play the tennis game? Or anything at all, for that matter.

As it turned out, he didn't have to finish it, although it was after lunch before he was finally allowed to quit. His mother called him in and made him wash for lunch (exclaiming over how dirty he always managed to get, to which he of course said nothing) and fed him and then sent him back out to work on it another hour. But then she let him quit and made him take a bath because this afternoon she was having her Wisdom Club bridge ladies that she had to entertain once every two months, and she didn't want him coming in the house all messy and dirty while they were there. So he was free to play, reprieved, and the rest of the garden as well as the yard to mow was put back until tomorrow. Happy just simply to be free, and willing to let tomorrow take care of itself and not even think about it, he ran outside through the kitchen and the back door after he had dressed and across the driveway to the playhouse his father had bought for him and his baby sister a year ago, wanting only to get away and out of sight before she changed her mind maybe, as she often did.

Listening to the Wisdom Club bridge ladies as they began to arrive, and feeling like a rich man, he sat in the little chair on the porch of the playhouse and went over in his mind the various games he could play. The tickle of secretive pleasure had come back into his stomach again. He knew of course what he was going to play. The tennis game. But he enjoyed going over his possibilities and pretending he was making his choice. For instance, there was the tree house and Tarzan, for which he would have to take off his shirt and put on his hunting knife, and he could carry her there, Jane, and make her play with his peepee. Or he could get out his sun helmet and play jungle explorers and how they found the lost tribe of naked white women Amazons who captured them and tortured them. He could, if he wanted to, go on with the lead-soldier battle he had in progress in the playhouse. He sat on the porch of the playhouse luxuriously, and thoughtfully studied all of these.

The playhouse where he sat was a regular little house with a regular roof that sloped two ways like a real house and a front door and back door and windows that opened; it was very realistic, and the floor of the single room interior was the scene of the lead-soldier battle. It had been going on almost three weeks now. First he had fixed up the floor with pillows for mountains and piles of Big Little Books for hills and long strips of blue paper for the river, and then later two lines of Big Little Books for the trenches in front of the big plaster fort. From one end of the room the bad side was advancing upon and trying to capture the good side who were gradually being forced back to take refuge in their fort. At present, the good side had had to abandon two whole lines of trenches. Trenches which the bad side, naturally, had taken over to use against them. With it arranged this way, and the attack moving from one end of the room toward the other, he could shoot for both sides through the open windows at either end of the playhouse. Only just yesterday he had killed a colonel of the good side who was leading a counterattack against the steadily encroaching trenches in an attempt to break through and split the line. The BB had struck the colonel's horse, breaking off both of its front legs, and that particular soldier was ruined forever, which made John feel curiously and pleasantly sad, and the colonel's force had been driven back in confusion, losing two more killed before they could get back to their own lines. The counterattack had failed. It was a bad blow for the good side. The colonel had been one of their best field commanders and they had counted a great deal on that attack and now things didn't look good for them at all. Steadily they were being forced further and further back, ringed in into a smaller and smaller maneuvering space. It gave John a strange delicious feeling of tragic fatalisticness, to see them fighting so hard and bravely and being gradually beaten back. On the other hand, as the bad side steadily advanced into the good side's territory, they came more and more into dead range of the BB gun in the window, and consequently were now losing a great many more men than they had before. It even appeared at times that they might not have sufficient forces to capture the fort once they got there. Also, John had contemplated putting a relieving force of reinforcements in the field behind the bad side to aid the beleaguered garrison. He had the men. And if he did that, it would turn into a real blood bath, a regular rout, for the bad side. And in fact John was not sure yet just which side was going to win. Sometimes he could hardly wait to find out.

The deciding factor of course was himself, and he knew this, and understood it fully and completely in all its implications, and accepted the responsibility. Just as he accepted the responsibility of destroying his own soldiers, which he loved and valued, every time he levered his BB gun against his leg and shot a big ugly hole in one, or knocked off its head, or broke it off from its stand. He understood this too and it made him sad when he had to do it. But there wasn't any choice. It was necessary in the cause of reality. Otherwise the battle wouldn't be real or realistic at all. And every time he got one of his better soldiers he particularly loved in his sights, the old sad fatalistic secret tickle of almost hurtful pleasure would arise in his stomach. Of course, he didn't shoot these better ones very often, like the colonel, and saved them back for special occasions.

Nevertheless, though he knew what the deciding factor would be, in other words himself, and it was a great responsibility, he still didn't know which side would win. Naturally, he wanted the good side to win, because they were the good guys. But in some ways he wanted the bad side to win too, and tear the good side all to shreds and kill them to the last man like the Arabs did at the fort in *Beau Geste* when he read it, or like at the Alamo. So he could not be sure which side would win because he wasn't sure which side he *wanted* to win. His opinions changed with his moods. He was not above cheating a little, either, and making a greater percentage of his shots miss one side or the other depending upon what mood he was in and who he was for at the moment, but he didn't really feel that that was really cheating. One day, in a fit of mood, he had organized an all-out attack by the good side which in an hour had the bad side in full retreat and which before it was done had swept away and destroyed almost all the gains the bad side had so laboriously built up since the battle started, and in fact the only thing that saved them from complete defeat was a last ditch stand by a small group of French Foreign Legionnaires, tough fighters all, who were fighting with the bad side this battle. That time almost all the shots the bad side made either missed or went astray, and when it was all over and he looked around at the carnage and havoc and the ruptured plans he felt half sick and strangely astonished, although he had known all along what he was doing and was going to do. Why had he done it? Now they would have to start all over.

Sitting on the little porch and hearing the high-pitched cackling chatter of the Wisdom Club bridge ladies in the house, John looked in through the window at the battlefield of the floor. The bad side had by now of course regained all of the lost ground that the good side's attack had wrested from them and were once again encroaching upon the fort. Maybe tomorrow he would start a feeling attack by the bad side with the objective maybe of driving a salient into the good side's line and breaking it. If it did, if it succeeded, did break the line, it would be nearly the end. The good side would have to retire into their fort, the fort would be invested, and from then on it would only be a matter of time. There wasn't anywhere behind them to fall back to; the fort was right back against the end wall of the playhouse. It gave John a strange excited sad feeling. And now would be a good time to start off such a feeling attack, while the good side was still shaken up and in distress over the failure of their counterattack, and the loss of their fine colonel. Yes, that was what he would do. But not today. Today he was going to play the tennis game.

Getting up from the little porch, excited, and tingly all over at the prospect, and with the high-pitched cackle of the Wisdom Club bridge ladies still irritably in his ears (the boobs), he went to the garage to get the racket and balls. The playhouse which served as battlefield for the lead-soldiers also doubled as grandstand for the tennis game, and he brought the equipment back to where the umpires waited, to be introduced to his opponent. Although, of course, they knew each other, and had in fact played against each other many times at Wimbledon and Forest Hills and in many other tournaments. The introduction was only a formality.

But first, before beginning to play, he laid the equipment on the little porch and went around to the side of the garage to pee, and suddenly for no reason, but with his heartbeat rising in his ears frightenedly and causing his excitement over the game to dissipate and leave him feeling hollow and empty, found himself thinking of that day a month or so ago when Alice Pringle from the other side of town had been here to play.

He knew, of course, why he suddenly thought of Alice, whom he hardly knew; it was because of what had happened right here around the side of the garage, right where he was standing now, when Alice had been here. It was a secluded spot here, out of sight of his house, and the spot where all the guys came to pee when they played here or in the vacant lot behind the playhouse. A neighbor's garage which faced the other way from his own toward the other street was built right alongside John's garage, so close their eaves were only a few feet apart and you could jump from one garage roof to the other and there was almost like a tunnel between them, a sort of passageway between the yards, from one side of the block to the other, and right at the back end of it a big young locust tree that partly shaded the playhouse. This was where he brought Alice to pee too, when she had asked him to take her some place. He had offered to take her in the house, first, but looking at him with a funny strange grin that made her eyes seem to get littler, the same kind of grin he could feel beginning to come over his own face, she had said no she would rather go somewhere close outside instead of in the house.

Alice was just exactly his own age, but he didn't know her very well because she wasn't from his town and was only visiting here for the summer with her mother. She did every summer. And her mother had brought her by for the afternoon because she had to go somewhere. So feeling strangely scared and embarrassed, though he didn't want to, he had taken Alice in between the garages where all the guys always went, and then had turned to go away until she was through, as he knew he was supposed to.

But she had said in a funny voice didn't he want to stay, maybe he had to pee too, and it was all right as long as he turned his back and didn't look, and then she would turn her back and not look, that was the way the boys and girls all always did in her town where she came from.

And so that was what they had done, and the sequence they followed—except for one thing: when she asked him if he was done and he should have said no he said yes instead and she turned around and saw him still peeing, while his heart was beating in his throat like a triphammer. Alice had giggled and slapped his arm, and then she frowned and looked angry and turned back around and said in an angry voice that he shouldn't have done that, that was bad. It was not exactly the reaction he was expecting. Or even why he had done it, really. Anyway, it didn't matter because that was when his mother's voice, shrill, strident, demanding and insistent, like some all-seeing all-knowing powerful dark angel of God, had come out sharply at him from the upstairs bedroom window over the back porch where she was supposed to be lying down taking a nap. *Johnnnnyy! What are you children doing? Where are you? Come here!* Hastily buttoning his pants, his mind fumbling and balking on him frightenedly, he walked slowly around from between the garages to stand looking up under the upstairs bedroom window, feeling like a criminal caught in the act and brought before the high bench of the stern judges of the bar of justice. And when she asked him again what they had been doing, he simply told her, his mind floundering and fumbling so badly that there wasn't even any question of thinking of an excuse. Later he would wonder why he hadn't lied; she couldn't prove anything. Alice wondered why he hadn't lied, too.

"What did you do that for? What did you tell her the truth for?" she whispered furiously, while they waited for her to come down. "Now you've got us both into trouble."

He didn't know what trouble Alice got into, when her mother came to take her home, but she had certainly been right about him anyway. His mother had separated them and made Alice stay in the livingroom and him in the bedroom upstairs. Then she had, first, washed his mouth out with soap on a wet washcloth (although he didn't know why she had to do that to him; that was usually his punishment for lying, not for telling the truth) and then, second, she had given him a whale of a whipping on his bare bottom while she glared at him with angrily narrowed eyes and made it plain to him in no uncertain terms what a filthy, dirty thing it was he had done.

He never did find out what happened to Alice when she got home, because she never came back any more and he hadn't seen her since.

Standing there between the garages to pee, where it had all happened, his heart beating dully with fright and fear again in his ears just as it had that day (although at least he didn't have to listen to the high-pitched cackle of the Wisdom Club bridge ladies around here where you couldn't hear it), he finished and then went back to the little porch, the enthusiasm for the tennis game all gone. And it was quite a while, sitting there hollow and empty and dandling the tennis racket lethargically, before he could work himself up to starting to play it.

The tennis game was a new one, one that he had invented only a few weeks ago, when he read a story about a championship tennis match in a *Collier's* magazine that his mother had brought home. The idea for the story obviously came from Don Budge's victory over Baron von Cramm in the Davis Cup and the Wimbledon, which John had followed in the sports pages with interest. The writer had taken that for his starter, and then had made up a story about this championship match, and these two men, both of whom had to win it. It was a real battle of wills. Everything both men wanted from the world was at stake. The young American would lose his girl he wanted to marry and the big job her father had offered him if he lost the match; and the German Baron had been told by the Fuhrer that if he did not win for Germany all his estates would be confiscated and himself imprisoned. All this came out in the story as the two men played the match, and you could read it tensely, liking both men, hoping both could win, but knowing only one could. In the end, in this great test of wills, the young American had won over the older German sportsman, and the Baron, rather than return to Germany and what he knew waited there, had shut the garage door and turned on his car motor, thinking he had been an adventurer all his life and now he was embarking upon the greatest adventure of all. It was a gripping story and John, who would be twelve before too long, in some strange way that he couldn't describe was able to sense out and associate with the German's sad but strong feelings his tragic courage. And in fact, in the story, he had liked the Baron much more than he had liked the young American who won.

And that was the story of his tennis game. Sometimes, when he played the match through against the garage doors, he would become so involved in it and its struggle that the play of emotions which ran through him became unbelievably intense, almost unbearable, exquisitely powerful. He *became* the German, and the young American too. Of course, he never played it when any of the other kids were around; and he never told anybody about it. He would have felt silly and embarrassed. So to all intents and purposes he was merely practicing tennis strokes against the garage. But the very secrecy itself added to the excitement of it, and even before he would begin to play out the match that secret, completely contained, private pleasure which caused his stomach to spin, would steal over him, as he marched out onto the court.

He had arranged it all so it would be very realistic. The playhouse was the grandstand, and the concrete driveway which was double for two car-lengths back from the double doors was the court. The garage doors, which were on rollers and slid from side to side one behind the other, were made with two-by-four braces that framed their edges and crisscrossed from corner to corner and were painted white, and the brace that ran across them cutting them in half horizontally across the middle was the net; every shot that hit below that was a lost point. And every shot that went off the concrete was an "out," and another lost point. The crisscross braces themselves, as well as the offset door joint, gave an added element of chance to it since at times the ball would hit one of them and squirt off out of bounds to the side, or else hit the concrete where he could not possibly get it back. In spite of this element of chance, however, the deciding factor was once again, of course, as with the lead-soldiers' battle, himself. He could make whichever one win he wanted to, and could *be* whichever one he wanted whether winning or losing, according to his mood. Usually he chose to be the Baron and to lose.

And today, after getting over the upset of the memory of Alice Pringle, that was who he was. After getting himself worked into it and beginning to get involved by the end of the first set (the Baron took the first one, building his tragic hopes unnaturally high), the cackling conversation of the Wisdom Club bridge ladies coming out to him from inside the house added a strange, new, exciting element. They were the crowd, chattering and talking excitedly among themselves as they sat happily in the grandstand. What did they know about the tragedy that was being enacted out here on the court as the Baron fought desperately to win? What did they know of his desperate effort to keep all his estates and keep himself from being put in a Nazi concentration camp? It was only a game to them, an exciting match to be enjoyed while they drank Cokes and ate sandwiches. Just for spite, as if Fate itself were playing nasty tricks on the plucky German, he let the Baron take the second set too. Now he was all set up. Just one more set to win, out of three, and he would have the championship and all it meant to him. But then, just as the German thought he had it, thought he was safe at last, he switched sides to the young American and really began to go to work.

Cold, calm, collected, the young American (he had always been noted as a pressure player) began to play tennis like he had never played in his life before. Ferocious drop shots, sizzling volleys, high lobs in the very corners, everything. He, and John with him, was everywhere on the court, growing steadily and relentlessly stronger in confidence and power. Even the crowd hushed and became quiet at such a brilliant exhibition. And slowly the score crept up on the weakening German. The American, playing brilliantly, took the third set 6-4. Then came back to take the fourth set 6-2.

And then, as the two of them stood staring implacably at each other across the net after their rest, John switched back to the Baron for the fifth and final set and the climax. The Baron already knew it was a lost cause now. Several years older than his opponent, weakening, tired, winded, his knees shaky, he fought on grimly, the handkerchief tied around his forehead to keep the sweat out of his eyes. Several times he, and John with him, staggered on the court going after impossible placements. But he did not go down. He lost the first two games without even a deuce. But then, almost completely exhausted, in actual physical pain almost, he rallied and took the next three straight games, all of them with at least two deuces, making one supreme effort, which was his last. Then, with the game score 3-2 in his favor, the American broke through his service, and on the last point he, and John with him, staggered and fell, trying to reach an impossibly brilliant drop shot, and he knew it was all over. Lying stretched out on the court, his racket still reaching across the concrete after that irretrievably lost ball, breathing convulsively, he rolled over, then got wearily up to one knee and looked across the net at the man who had defeated him. There would be no going back to Germany for him now. There was almost a luxury in knowing it, in knowing it was over, in embracing his defeat he had fought so hard against, a real happiness and pleasure almost. And, his stomach spinning almost sickly with excitement and emotion, John climbed back slowly to his feet.

The rest was an anticlimax. Everybody, even the crowd, knew it was over. For the next three games the Baron played grimly. Several times he staggered and nearly fell, and twice he, and John with him, went down on one knee. But it was all only a formality. And then it was finally over. Knowing what he must do, now, he walked slowly over to the umpire's stand on the little porch in front of the grandstand to congratulate his opponent. And almost physically sick with excitement and emotion, the nerves in his arms and legs tingling with it, John dropped the racket and balls on the porch in beaten defeat and started around the garage to where the tree house was, out in back of it, to do what he always wanted to do when he felt like this. He wanted to play with himself. It was then that his mother's voice followed him from out of the kitchen, where she was fixing the refreshments.

"Johnny! Johnny! What are you doing out there, falling around like that?"

"Playing," he said grimly, his face a mask of German iron control, as became a Prussian.

And as he went on to the tree house, his peepee throbbing in his pants, behind him he heard his mother say laughingly to the Wisdom Club bridge lady who was helping her:

"Playing! Oh, well, you know how children are. They're always playing some little game or other when they're by themselves."

Tennis by Cable

RING LARDNER

Here is an idea that was suggested by my 2d. son Jimmie as
we was setting at some meal the day after the tennis boys
played for the east and west championship. I made the remark
that Vincent Richards had beat Bill Johnston in straight sets
and he says where was the matches played and I says right
here on Long Island and he says well was he here on Long Island yesterday.

So I give him a sarcastic answer, namely, Oh no, he was out
in San Francisco and they played by telegraph like they play
the international chess matches sometimes. So then I had to
exclaim to him about the international chess matches that is
sometimes played by cable and he says why don't they play
the international golf matches and tennis matches and etc. by
cable instead of them taking all the trouble to make the trips
back and forth.

So I thought it over a long wile and come to the conclusion
that maybe after all he was right and why should people cross
the ocean just for a friendly game that they don't get no money
out of it and we will take for inst. the Australian tennis team
who I have nicknamed the anzacs and it must cost them a mint

of money to come here from clear over there and what does it get them outside of the exercise which they could just as well of had over there and not take no chances of being seasick and I don't know how much it costs to get here from Australia, but it certainly would not cost nowheres near as much if they played tennis by cable.

For example suppose Tilden was playing Gerald Patterson and it happened to be Tilden's first serve, why he would cable to Patterson that he had got his first service over and it was a terrific hard hit ball and what are you going to do about it, why Patterson would cable back, it did not look so hard hit to me. I returned it way into the upper corner of the court on your back-hand where it was pretty near impossible for you to get it. Then Tilden would reply, well I did get it on my back-hand and as you was close up to the net, I made a passing shot which you couldn't possibly get. Then Patterson would reply, it may of seemed to you like I couldn't possibly get it, but as a matter of fact I did get it by a phenomenal stab and I returned it where you couldn't get it in a week.

Then Tilden would wait a wile and send back the following answer. It ain't only five days since your last shot came back and I managed to get a hold of it and lob it over your head to pretty close to the base line where I doubt if you could get a racket on it unless you used a airship.

Patterson's reply would be, I bought a airship as soon as I received your cable and managed to get back and hit that ball and I hit it with such force that even if you do get your racket on it, it will probably break your racket. Tilden would answer: Well, I seen that ball was going to break my racket as the last named is a old racket that has stood lots of wear and tear, so I bought myself a new racket and returned your shot to one inch from the base line where no living being could get their racket on it.

In this way the game could be carried on indefinitely and would probably be the closest tennis game ever played and still not cost near as much as if Mr. Patterson had come over here to play it and further and more we would not half to set out in the boiling sun on hot seats to watch it. To say nothing about how much more chance Patterson would have to win.

The Olympic games could be pulled off in the same way. Like for inst. Hubbard of Michigan was broad jumping vs. who ever broad jumps for France who we will call Lafayette and Hubbard makes the first jump and cables I just jumped 26 ft., try and laugh that off. So Lafayette wires back, you look silly to me, I just took my first leap and done 27 ft. They could keep this up till all records was broke and themselfs too.

But the best game that could be played by cable would be a bridge game because a person could bid pretty near as high as they wanted to and for inst. say they was bidding 6 spades, why when they come to play the hand the declarer could say I have got 12 spades in my hand and the ace of diamonds and the dummy has got the other spade and no diamonds and of course the oppts. could not see what was in either hand and it is bound to be a grand slam.

An FBI Story

PETER LASALLE

In only his second year of playing the game, Riley won the plated plaque for the senior division in the FBI New York office tournament held every September at a country club in Westchester. For him, it simply was the most important thing that had happened to him in the last ten years. He regarded his work at the Bureau as a job, and a rather boring one at that. But at thirty-four he already was on the $20,000 step and at forty-four he could retire.

With the victory in that tournament, he immersed himself in the sport with even more fervor. That winter he spent long hours at night not really reading the several glossy tennis magazines he subscribed to, but actually studying them as he used to pore over the fine-print legal texts when he was at Villanova Law. He sometimes stayed up late in his studio apartment on East Sixty-ninth Street with the yellow felt-tipped marker in his hand. The thing smelled chemical and squeaked. He overlined complete paragraphs of instruction while leaning back with his feet up on the footrest of the black Naugahyde recliner. Before bed he always did sixty squeezes with the chrome-plated wrist exerciser on his right racket hand. The exerciser looked like a giant hairpin with blue-painted handles, and he always did twenty squeezes on his left hand for what one magazine called "muscular balance." Occasionally he played at an indoor court on Long Island that was very expensive. He looked forward to the summer and weekends at a cottage he planned to rent with Gogarty, another bachelor agent.

The day they first moved into the place by the shore in eastern Connecticut, Riley played random games with various members of the group who said they were all regulars at the asphalt courts at the town's public recreation area. The last of these was a New York salesman Riley's own age. They sat on the splintery bench and drank the Gatorade Riley had brought in a thermos. The mosquitoes were starting to come out and the leaves on the big maples were that deep emerald of early July. The salesman was prematurely bald. He fiddled with the terry-cloth headband—it was striped red, white, and blue—that he had just tugged off.

"The FBI, huh," said the salesman.

"Yes," said Riley. "What about doubles? Do you think we can get some doubles in tomorrow?"

"I bet that's some interesting job."

"It's a job. Heh, how about some more of this Gatorade? I've got half the thermos left."

"Is it exciting? I mean, is it really like that Efrem Zimbalist Junior stuff on television?"

Of course it wasn't. Not for Riley, anyway. Riley went to "basic training" for the Bureau at the camp in Louisiana right after law school maybe because he did think FBI life would be more interesting than working for a firm. Then, in the midsixties he was accepted immediately because of the Bureau's tendency to take in upstanding boys from Catholic colleges with Irish last names. His first assignment was Kansas City and when he was sent there, at least he was pleased it was a "major-league town." Riley had been a high-school and college second baseman who got an invitation on stationery with a little red cardinal embossed on the top to try out with the St. Louis team after his senior year. He never did. He spent almost three years in Kansas City and he would remember it as being the only place where he ever shot at a man. The fugitive had just robbed a local bank and at least two dozen agents surrounded the woodframe flophouse with peeling paint where he was holed up. Riley squeezed the blue metal trigger of his .38 twice while aiming at the open window of the room the man supposedly was in. A lot of agents were still shooting for a good five minutes after the stubble-faced criminal had surrendered at the back alley and already had his arms on the hood of the tan government Chevrolet for frisking.

Maybe Riley wanted adventure. Maybe he just wanted to be in the thick of something. He applied for a transfer to Chicago, convinced the office there was bound to be busy. He was assigned to the truck-hijacking squad when truck hijacking in the city was at a low ebb. He worked mostly nights on stake-outs. They entailed little more than being a glorified night watchman at some bleak factory on the West Side. He and another agent would gawk for hours at the sooty parked trailers in the lots surrounded with chain-link fence as nothing happened. Riley became an enthusiastic Cubs fan for a while and was a regular at Wrigley Field during the couple of seasons the Cubs were pennant contenders. But after a few years, he again hoped a transfer would mean something more exciting. The problem was that once the Bureau put you on a force in one office, you were apt to be on that same squad for most of your career. Just before his transfer to New York came through, Riley helped out, as did most of the Chicago agents, at the 1968 Democratic Convention. The office fully mobilized for the event and Riley's squad boss told him to wear casual clothes and spend time in Grant Park to see if he could pick up any "interesting" information. In desert boots and corduroy jeans, Riley put in three days doing just that. Nothing happened except for a stringy-haired kid offering to sell him a few sticks of what the kid liked to call "whacky tabacky."

Somebody in the big New York office must have noticed on Riley's dossier that he had done work in the field of "activism." He was assigned to a newly formed Weatherman-bombing squad. It had come into being shortly after the explosion of a supposed Weatherman bomb factory in the Village. After that there was no more Weatherman bombing, though the squad remained intact. Riley worked days. He spent most of his time tramping up creaky stairs in urine-stinking East Village flophouses to find stoned kids in rooms splattered with psychedelic posters and checking if they had any leads on the whereabouts of suspected bombers. At about this time, Riley thought of maybe leaving the Bureau altogether and finding a job in private practice. But he knew it would be a shame to have wasted those several years he already had invested toward his pension fund. And again, he could retire at forty-four with two-thirds salary for the rest of his days. A man was still young at forty-four, he thought. He became a Mets fan.

Before he discovered tennis, he probably was in the lowest spirits he ever had been in. The Mets were losing and he lost interest in them easily. Rather than go out to Shea Stadium, he was content to watch the color set in his apartment, where he got excellent reception because of the cable-system hookup. He even made little effort to date women. In Chicago he had met a lot of stewardesses and secretaries in dating bars on Division Street who seemed impressed that he was an agent.

But in New York an agent was only another government employee at a time when the government itself wasn't very popular. The girls he would meet often turned cold—almost gagging on their Harvey Wallbangers and Bloody Marys—when he sheepishly announced his trade. One in black leather pants and jacket simply called him a "pig," a name Riley never before had been called.

The tennis, though, made all the difference. He picked it up very quickly and playing, he remembered the satisfaction of athletics. He remembered what it was like when he played baseball himself and could scoop a hot bouncer with a swipe of his oiled glove, tag the dirty canvas bag, bullet a throw to first for the double play—in one uninterrupted motion.

So, that summer when it happened, Riley lived for those weekends. He usually would manage to knock off on Friday afternoon to get on the FDR Drive along the East River and out

of the steamy city before the rush-hour traffic. Gogarty usually took the train up on Saturday morning. Gogarty couldn't
even coax Riley into going out to the roadside bar off old
Route 1. The place had a pink neon glass on a sign outside
that tipped back and forth as if it suffered from palsy.

"Relax a little," said Gogarty. "You should see this bar, Riley.
Crawling with women."

"No, I think I better relax here. Get a good night's sleep. I
got a full game schedule tomorrow."

"You played all day today."

"I can't help it. I like it."

Riley even ate like a man in serious training. He shied away
from starches and concentrated on meat and vegetables. He
ate fruit to get the sugar he needed and kept the white-painted
refrigerator in the wood-shingled cottage stocked with Gatorade. He liked the way the somewhat salty Gatorade seemed to
be absorbed by his system even before it reached his stomach. He told himself the drink was the greatest boon to athletics since water. And water had the obvious shortcoming of
leaving you bloated. On Saturday nights he did little more than
watch a Red Sox game televised by a Rhode Island station.

Once he had a dream that he was being carried into the
packed Astrodome on a pallet borne by a half-dozen slim
blondes. It was as if he were Bobby Riggs in the supposed
match of the century against Billie Jean King. Maybe he wore
a yellow windbreaker advertising Sugardaddy candy, as Bobby
Riggs had worn that night in Texas. Riley kept trying to tell
the sportscasters who leaned over the crowd to hand him their

microphones that this was all ridiculous. "I'm really not that good. I've only been playing two years." He laughed modestly and was embarrassed to receive so much attention.

"You'll lick her good, Riley," said one commentator, slapping him on the windbreaker. The crowd roared as the blondes carried him on. He dreamed of tennis often.

By August he thought he was within striking distance of Ted Smith. Smith was a twenty-one-year-old recent graduate of Amherst, where he had been captain of the tennis team. Smith, with his hip waterfall haircut and youthful tanned physique, also had been a national junior champion in high school. He was spending the summer after graduation instructing privately and living at his parents' summer place while he tried to decide whether to give the pro circuit a try for a year. Riley had made short work of all the salesmen and vacationing lawyers at the recreation-area courts. Occasionally he played with one of them—or even with half-able Gogarty once in a while— out of politeness. But Smith was his target.

"You've only been playing *two* years?" Smith once asked, disbelieving.

"Well, closer to two and a half now."

"Wow. Too bad you didn't start earlier. You know you're a natural," said the professional prospect. "Yeah, it's too bad."

By the end of August, when he took his vacation, Riley knew he was getting close. One scorching weekday afternoon—not at the town courts, but at a private club two towns over where Smith instructed—Riley almost succeeded. It was hot and most of the golfers had abandoned the brown fairways and congregated under umbrellas on the flagstone patio overlooking the courts. They sipped cool rum and gin drinks and watched. The long match went on and on. The court's red clay puffed like magician's smoke as the rubber soles pounded over it, and the dust settled slowly in distinct particles. The golfers in their bright slacks and open-necked shirts moved down from the patio for the last couple of games and lined the sidelines to see Smith finally win. There was applause and somebody was ribbing Smith.

"A club pro is supposed to win, Ted—win easily." Handsome Smith smiled. Wiping the grit from his forehead, Riley smiled too. He beamed. He wasn't sure, but he thought that maybe he had let Smith win the final, deciding points. He knew then that he could beat him. And he wanted to do it decisively.

"I just thought you would be more enthusiastic," said the man on the phone. It was the week after his vacation when he had almost beaten Smith, and Riley was back in New York. The air conditioner in his apartment hummed. The man had identified himself as a reporter for one of the Chicago papers.

"Do you realize what you're saying?" Riley said, squinting. The black plastic telephone seemed to sweat in his hand.

"Ah, come on. I tell you I just didn't expect this. Stedder has been giving me all he can from out here." Stedder was an agent with whom Riley had shared an apartment when he was assigned to Chicago. "I just need to get a contact in the New York office. He said you would be perfect. I don't want any accusatory stuff. Just document some examples of bureaucratic bogdown or stupidity. The waste of the taxpayers' money, as they say. The way the Bureau keeps task forces like your bomb

squad when everybody knows there hasn't been a Weatherman bombing in years. The way half your bomb squad plays
that basketball game all afternoon."

"Basketball game?"

"The thing with the little backboard and hoop you attach
to the wastebasket to toss crumpled paper. That's a riot. Stedder said you told him about it. How the office was going to or-
ganize a league. That's the kind of thing I need. Did somebody
send away for it? I've seen them advertised."

"What?"

"The little backboard and hoop. Did somebody send away?"

"Who's been telling you this?"

"Stedder, I said. And Stedder told me you'd be glad to talk.
Really. Stedder and I went to college together. Now I don't
mean to offend you, but Stedder said you were a perfect case
to cite in the FBI's wasting of personnel. A man with a law degree from a good university sitting in a car in Chicago waiting
for some trucker to pilfer a case of whiskey from his rig."

"I want your name."

"What?"

"You heard me. Your name. I didn't get it."

"Come on. Let's talk like two adults. If this isn't for you,
just tell me."

"Your name. I can track you down easily enough, you know."

"Riley. Mr. Riley, Stedder just said that . . ."

"I don't care what the hell Stedder said to you or any other
lousy hack."

"Lousy hack, huh. Oh, I see. I'm a lousy hack. I'm a lousy
hack to want to tell people what's going on with their money.

We both know what the story is. I just hoped that you had the guts to be honest. I'm sorry. And I told you what my name is before and I'll tell you again. I'm John Mayer, for God's sake. Get in touch care of my paper. What are you going to do, bug my jockey shorts?" Riley could hear a sigh. "Stedder told me you had some intelligence. He said he knew you had your bellyful yourself and were thinking about leaving the Bureau anyway."

"Stedder," Riley said very slowly. "Stedder." The reporter suddenly was less assuming.

"Now wait a minute. Don't you go dragging Stedder into this. Forget I ever called. We're friends, Stedder and I. Stedder is your friend. I mean you wouldn't do something like that."

"Good-bye, Mr. Mayer."

"Heh, wait a minute. Look, Stedder is a source. A source whom I must protect professionally. I don't want to be responsible for getting him into a jam."

"That's the old story. And that's what's wrong with all you hacks. You have no responsibility for anything."

"Wait a minute, Riley."

"Good-bye."

"Riley!" Shaking, Riley planted the receiver back on the base. No sooner did he hang up, than the phone rang again. He lifted the receiver to break the connection and once more hung up. Riley dropped himself to the black Naugahyde recliner. The footrest popped up and the springs wheezed. He said Stedder's name several times out loud.

Stedder.

At his green metal desk topped with green linoleum in the

New York office the next morning, Riley put through a call to the Chicago office. Stedder confirmed his friendship with Mayer, the reporter, and after that Riley was very short with Stedder. Stedder pleaded, but it was no use. That same afternoon Riley approached his squad boss and asked him how he would go about seeing the Director himself. At first the sleepy-eyed man with cataracts thought he had heard wrong.

"The Director." He pronounced director very distinctly, emphasizing each syllable. He straightened his food-splattered wide tie.

"That's what I said. The sooner, the better."

"Maybe you better tell me about this."

"I have to talk to the Director. It's like that."

"Hmmm. I mean you really want to talk to the Director."

"God!" yelled Riley. "Doesn't anybody do anything around here at all!"

"All right. Sure. Take it easy, Riley. Let's see. The Director."

Riley defeated Smith on a damp Saturday in early October. Riley and Gogarty no longer had the rented cottage and Riley drove up by himself to play Smith, again at the country-club courts. He had worried that it would rain and the match would have to be canceled altogether. Smith wore his sweat clothes and obviously wasn't playing his best. Riley never had had delusions that he could consistently beat the twenty-one-year-old who was about to go on the pro circuit. But he had wanted to beat him at least once and that had given him a summer-long goal.

He left the club without changing. There had been no crowd on hand to watch and when it was over, Smith simply shook his hand. Not much more was said besides congratulations and Riley was markedly cool. On Labor Day weekend Riley had overheard Smith's girl—a New York model with wispy auburn hair—call Riley "strange" when neither she nor Smith knew he was in the club pro shop at the time.

Riley could have driven back to New York in less than three hours. But he started on the coast road, the old Route 1, and didn't bother taking the connecting route to the turnpike. The Volkswagen's heat smelled stale, as car heat does smell the first few times you use it every season. It had started to rain lightly. The stubby windshield wipers squeaked back and forth on the flat windshield like sluggish metro-nomes. He felt a chill and fiddled with the heater handle beside the seat up-holstered with plastic supposed to look like cloth tweed. He stared blankly ahead. For an instant he saw his face in the oval of the rearview mirror and looked away quickly. He tried to lose himself in the passing blur of roadside bars and ham-burger places.

He had feared this letdown. He had beaten Smith and he felt no different. He had only the fact that he had fingered Stedder, who was about to be asked to resign from the Bureau, to think about for the whole coming winter. The tennisless winter. It wasn't fair. He had beaten a pro. There should be more to it.

He turned down a buckled asphalt road. The sea grass in the marshes looked combed. There were a few one-story summer houses with boarded-up windows. The wooden telephone poles had single crosspieces and the wires drooped from one to the next in graceful crescents. The sky was a very dull green and the twin yellow stripes in the road only stressed the dreariness of everything else in the scene. He could see the water in the distance. He parked the red Volkswagen in the bathing pavilion's empty huge lot. If only that damn reporter hadn't called him, he thought. If only he had been out at the time.

Riley twisted the black ridged knob on the glove compartment. Inside was stuffed his .38 in its mahogany leather shoulder holster. He unsnapped the button clasp and took only the oily-smelling blue thing with its handle that had a crisscross pattern on the wood grip. There was something strangely jarring about having the gun and being alone like that. He always carried the pistol on duty, though, outside of that once in Kansas City, he only fired it at the once-a-month target practice the agents had to put in at a field on Long Island. His stomach jumped.

With the gun hanging from his limp arm, he started onto the beach and seemed almost programmed to do so. He could have been sleepwalking through the sand and his Adidas sank with each step till he got to the hard part where the tide had been up that morning. The rain was heavier and a few seagulls with black-tipped wings and orange beaks congregated fifty yards ahead of him. They took off as he approached. In the middle of the beach of the cove, he stopped and looked out to where the flat horizon met that green sky. He closed his eyes to see the purple screen of his lids. He listened to the water lapping and everything smelled seaweedy. He opened his eyes. Then came the strangest part.

It was as if he were outside of himself and saw himself from a distance. It was as if he were watching a movie of all of this— a movie of himself. He saw a man alone on a beach. The man wore a track warm-up suit and he held a gun at his side. The man slowly lifted the gun with his arm straight out. Behind the man was a raised boardwalk and a long row of cabanas planked with weathered boards that looked black in the rain. He watched the man just standing there with his arm out for what seemed a long while. Finally, he heard the shots as the man emptied the revolver's contents out over the ocean. One, two, three, four, five, six.

And after his ears stopped echoing with the deafening cracks, the full impact of what had happened that day at last sunk in. Riley was inside himself again. Suddenly he knew that at thirty-four, and after playing tennis for only two and a half years, he, Riley, had beaten Ted Smith the professional. It was amazing. Absolutely amazing!

He jogged back to the parking lot and told himself it wasn't a sound idea to stand around any longer in that dampness. He would catch a cold and a cold would mean lost tennis time. Excited, Riley told himself he would join the indoor club on Long Island that Monday.

He got back into the Volkswagen and shoved the vaguely warm gun back in the glove compartment. He leaned over the seat to tug a terry-cloth towel from his equipment bag and vigorously dry his dripping short-cut hair, which already was graying a bit. Shifting out of the parking lot, he thought that the indoor club would be expensive, that it would take as much of his salary as he paid for his apartment. But what the hell. Tennis was all there was. Tennis.

"TENNIS! TENNIS! TENNIS!" he yelled out the open window as loud as he could. He quickly rolled up the window because a draft like that was dangerous for a man in training too.

The Facts of Life

W. SOMERSET MAUGHAM

It was Henry Garnet's habit on leaving the city of an afternoon to drop in at his club and play bridge before going home
to dinner. He was a pleasant man to play with. He knew the
game well and you could be sure that he would make the best
of his cards. He was a good loser; and when he won was more
inclined to ascribe his success to his luck than to his skill. He
was indulgent, and if his partner made a mistake could be
trusted to find an excuse for him. It was surprising then on
this occasion to hear him telling his partner with unnecessary
sharpness that he had never seen a hand worse played; and it
was more surprising still to see him not only make a grave error
himself, an error of which you would never have thought him
capable, but when his partner, not unwilling to get a little of
his own back, pointed it out, insist against all reason and with
considerable heat that he was perfectly right. But they were all
old friends, the men he was playing with, and none of them
took his ill-humour very seriously. Henry Garnet was a broker,
a partner in a firm of repute, and it occurred to one of them
that something had gone wrong with some stock he was interested in.

"How's the market today?" he asked.

"Booming. Even the suckers are making money."

It was evident that stocks and shares had nothing to do with Henry Garnet's vexation; but something was the matter; that was evident too. He was a hearty fellow, who enjoyed excellent health; he had plenty of money; he was fond of his wife and devoted to his children. As a rule he had high spirits, and he laughed easily at the nonsense they were apt to talk while they played; but today he sat glum and silent. His brows were crossly puckered and there was a sulky look about his mouth. Presently, to ease the tension, one of the others mentioned a subject upon which they all knew Henry Garnet was glad to speak.

"How's your boy, Henry? I see he's done pretty well in the tournaments."

Henry Garnet's frown grew darker.

"He's done no better than I expected him to."

"When does he come back from Monte?"

"He got back last night."

"Did he enjoy himself?"

"I suppose so; all I know is that he made a damned fool of himself."

"Oh. How?"

"I'd rather not talk about it if you don't mind."

The three men looked at him with curiosity. Henry Garnet scowled at the green baize.

"Sorry, old boy. Your call."

The game proceeded in a strained silence. Garnet got his bid, and when he played his cards so badly that he went three down not a word was said. Another rubber was begun and in the second game Garnet denied a suit.

"Having none?" his partner asked him.

Garnet's irritability was such that he did not even reply, and when at the end of the hand it appeared that he had revoked, and that his revoke cost the rubber, it was not to be expected that his partner should let his carelessness go without remark.

"What the devil's the matter with you, Henry?" he said. "You're playing like a fool."

Garnet was disconcerted. He did not so much mind losing a big rubber himself, but he was sore that his inattention should have made his partner lose too. He pulled himself together.

"I'd better not play any more. I thought a few rubbers would calm me, but the fact is I can't give my mind to the game. To tell you the truth I'm in a hell of a temper."

They all burst out laughing.

"You don't have to tell us that, old boy. It's obvious."

Garnet gave them a rueful smile.

"Well, I bet you'd be in a temper if what's happened to me had happened to you. As a matter of fact I'm in a damned awkward situation, and if any of you fellows can give me any advice how to deal with it I'd be grateful."

"Let's have a drink and you tell us about it. With a K.C., a Home Office official and an eminent surgeon—if we can't tell you how to deal with a situation, nobody can."

The K.C. got up and rang the bell for a waiter.

"It's about that damned boy of mine," said Henry Garnet.

Drinks were ordered and brought. And this is the story that Henry Garnet told them.

The boy of whom he spoke was his only son. His name was Nicholas and of course he was called Nicky. He was eighteen. The Garnets had two daughters besides, one of sixteen and the other of twelve, but however unreasonable it seemed, for a father is generally supposed to like his daughters best, and though he did all he could not to show his preference, there was no doubt that the greater share of Henry Garnet's affection was given to his son. He was kind, in a charming, casual way, to his daughters, and gave them handsome presents on their birthdays and at Christmas; but he doted on Nicky. Nothing was too good for him. He thought the world of him. He could hardly take his eyes off him. You could not blame him, for Nicky was a son that any parent might have been proud of. He was six foot two, lithe but muscular, with broad shoulders and a slim waist, and he held himself gallantly erect; he had a charming head, well placed on the shoulders, with pale brown hair that waved slightly, blue eyes with long dark lashes under well-marked eyebrows, a full red mouth and a tanned, clean skin. When he smiled he showed very regular and very white teeth. He was not shy, but there was a modesty in his demeanour that was attractive. In social intercourse he was easy, polite and quietly gay. He was the offspring of nice, healthy, decent parents, he had been well brought up in a good home, he had been sent to a good school, and the general result was as engaging a specimen of young manhood as you were likely to find in a long time. You felt that he was as honest, open and virtuous as he looked. He had never given his parents a moment's uneasiness. As a child he was seldom ill and never naughty. As a boy he did everything that was expected of him. His school reports were excellent. He was wonderfully popular, and he ended his career, with a creditable number of prizes, as head of the school and captain of the football team. But this was not all. At the age of fourteen Nicky had developed an unexpected gift for lawn tennis. This was a game that his father not only was fond of, but played very well, and when he discerned in the boy the promise of a tennis player he fostered it. During the holidays he had him taught by the best professionals and by the time he was sixteen he had won a number of tournaments for boys of his age. He could beat his father so badly that only parental affection reconciled the older player to the poor show he put up. At eighteen Nicky went to Cambridge and Henry Garnet conceived the ambition that before he was through with the university he should play for it. Nicky had all the qualifications for becoming a great tennis-player. He was tall, he had a long reach, he was quick on his feet and his timing was perfect. He realized instinctively where the ball was coming and, seemingly without hurry, was there to take it. He had a powerful serve, with a nasty break that made it difficult to return, and his forehand drive, low, long and accurate, was deadly. He was not so good on the backhand and his volleying was wild, but all through the summer before he went to Cambridge Henry Garnet made him work on these points under the best teacher in England. At the back of his mind, though he did not even mention it to Nicky, he cherished a further ambition, to see his son play at Wimbledon, and who could tell, perhaps be chosen to represent his country in the

Davis Cup. A great lump came into Henry Garnet's throat as he saw in fancy his son leap over the net to shake hands with the American champion whom he had just defeated, and walk off the court to the deafening plaudits of the multitude.

As an assiduous frequenter of Wimbledon Henry Garnet had a good many friends in the tennis world, and one evening he found himself at a City dinner sitting next to one of them, a Colonel Brabazon, and in due course began talking to him of Nicky and what chance there might be of his being chosen to play for his university during the following season.

"Why don't you let him go down to Monte Carlo and play in the spring tournament there?" said the Colonel suddenly.

"Oh, I don't think he's good enough for that. He's not nineteen yet, he only went up to Cambridge last October; he wouldn't stand a chance against all those cracks."

"Of course, Austin and von Cramm and so on would knock spots off him, but he might snatch a game or two; and if he got up against some of the smaller fry there's no reason why he shouldn't win two or three matches. He's never been up against any of the first-rate players and it would be wonderful practice for him. He'd learn a lot more than he'll ever learn in the seaside tournaments you enter him for."

"I wouldn't dream of it. I'm not going to let him leave Cambridge in the middle of a term. I've always impressed upon him that tennis is only a game and it mustn't interfere with work."

Colonel Brabazon asked Garnet when the term ended.

"That's all right. He'd only have to cut about three days. Surely that could be arranged. You see, two of the men we were depending on have let us down, and we're in a hole. We want to send as good a team as we can. The Germans are sending their best players and so are the Americans."

"Nothing doing, old boy. In the first place Nicky's not good enough, and secondly, I don't fancy the idea of sending a kid like that to Monte Carlo without anyone to look after him. If I could get away myself I might think of it, but that's out of the question."

"I shall be there. I'm going as the non-playing captain of the English team. I'll keep an eye on him."

"You'll be busy, and besides, it's not a responsibility I'd like to ask you to take. He's never been abroad in his life, and to tell you the truth, I shouldn't have a moment's peace all the time he was there."

They left it at that and presently Henry Garnet went home. He was so flattered by Colonel Brabazon's suggestion that he could not help telling his wife.

"Fancy his thinking Nicky's as good as that. He told me he'd seen him play and his style was fine. He only wants more practice to get into the first flight. We shall see the kid playing in the semi-finals at Wimbledon yet, old girl."

To his surprise Mrs. Garnet was not so much opposed to the notion as he would have expected.

"After all the boy's eighteen. Nicky's never got into mischief yet and there's no reason to suppose he will now."

"There's his work to be considered; don't forget that. I think it would be a very bad precedent to let him cut the end of term."

"But what can three days matter? It seems a shame to rob him of a chance like that. I'm sure he'd jump at it if you asked him."

"Well, I'm not going to. I haven't sent him to Cambridge just to play tennis. I know he's steady, but it's silly to put temptation in his way. He's much too young to go to Monte Carlo by himself."

"You say he won't have a chance against these crack players, but you can't tell."

Henry Garnet sighed a little. On the way home in the car it had struck him that Austin's health was uncertain and that von Cramm had his off-days. Supposing, just for the sake of argument, that Nicky had a bit of luck like that—then there would be no doubt that he would be chosen to play for Cambridge. But of course that was all nonsense.

"Nothing doing, my dear. I've made up my mind and I'm not going to change it."

Mrs. Garnet held her peace. But next day she wrote to Nicky, telling him what had happened, and suggested to him what she would do in his place if, wanting to go, he wished to get his father's consent. A day or two later Henry Garnet received a letter from his son. He was bubbling over with excitement. He had seen his tutor, who was a tennis-player himself, and the Provost of his college, who happened to know Colonel Brabazon, and no objection would be made to his leaving before the end of term; they both thought it an opportunity that shouldn't be missed. He didn't see what harm he could come to, and if only, just this once, his father would stretch a point, well, next term, he promised faithfully, he'd work like blazes. It was a very pretty letter. Mrs. Garnet watched her husband read it at the breakfast table; she was undisturbed by the frown on his face. He threw it over to her.

"I don't know why you thought it necessary to tell Nicky something I told you in confidence. It's too bad of you. Now you've thoroughly unsettled him."

"I'm sorry. I thought it would please him to know that Colonel Brabazon had such a high opinion of him. I don't see why one should only tell people the disagreeable things that are said about them. Of course I made it quite clear that there could be no question of his going."

"You've put me in an odious position. If there's anything I hate it's for the boy to look upon me as a spoil-sport and a tyrant."

"Oh, he'll never do that. He may think you are rather silly and unreasonable, but I'm sure he'll understand that it's only for his own good that you're being so unkind."

"Christ," said Henry Garnet.

His wife had a great inclination to laugh. She knew the battle was won. Dear, oh dear, how easy it was to get men to do what you wanted. For appearance sake Henry Garnet held out for forty-eight hours, but then he yielded, and a fortnight later Nicky came to London. He was to start for Monte Carlo next morning, and after dinner, when Mrs. Garnet and her elder daughter had left them, Henry took the opportunity to give his son some good advice.

"I don't feel quite comfortable about letting you go off to a place like Monte Carlo at your age practically by yourself," he finished, "but there it is and I can only hope you'll be sensible. I don't want to play the heavy father, but there are three things especially that I want to warn you against: one is gambling, don't gamble; the second is money, don't lend anyone money; and the third is women, don't have anything to do with women. If you don't do any of those three things you can't come to much harm, so remember them well."

"All right, father," Nicky smiled.

"That's my last word to you. I know the world pretty well and believe me, my advice is sound."

"I won't forget it. I promise you."

"That's a good chap. Now let's go up and join the ladies."

Nicky beat neither Austin nor von Cramm in the Monte Carlo tournament, but he did not disgrace himself. He snatched an unexpected victory over a Spanish player and gave one of the Austrians a closer match than anyone had thought possible. In the mixed doubles he got into the semi-finals. His charm conquered everyone and he vastly enjoyed himself. It was generally allowed that he showed promise, and Colonel Brabazon told him that when he was a little older and had had more practice with first-class players he would be a credit to his father. The tournament came to an end and the day following he was to fly back to London. Anxious to play his best he had lived very carefully, smoking little and drinking nothing, and going to bed early; but on his last evening he thought he would like to see something of the life in Monte Carlo of which he had heard so much. An official dinner was given to the tennis-players and after dinner with the rest of them he went into the Sporting Club. It was the first time he had been there. Monte Carlo was very full and the rooms were crowded. Nicky had never before seen roulette played except in the pictures; in a maze he stopped at the first table he came to; chips of different sizes were scattered over the green cloth in what looked like a hopeless muddle; the croupier gave the wheel a sharp turn and with a flick threw in the little white ball. After what seemed an endless time the ball stopped and another croupier with a broad, indifferent gesture raked in the chips of those who had lost.

Presently Nicky wandered over to where they were playing *trente et quarante,* but he couldn't understand what it was all about and he thought it dull. He saw a crowd in another room and sauntered in. A big game of baccara was in progress and he was immediately conscious of the tension. The players were protected from the thronging bystanders by a brass rail; they sat round the table, nine on each side, with the dealer in the middle and the croupier facing him. Big money was changing hands. The dealer was a member of the Greek Syndicate. Nicky looked at his impassive face. His eyes were watchful, but his expression never changed whether he won or lost. It was a terrifying, strangely impressive sight. It gave Nicky, who had been thriftily brought up, a peculiar thrill to see someone risk a thousand pounds on the turn of a card and when he lost make a little joke and laugh. It was all terribly exciting. An acquaintance came up to him.

"Been doing any good?" he asked.

"I haven't been playing."

"Wise of you. Rotten game. Come and have a drink."

"All right."

While they were having it Nicky told his friend that this was the first time he had ever been in the rooms.

"Oh, but you must have one little flutter before you go. It's idiotic to leave Monte without having tried your luck. After all it won't hurt you to lose a hundred francs or so."

"I don't suppose it will, but my father wasn't any too keen on my coming at all and one of the three things he particularly advised me not to do was to gamble."

But when Nicky left his companion he strolled back to one of the tables where they were playing roulette. He stood for a while looking at the losers' money being raked in by the croupier and the money that was won paid out to the winners. It was impossible to deny that it was thrilling. His friend was right, it did seem silly to leave Monte without putting something on the table just once. It would be an experience, and at his age you had to have all the experience you could get. He reflected that he hadn't promised his father not to gamble, he'd promised him not to forget his advice. It wasn't quite the same, was it? He took a hundred-franc note out of his pocket and rather shyly put it on number eighteen. He chose it because that was his age. With a wildly beating heart he watched the wheel turn; the little white ball whizzed about like a small demon of mischief; the wheel went round more slowly, the little white ball hesitated, it seemed about to stop, it went on again; Nicky could hardly believe his eyes when it fell into number eighteen. A lot of chips were passed over to him and his hands trembled as he took them. It seemed to amount to a lot of money. He was so confused that he never thought of putting anything on the following round; in fact he had no intention of playing any more, once was enough; and he was surprised when eighteen again came up. There was only one chip on it.

"By George, you've won again," said a man who was standing near to him.

"Me? I hadn't got anything on."

"Yes, you had. Your original stake. They always leave it on unless you ask for it back. Didn't you know?"

Another packet of chips was handed over to him. Nicky's head reeled. He counted his gains: seven thousand francs. A queer sense of power seized him; he felt wonderfully clever. This was the easiest way of making money that he had ever heard of. His frank, charming face was wreathed in smiles. His bright eyes met those of a woman standing by his side. She smiled.

"You're in luck," she said.

She spoke English, but with a foreign accent.

"I can hardly believe it. It's the first time I've ever played."

"That explains it. Lend me a thousand francs, will you? I've lost everything I've got. I'll give it you back in half an hour."

"All right."

She took a large red chip from his pile and with a word of thanks disappeared. The man who had spoken to him before grunted.

"You'll never see that again."

Nicky was dashed. His father had particularly advised him not to lend anyone money. What a silly thing to do! And to somebody he'd never seen in his life. But the fact was, he felt at that moment such love for the human race that it had never occurred to him to refuse. And that big red chip, it was almost impossible to realize that it had any value. Oh well, it didn't matter, he still had six thousand francs, he'd just try his luck once or twice more and if he didn't win he'd go home. He put a chip on sixteen, which was his elder sister's age, but it didn't come up; then on twelve, which was his younger sister's, and that didn't come up either; he tried various numbers at random, but without success. It was funny, he seemed to have lost his knack. He thought he would try just once more and then stop; he won. He had made up all his losses and had something left over. At the end of an hour, after various ups and downs, having experienced such thrills as he had never known in his life, he found himself with so many chips that they would hardly go in his pockets. He decided to go. He went to the changers' office and he gasped when twenty thousand-franc notes were spread out before him. He had never won so much money in his life. He put it in his pocket and was turning away when the woman to whom he had lent the thousand francs came up to him.

"I've been looking for you everywhere," she said. "I was afraid you'd gone. I was in a fever, I didn't know what you'd think of me. Here's your thousand francs and thank you so much for the loan."

Nicky, blushing scarlet, stared at her with amazement. How he had misjudged her! His father had said, don't gamble; well, he had, and he'd made twenty thousand francs; and his father had said, don't lend anyone money; well, he had, he'd lent quite a lot to a total stranger, and she'd returned it. The fact was that he wasn't nearly such a fool as his father thought: he'd had an instinct that he could lend her money with safety, and you see, his instinct was right. But he was so obviously taken aback that the little lady was forced to laugh.

"What is the matter with you?" she asked.

"To tell you the truth I never expected to see the money back."

"What did you take me for? Did you think I was a—cocotte?" Nicky reddened to the roots of his wavy hair.

"No, of course not."

"Do I look like one?"

"Not a bit."

She was dressed very quietly, in black, with a string of gold beads round her neck; her simple frock showed off a neat, slight figure; she had a pretty little face and a trim head. She was made up, but not excessively, and Nicky supposed that she was not more than three or four years older than himself She gave him a friendly smile.

"My husband is in the administration in Morocco, and I've come to Monte Carlo for a few weeks because he thought I wanted a change."

"I was just going," said Nicky because he couldn't think of anything else to say.

"Already!"

"Well, I've got to get up early tomorrow. I'm going back to London by air."

"Of course. The tournament ended today, didn't it? I saw you play, you know, two or three times."

"Did you? I don't know why you should have noticed me."

"You've got a beautiful style. And you looked very sweet in your shorts."

Nicky was not an immodest youth, but it did cross his mind that perhaps she had borrowed that thousand francs in order to scrape acquaintance with him.

"Do you ever go to the Knickerbocker?" she asked.

"No. I never have."

"Oh, but you mustn't leave Monte Carlo without having been there. Why don't you come and dance a little? To tell you the truth, I'm starving with hunger and I should adore some bacon and eggs."

Nicky remembered his father's advice not to have anything to do with women, but this was different; you had only to look at the pretty little thing to know at once that she was perfectly respectable. Her husband was in what corresponded, he supposed, to the Civil Service. His father and mother had friends who were Civil Servants and they and their wives sometimes came to dinner. It was true that the wives were neither so young nor so pretty as this one, but she was just as ladylike as they were. And after winning twenty thousand francs he thought it wouldn't be a bad idea to have a little fun.

"I'd love to go with you," he said. "But you won't mind if I don't stay very long. I've left instructions at my hotel that I'm to be called at seven."

"We'll leave as soon as ever you like."

Nicky found it very pleasant at the Knickerbocker. He ate his bacon and eggs with appetite. They shared a bottle of champagne. They danced, and the little lady told him he danced beautifully. He knew he danced pretty well, and of course she was easy to dance with. As light as a feather. She laid her cheek against his and when their eyes met there was in hers a smile that made his heart go pit-a-pat. A coloured woman sang in a throaty, sensual voice. The floor was crowded.

"Have you ever been told that you're very good-looking?" she asked.

"I don't think so," he laughed. "Gosh," he thought, "I believe she's fallen for me."

Nicky was not such a fool to be unaware that women often liked him, and when she made that remark he pressed her to him a little more closely. She closed her eyes and a faint sigh escaped her lips.

"I suppose it wouldn't be quite nice if I kissed you before all these people," he said.

"What do you think they would take me for?"

It began to grow late and Nicky said that really he thought he ought to be going.

"I shall go too," she said. "Will you drop me at my hotel on your way?"

Nicky paid the bill. He was rather surprised at its amount, but with all that money he had in his pocket he could afford not to care, and they got into a taxi. She snuggled up to him and he kissed her. She seemed to like it.

"By Jove," he thought, "I wonder if there's anything doing."

It was true that she was a married woman, but her husband was in Morocco, and it certainly did look as if she'd fallen for him. Good and proper. It was true also that his father had warned him to have nothing to do with women, but, he reflected again, he hadn't actually promised he wouldn't, he'd only promised not to forget his advice. Well, he hadn't; he was bearing it in mind that very minute. But circumstances alter cases. She was a sweet little thing; it seemed silly to miss the chance of an adventure when it was handed to you like that on a tray. When they reached the hotel he paid off the taxi.

"I'll walk home," he said. "The air will do me good after the stuffy atmosphere of that place."

"Come up a moment," she said. "I'd like to show you the photo of my little boy."

"Oh, have you got a little boy?" he exclaimed, a trifle dashed.

"Yes, a sweet little boy."

He walked upstairs after her. He didn't in the least want to see the photograph of her little boy, but he thought it only civil to pretend he did. He was afraid he'd made a fool of himself; it occurred to him that she was taking him up to look at the photograph in order to show him in a nice way that he'd made a mistake. He'd told her he was eighteen.

"I suppose she thinks I'm just a kid."

He began to wish he hadn't spent all that money on champagne at the night-club.

But she didn't show him the photograph of her little boy after all. They had no sooner got into her room than she turned to him, flung her arms round his neck, and kissed him full on the lips. He had never in all his life been kissed so passionately.

"Darling," she said.

For a brief moment his father's advice once more crossed Nicky's mind and then he forgot it.

Nicky was a light sleeper and the least sound was apt to wake him. Two or three hours later he awoke and for a moment could not imagine where he was. The room was not quite dark, for the door of the bathroom was ajar, and the light in it had been left on. Suddenly he was conscious that someone was moving about the room. Then he remembered. He saw that it was his little friend, and he was on the point of speaking when something in the way she was behaving stopped him. She was walking very cautiously, as though she were afraid of waking him; she stopped once or twice and looked over at the bed. He wondered what she was after. He soon saw. She went over to the chair on which he had placed his clothes and once more looked in his direction. She waited for what seemed to him an interminable time. The silence was so intense that Nicky thought he could hear his own heart beating. Then, very slowly, very quietly, she took up his coat, slipped her hand into the inside pocket and drew out all those beautiful thousand-franc notes that Nicky had been so proud to win. She put the coat back and placed some other clothes on it so that it should look as though it had not been disturbed, then, with the bundle of notes in her hand, for an appreciable time stood once more stock-still. Nicky had repressed an instinctive impulse to jump up and grab her; it was partly surprise that had kept him quiet, partly the notion that he was in a strange hotel, in a foreign country, and if he made a row he didn't know what might happen. She looked at him. His eyes were partly closed and he was sure that she thought he was asleep. In the silence she could hardly fail to hear his regular breathing. When she had reassured herself that her movements had not disturbed him she stepped, with infinite caution, across the room. On a small table in the window a cineraria was growing in a pot. Nicky watched her now with his eyes wide open. The plant was evidently placed quite loosely in the pot, for taking it by the stalks she lifted it out; she put the banknotes in the bottom of the pot and replaced the plant. It was an excellent hiding-place. No one could have guessed that anything was concealed under that richly flowering plant. She pressed the earth down with her fingers and then, very slowly, taking care not to make the smallest noise, crept across the room, and slipped back into bed.

"Cheri," she said, in a caressing voice.

Nicky breathed steadily, like a man immersed in deep sleep. The little lady turned over on her side and disposed herself to slumber. But though Nicky lay so still his thoughts worked busily. He was extremely indignant at the scene he had just witnessed, and to himself he spoke his thoughts with vigour.

"She's nothing but a damned tart. She and her dear little boy and her husband in Morocco. My eye! She's a rotten thief, that's what she is. Took me for a mug. If she thinks she's going to get away with anything like that, she's mistaken."

He had already made up his mind what he was going to do with the money he had so cleverly won. He had long wanted a car of his own, and had thought it rather mean of his father not to have given him one. After all, a feller doesn't always want to drive about in the family bus. Well, he'd just teach the old man a lesson and buy one himself. For twenty thousand francs, two hundred pounds roughly, he could get a very decent sec- ondhand car. He meant to get the money back, but just then he didn't know how. He didn't like the idea of kicking up a row, he was a stranger, in an hotel he knew nothing of; it might very well be that the beastly woman had friends there, he didn't mind facing anyone in a fair fight, but he'd look pretty foolish if someone pulled a gun on him. He reflected besides, very sensibly, that he had no proof the money was his. If it came to a showdown and she swore it was hers, he might very easily find himself hauled off to a police-station. He really didn't know what to do. Presently by her regular breathing he knew that the little lady was asleep. She must have fallen asleep with an easy mind, for she had done her job without a hitch. It infuriated Nicky that she should rest so peacefully while he lay awake worried to death. Suddenly an idea occurred to him. It was such a good one that it was only by the exercise of all his self-control that he prevented himself from jumping out of bed and carrying it out at once. Two could play at her game. She'd stolen his money; well, he'd steal it back again, and they'd be all square. He made up his mind to wait quite quietly until he was sure that deceitful woman was sound asleep. He waited for what seemed to him a very long time. She did not stir. Her breathing was as regular as a child's.

"Darling," he said at last.

No answer. No movement. She was dead to the world. Very slowly, pausing after every movement, very silently, he slipped out of bed. He stood still for a while, looking at her to see whether he had disturbed her. Her breathing was as regular as before. During the time he was waiting he had taken note carefully of the furniture in the room so that in crossing it he should not knock against a chair or a table and make a noise. He took a couple of steps and waited, he took a couple of steps more; he was very light on his feet and made no sound as he walked; he took fully five minutes to get to the window, and here he waited again. He started, for the bed slightly creaked, but it was only because the sleeper turned in her sleep. He forced himself to wait till he had counted one hundred. She was sleeping like a log. With infinite care he seized the cineraria by the stalks and gently pulled it out of the pot; he put his other hand in, his heart beat nineteen to the dozen as his fingers touched the notes, his hand closed on them and he slowly drew them out. He replaced the plant and in his turn carefully pressed down the earth. While he was doing all this he had kept one eye on the form lying in the bed. It remained still. After another pause he crept softly to the chair on which his clothes were lying. He first put the bundle of notes in his coat pocket and then proceeded to dress. It took him a good quarter of an hour, because he could afford to make no sound. He had been wearing a soft shirt with his dinner jacket, and he congratulated himself on this, because it was easier to put on silently than a stiff one. He had difficulty in tying his tie without a looking-glass, but he very wisely reflected that it didn't really matter if it wasn't tied very well. His spirits were rising. The whole thing now began to seem rather a lark. At length he was completely dressed except for his shoes, which he took in his hand; he thought he would put them on when he got into the passage. Now he had to cross the room to get to the door. He reached it so quietly that he could not have disturbed the lightest sleeper. But the door had to be unlocked. He turned the key very slowly; it creaked.

"Who's that?"

The little woman suddenly sat up in bed. Nicky's heart jumped to his mouth. He made a great effort to keep his head.

"It's only me. It's six o'clock and I've got to go. I was trying not to wake you."

"Oh, I forgot."

She sank back on to the pillow.

"Now that you're awake I'll put on my shoes." He sat down on the edge of the bed and did this.

"Don't make a noise when you go out. The hotel people don't like it. Oh, I'm so sleepy."

"You go right off to sleep again."

"Kiss me before you go." He bent down and kissed her. "You're a sweet boy and a wonderful lover. *Bon voyage.*"

Nicky did not feel quite safe till he got out of the hotel. The dawn had broken. The sky was unclouded, and in the harbour the yachts and the fishing-boats lay motionless on the still water. On the quay fishermen were getting ready to start on their day's work. The streets were deserted. Nicky took a long breath of the sweet morning air. He felt alert and well. He also felt as pleased as Punch. With a swinging stride, his shoulders well thrown back, he walked up the hill and along the gardens in front of the Casino—the flowers in that clear light had a dewy brilliance that was delicious—till he came to his hotel. Here the day had already begun. In the hall porters with mufflers round their necks and berets on their heads were busy sweeping. Nicky went up to his room and had a hot bath. He lay in it and thought with satisfaction that he was not such a mug as some people might think. After his bath he did his exercises, dressed, packed and went down to breakfast. He had a grand appetite. No continental breakfast for him! He had grape-fruit, porridge, bacon and eggs, rolls fresh from the oven, so crisp and delicious they melted in your mouth, marmalade and three cups of coffee. Though feeling perfectly well before, he felt better after that. He lit the pipe he had recently learnt to smoke, paid his bill and stepped into the car that was waiting to take him to the aerodrome on the other side of Cannes. The road as far as Nice ran over the hills and below him was the blue sea and the coastline. He couldn't help thinking it damned pretty. They passed through Nice, so gay and friendly in the early morning, and presently they came to a long stretch of straight road that ran by the sea. Nicky had paid his bill, not with the money that he had won the night before, but with the money his father had given him; he had changed a thousand francs to pay for supper at the Knickerbocker, but that deceitful little woman had returned him the thousand francs he had lent her, so that he still had twenty thousand-franc notes in his pocket. He thought he would like to have a look at them. He had so nearly lost them that they had a double value for him. He took them out of his hip-pocket into which for safety's sake he had stuffed them when he put on the suit he was travelling in, and counted them one by one. Something very strange had happened to them. Instead of there being twenty notes as there should have been there were twenty-six. He couldn't understand it at all. He counted them twice more. There was no doubt about it; somehow or other he had twenty-six thousand francs instead of the twenty he should have had. He couldn't make it out. He asked himself if it was possible that he had won more at the Sporting Club than he had realized. But no, that was out of the question; he distinctly remembered the man at the desk laying the notes out in four rows of five, and he had counted them himself.

Suddenly the explanation occurred to him; when he had put his hand into the flower-pot, after taking out the cineraria, he had grabbed everything he felt there. The flower-pot was the little hussy's money-box and he had taken out not only his own money, but her savings as well. Nicky leant back in the car and burst into a roar of laughter. It was the funniest thing he had ever heard in his life. And when he thought of her going to the flower-pot some time later in the morning when she awoke, expecting to find the money she had so cleverly got away with, and finding, not only that it wasn't there, but that her own had gone too, he laughed more than ever. And so far as he was concerned there was nothing to do about it; he neither knew her name, nor the name of the hotel to which she had taken him. He couldn't return her money even if he wanted to.

"It serves her damned well right," he said.

This then was the story that Henry Garnet told his friends over the bridge-table, for the night before, after dinner when his wife and daughter had left them to their port, Nicky had narrated it in full.

"And you know what infuriated me is that he's so damned pleased with himself. Talk of a cat swallowing a canary. And d'you know what he said to me when he'd finished? He looked at me with those innocent eyes of his and said: 'You know, father, I can't help thinking there was something wrong with the advice you gave me. You said, don't gamble; well, I did, and I made a packet; you said, don't lend money; well, I did, and I got it back; and you said don't have anything to do with women; well, I did, and I made six thousand francs on the deal.'"

It didn't make it any better for Henry Garnet that his three companions burst out laughing.

"It's all very well for you fellows to laugh, but you know, I'm in a damned awkward position. The boy looked up to me, he respected me, he took whatever I said as gospel truth, and now, I saw it in his eyes, he just looks on me as a drivelling old fool. It's no good my saying that one swallow doesn't make a summer; he doesn't see that it was just a fluke, he thinks the whole thing was due to his own cleverness. It may ruin him."

"You do look a bit of a damned fool, old man," said one of the others. "There's no denying that, is there?"

"I know I do, and I don't like it. It's so dashed unfair. Fate has no right to play one tricks like that. After all, you must admit that my advice was good."

"Very good."

"And the wretched boy ought to have burnt his fingers. Well, he hasn't. You're all men of the world, you tell me how I'm to deal with the situation now."

But they none of them could.

"Well, Henry, if I were you, I wouldn't worry," said the lawyer. "My belief is that your boy's born lucky, and in the long run that's better than to be born clever or rich."

Pat-Ball

A. A. MILNE

"You'll play tennis?" said my hostess absently. "That's right. Let me introduce you to Miss—er—um."

"Oh, we've met before," smiled Miss—I've forgotten the name again now.

"Thank you," I said gratefully. I thought it was extremely nice of her to remember me. Probably I had spilt lemonade over her at a dance, and in some way the incident had fixed itself in her mind. We do these little things, you know, and think nothing of them at the moment, but all the time—

"Smooth," said a voice.

I looked up and found that a pair of opponents had mysteriously appeared, and that my partner was leading the way on to the court.

"I'll take the right-hand side, if you don't mind," she announced. "Oh, and what about apologizing?" she went on. "Shall we do it after every stroke, or at the end of each game, or when we say good-bye, or never? I get so tired of saying 'sorry.'"

"Oh, but we shan't want to apologize; I'm sure we're going to get on beautifully together."

"I suppose you've played a lot this summer?"

"No, not at all yet, but I'm feeling rather strong, and I've got a new racket. One way and another, I expect to play a very powerful game."

Our male opponent served. He had what I should call a nasty swift service. The first ball rose very suddenly and took my partner on the side of the head. ("Sorry," she apologized. "It's all right," I said magnanimously.) I returned the next into the net; the third clean bowled my partner; and off the last I was caught in the slips. (*One, love.*)

"Will you serve?" said Miss—I wish I could remember her surname. Her Christian name was Hope or Charity or something like that; I know, when I heard it, I thought it was just as well. If I might call her Miss Hope for this once? Thank you.

"Will you serve?" said Miss Hope.

In the right-hand court I use the American service, which means that I never know till the last moment which side of the racket is going to hit the ball. On this occasion it was a dead heat—that is to say, I got it in between with the wood; and the ball sailed away over beds and beds of the most beautiful flowers.

"Oh, is *that* the American service?" said Miss Hope, much interested.

"South American," I explained. "Down in Peru they never use anything else."

In the left-hand court I employ the ordinary Hampstead Smash into the bottom of the net. After Four Hampstead Smashes and four Peruvian Teasers (*love, two*) I felt that another explanation was called for.

"I've got a new racket I've never used before," I said. "My old one is being pressed; it went to the shop yesterday to have the creases taken out. Don't you find that with a new racket you—er—exactly."

In the third game we not only got the ball over, but kept it between the white lines on several occasions—though not so often as our opponents (*three, love*); and in the fourth game Miss Hope served gentle lobs, while I, at her request, stood close up to the net and defended myself with my racket. I warded off the first two shots amidst applause (*thirty, love*), and dodged the next three (*thirty, forty*), but the last one was too quick for me and won the coco-nut with some ease. (*Game. Love, four.*)

"It's all right, thanks," I said to my partner, "it really doesn't hurt a bit. Now then, let's buck up and play a simply dashing game."

Miss Hope excelled herself in that fifth game, but I was still unable to find a length. To be more accurate, I was unable to find a shortness—my long game was admirable, strong and lofty.

"Are you musical?" said my partner at the end of it. (*Five, love*.) She had been very talkative all through.

"Come, come," I said impatiently, "you don't want a song at this very moment. Surely you can wait till the end of the set?"

"Oh, I was only just wondering."

"I quite see your point. You feel that Nature always compensates us in some way, and that as—"

"Oh, no!" said Miss Hope in great confusion. "I didn't mean that at all."

She must have meant it. You don't talk to people about singing in the middle of a game of tennis; certainly not to comparative strangers who have only spilt lemonade over your frock once before. No, no. It was an insult, and it nerved me to a great effort. I discarded—for it was my serve—the Hampstead Smash; I discarded the Peruvian Teaser. Instead, I served two Piccadilly Benders from the right-hand court and two Westminster Welts from the left-hand. The Piccadilly Bender is my own invention. It can only be served from the one court, and it must have a wind against it. You deliver it with your back to the net, which makes the striker think that you have either forgotten all about the game, or else are apologizing to the spectators for your previous exhibition. Then with a violent contortion you slue your body round and serve, whereupon your opponent perceives that you *are* playing, and that it is just one more ordinary fault into the wrong court. So she calls "Fault!" in a contemptuous tone and drops her racket . . . and then adds hurriedly, "Oh, no, sorry, it wasn't a fault, after all." That being where the wind comes in.

The Westminster Welt is in theory the same as the Hampstead Smash, but goes over the net. One must be in very good form (or have been recently insulted) to bring this off.

Well, we won that game, a breeze having just sprung up; and, carried away by enthusiasm and mutual admiration, we collected another. (*Five, two.*) Then it was Miss Hope's serve again.

"Good-bye," I said. "I suppose you want me in the forecourt again?"

"Please."

"I don't mind *her* shots—the bottle of scent is absolutely safe; but I'm afraid he'll win another packet of Woodbines."

Miss Hope started off with a double, which was rather a pity, and then gave our masculine adversary what is technically called "one to kill." I saw instinctively that I was the one, and I held my racket ready with both hands. Our opponent, who had been wanting his tea for the last two games, was in no mood of dalliance; he fairly let himself go over this shot. In a moment I was down on my knees behind the net . . . and the next moment I saw through the meshes a very strange thing. The other man, with his racket on the ground, was holding his eye with both hands!

"Don't you think," said Miss Hope (*two, five—abandoned*), "that your overhead volleying is just a little severe?"

Lolita
(excerpt)

VLADIMIR NABOKOV

By permitting Lolita to study acting, I had, fine fool, suffered her to cultivate deceit. It now appeared that it had not only been a matter of learning the answers to such questions as what is the basic conflict in "Hedda Gabler," or where are the climaxes in "Love Under the Lindens," or analyze the prevailing mood of "Cherry Orchard"; it was really a matter of learning to betray me. How I deplored the exercises in sensual simulation that I had so often seen her go through in our Beardsley parlor when I would observe her from some strategic point while she, like a hypnotic subject or a performer in a mystic rite, produced sophisticated versions of infantile make-believe by going through the mimetic actions of hearing a moan in the dark, seeing for the first time a brand new young stepmother, tasting something she hated, such as buttermilk, smelling crushed grass in a lush orchard, or touching mirages of objects with her sly, slender, girl-child hands. Among my papers I still have a mimeographed sheet suggesting:

> Tactile drill. Imagine yourself picking up and hold-
> ing: a pingpong ball, an apple, a sticky date, a new

flannel-fluffed tennis ball, a hot potato, an ice cube, a kitten, a puppy, a horseshoe, a feather, a flashlight.

Knead with your fingers the following imaginary things: a piece of bread, india rubber, a friend's aching temple, a sample of velvet, a rose petal.

You are a blind girl. Palpate the face of: a Greek youth, Cyrano, Santa Claus, a baby, a laughing faun, a sleeping stranger, your father.

But she had been so pretty in the weaving of those delicate spells, in the dreamy performance of her enchantments and duties! On certain adventurous evenings, in Beardsley, I also had her dance for me with the promise of some treat or gift, and although these routine leg-parted leaps of hers were more like those of a football cheerleader than like the languorous and jerky motions of a Parisian *petit rat,* the rhythms of her not quite nubile limbs had given me pleasure. But all that was nothing, absolutely nothing, to the indescribable itch of rapture that her tennis game produced in me—the teasing delirious feeling of teetering on the very brink of unearthly order and splendor.

Despite her advanced age, she was more of a nymphet than ever, with her apricot-colored limbs, in her sub-teen tennis togs! Winged gentlemen! No hereafter is acceptable if it does not produce her as she was then, in that Colorado resort between Snow and Elphin-stone, with everything right: the white wide little-boy shorts, the slender waist, the apricot midriff, the white breast-kerchief whose ribbons went up and encircled her neck to end behind in a dangling knot leaving bare her gaspingly young and adorable apricot shoulder blades with that pubescence and those lovely gentle bones, and the smooth, downward-tapering back. Her cap had a white peak. Her racket had cost me a small fortune. Idiot, triple idiot! I could have filmed her! I would have had her now with me, before my eyes, in the projection room of my pain and despair!

She would wait and relax for a bar or two of white-lined time before going into the act of serving, and often bounced the ball once or twice, or pawed the ground a little, always at ease, always rather vague about the score, always cheerful as she so seldom was in the dark life she led at home. Her tennis was the highest point to which I can imagine a young creature bringing the art of make-believe, although I daresay, for her it was the very geometry of basic reality.

The exquisite clarity of all her movements had its auditory counterpart in the pure ringing sound of her every stroke. The ball when it entered her aura of control became somehow whiter, its resilience somehow richer, and the instrument of precision she used upon it seemed inordinately prehensile and deliberate at the moment of clinging contact. Her form was, indeed, an absolutely perfect imitation of absolutely top-notch tennis—without any utilitarian results. As Edusa's sister, Electra Gold, a marvelous young coach, said to me once while I sat on a pulsating hard bench watching Dolores Haze toying with Linda Hall (and being beaten by her): "Dolly has a magnet in the center of her racket guts, but why the heck is she so polite?" Ali, Electra, what did it matter, with such grace! I remember at the very first game I watched being drenched with an almost painful convulsion of beauty assimilation. My

Lolita had a way of raising her bent left knee at the ample and springy start of the service cycle when there would develop and hang in the sun for a second a vital web of balance between toed foot, pristine armpit, burnished arm and far back-flung racket, as she smiled up with gleaming teeth at the small globe suspended so high in the zenith of the powerful and graceful cosmos she had created for the express purpose of falling upon it with a clean resounding crack of her golden whip.

It had, that serve of hers, beauty, directness, youth, a classical purity of trajectory, and was, despite its spanking pace, fairly easy to return, having as it did no twist or sting to its long elegant hop.

That I could have had all her strokes, all her enchantments, immortalized in segments of celluloid, makes me moan today with frustration. They would have been so much more than the snapshots I burned! Her overhead volley was related to her service as the envoy is to the ballade; for she had been trained, my pet, to patter up at once to the net on her nimble, vivid, white-shod feet. There was nothing to choose between her forehand and backhand drives: they were mirror images of one another—my very loins still tingle with those pistol reports repeated by crisp echoes and Electra's cries. One of the pearls of Dolly's game was a short half-volley that Ned Litam had taught her in California.

She preferred acting to swimming, and swimming to tennis; yet I insist that had not something within her been broken by me—not that I realized it then!—she would have had on the top of her perfect form the will to win, and would have become a real girl champion. Dolores, with two rackets under her arm, in Wimbledon. Dolores endorsing a Dromedary. Dolores turning professional. Dolores acting a girl champion in a movie. Dolores and her gray, humble, hushed husband-coach, old Humbert.

There was nothing wrong or deceitful in the spirit of her game—unless one considered her cheerful indifference toward its outcome as the feint of a nymphet. She who was so cruel and crafty in everyday life, revealed an innocence, a frankness, a kindness of ball-placing, that permitted a second-rate but determined player, no matter how uncouth and incompetent, to poke and cut his way to victory. Despite her small stature, she covered the one thousand and fifty-three square feet of her half of the court with wonderful ease, once she had entered into the rhythm of a rally and as long as she could direct that rhythm; but any abrupt attack, or sudden change of tactics on her adversary's part, left her helpless. At match point, her second serve, which—rather typically—was even stronger and more stylish than her first (for she had none of the inhibitions that cautious winners have), would strike vibrantly the harp-cord of the net—and ricochet out of court. The polished gem of her dropshot was snapped up and put away by an opponent who seemed four-legged and wielded a crooked paddle. Her dramatic drives and lovely volleys would candidly fall at his feet. Over and over again she would land an easy one into the net—and merrily mimic dismay by drooping in a ballet attitude, with her forelocks hanging. So sterile were her grace and whipper that she could not even win from panting me and my old-fashioned lifting drive.

I suppose I am especially susceptible to the magic of games. In my chess sessions with Gaston I saw the board as a square pool of limpid water with rare shells and stratagems rosily visible upon the smooth tessellated bottom, which to my confused adversary was all ooze and squid-cloud. Similarly, the initial tennis coaching I had inflicted on Lolita—prior to the revelations that came to her through the great Californian's lessons—remained in my mind as oppressive and distressful memories—not only because she had been so hopelessly and irritatingly irritated by every suggestion of mine—but because the precious symmetry of the court instead of reflecting the harmonies latent in her was utterly jumbled by the clumsiness and lassitude of the resentful child I mistaught. Now things were different, and on that particular day, in the pure air of Champion, Colorado, on that admirable court at the foot of steep stone stairs leading up to Champion Hotel where we had spent the night, I felt I could rest from the nightmare of unknown betrayals within the innocence of her style, of her soul, of her essential grace.

She was hitting hard and flat, with her usual effortless sweep, feeding me deep skimming balls—all so rhythmically coordinated and overt as to reduce my footwork to, practically, a swinging stroll—crack players will understand what I mean. My rather heavily cut serve that I had been taught by my father who had learned it from Decugis or Borman, old friends of his and great champions, would have seriously troubled my Lo, had I really tried to trouble her. But who would upset such a lucid dear? Did I ever mention that her bare arm bore the 8 of vaccination? That I loved her hopelessly? That she was only fourteen?

An inquisitive butterfly passed, dipping, between us.

Two people in tennis shorts, a red-haired fellow only about eight years my junior, with sunburnt bright pink shins, and an indolent dark girl with a moody mouth and hard eyes, about two years Lolita's senior, appeared from nowhere. As is common with dutiful tyros, their rackets were sheathed and framed, and they carried them not as if they were the natural and comfortable extensions of certain specialized muscles, but hammers or blunderbusses or wimbles, or my own dreadful cumbersome sins. Rather unceremoniously seating themselves near my precious coat, on a bench adjacent to the court, they fell to admiring very vocally a rally of some fifty exchanges that Lo innocently helped me to foster and uphold—until there occurred a syncope in the series causing her to gasp as her overhead smash went out of court, whereupon she melted into winsome merriment, my golden pet.

I felt thirsty by then, and walked to the drinking fountain; there Red approached me and in all humility suggested a mixed double. "I am Bill Mead," he said. "And that's Fay Page, actress. Maffy On Say"—he added (pointing with his ridiculously hooded racket at polished Fay who was already talking to Dolly). I was about to reply "Sorry, but—" (for I hate to have my filly involved in the chops and jabs of cheap bunglers), when a remarkably melodious cry diverted my attention: a bellboy was tripping down the steps from the hotel to our court and making me signs. I was wanted, if you please, on an urgent long distance call—so urgent in fact that the line was being held for me. Certainly. I got into my coat (inside pocket heavy with pistol) and told Lo I would be back in a minute. She was picking up a ball—in the continental foot-racket way which was one of the few nice things I had taught her,—and smiled—she smiled at me!

An awful calm kept my heart afloat as I followed the boy up to the hotel. This, to use an American term, in which discovery, retribution, torture, death, eternity appear in the shape of a singularly repulsive nutshell, was *it*. I had left her in mediocre hands, but it hardly mattered now. I would fight, of course. Oh, I would fight. Better destroy everything than surrender her. Yes, quite a climb.

At the desk, a dignified, Roman-nosed man, with, I suggest, a very obscure past that might reward investigation, handed me a message in his own hand. The line had not been held after all. The note said:

"Mr. Humbert. The head of Birdsley (sic!) School called. Summer residence—Birdsley 2-8282. Please call back immediately. Highly important."

I folded myself into a booth, took a little pill, and for about twenty minutes tussled with space-spooks. A quartet of propositions gradually became audible: soprano, there was no such number in Beardsley—alto, Miss Pratt was on her way to England; tenor, Beardsley School had not telephoned; bass, they could not have done so, since nobody knew I was, that particular day, in Champion, Colo. Upon my stinging him, the Roman took the trouble to find out if there had been a long distance call. There had been none. A fake call from some local dial was not excluded. I thanked him. He said: You bet.

After a visit to the purling men's room and a stiff drink at the bar, I started on my return march. From the very first terrace I saw, far below, on the tennis court which seemed the size of a school child's ill-wiped slate, golden Lolita playing in a double. She moved like a fair angel among three horrible Boschian cripples. One of these, her partner, while changing sides, jocosely slapped her on her behind with his racket. He had a remarkably round head and wore incongruous brown trousers. There was a momentary flurry—he saw me, and throwing away his racket—mine!—scuttled up the slope. He waved his wrists and elbows in would-be comical imitation of rudimentary wings, as he climbed, bow-legged, to the street, where his gray car awaited him. Next moment he and the grayness were gone. When I came down, the remaining trio were collecting and sorting out the balls.

"Mr. Mead, who was that person?"

Bill and Fay, both looking very solemn, shook their heads.

That absurd intruder had butted in to make up a double, hadn't he, Dolly?

Dolly. The handle of my racket was still disgustingly warm. Before returning to the hotel, I ushered her into a little alley half-smothered in fragrant shrubs, with flowers like smoke, and was about to burst into ripe sobs and plead with her imperturbed dream in the most abject manner for clarification, no matter how meretricious, of the slow awfulness enveloping me, when we found ourselves behind the convulsed Mead twosome—assorted people, you know, meeting among idyllic settings in old comedies. Bill and Fay were both weak with laughter—we had come at the end of their private joke. It did not really matter.

Speaking as if it really did not really matter, and assuming, apparently, that life was automatically rolling on with all its routine pleasures, Lolita said she would like to change into her bathing things, and spend the rest of the afternoon at the swimming pool. It was a gorgeous day. Lolita!

The Tennis Player

KENT NELSON

A simple motion made from the shoulder. His left hand, holding the ball, came to the left knee, and, as the weight of his body shifted forward over the baseline, Nicky's arm swung upward in an arc. Suddenly the tennis ball appeared against the blue sky, like a moon rising. Through years of practice, countless tosses, Nicky saw only the ball.

It hung there, poised, and in the precise moment before it fell again, the crack of his racquet sent it away. Nicky forced himself halfway to the net, but he lunged more than ran. Agee sliced the ball back. It came high and long, and Nicky paused a split second trying to decide whether it would go out. It had been too long since he had last played to know by instinct. His pause was his decision, and he let the ball sail. It struck the court just beyond the baseline, out.

He turned a moment in Agee's direction, smiled at luck, and then walked back to the fence where the ball had stopped rolling. His smile faded. With a familiar motion, he dribbled the ball from the court onto his racquet. He could still do it effortlessly, and no stranger could tell that he had been away.

He tossed the ball lightly from the racquet face to his left hand and stepped to the baseline left of center.

When he was younger, twelve and thirteen, Nicky had had tantrums on the court when the ball would not do as he wished. He cried when somebody cheated him. He remembered that well. He always read the lines honestly himself, and he could not keep other people's falseness from bothering him. Sometimes, when he lost on cheating, he broke his racquet on the ground, but it was only out of love for the game. That's how he explained it to his father.

"You can work out a new one in the store," his father said.

"But he cheated," Nicky protested.

"Two hours every day," his father answered. "You can still play your tournaments on the weekends."

Dressed in a black robe, he moved lights into position for sittings. He knew cameras inside out, knew every trick of freezing a face into a tedious smile. He knew the smells of the chemicals as the faces emerged onto cardboard in the trays. The ultraviolet lights, enlargers, dryers. He knew the faces of women and newlyweds when at last they returned to the store to collect their own images.

The ball hung, and Nicky served the first ball into the tape. The second, topspinned, turned oval in the air, thudded on the court, and bounced high and away to Agee's backhand. The return came to his left, and Nicky reached out awkwardly, out of position for such a hard shot. The ball skipped by, and he stopped short. Without expression, he turned and walked back again to the baseline. Agee lobbed a second ball over.

Nicky thought of his father's saying that the King of Sweden played tennis until he was eighty years old. His own movements came so strangely, dreamlike, as though he were so old. He told himself that he could not expect too much. But the last was an easy ball, one he should never miss.

He remembered Agee differently. Agee had seemed slower when they had played before, and he had been more cheerful. Now his friend seemed farther away, not certain anymore.

The ball always seemed beyond reach. He started to think of the way Agee had lured him out to play. Then, he thought, perhaps it had been Caroline.

"We all imagine what you've been through," Caroline had said to him.

They had sat on the swing in the warm spring night. Before they had often sat there. The terrace overlooked a long, wide swath of lawn which extended down in the dark trees and the night.

"We try to understand as best we can. All of us. But, Nicky, you can't close us out. You have to try as well. You have to try to come back to us."

He had closed his eyes and had thought then: And how did one go about coming back to everything? Yes, he wanted to come back. There was nothing he wished more than to come back into everything just as he had left it. But, happier. He had been so tired then.

He opened his eyes again to the night. "It's just that everyone has not moved at all, and I've moved a great distance," he said.

His mind went on, and he spoke as though she would know what he talked about.

"Suppose," he had said, "that I decide to do only one thing for my whole life. What happens then?"

"Why, then you become something," she said.

He remembered that he could not quite see her eyes as she had said this.

"At least you've started something," she went on, "if you make a decision like that."

"And what if the one thing you decide upon turns out to be without value?"

Caroline had looked at him. She stopped the movement of the swing by putting her foot on the ground. For a moment he thought she might be angry at such nonsense, but as she leaned forward into the light from the windows of the house, he could see in her eyes that she did not understand. She had never thought of such things. Hers was another world—one of application, restraint, and respect for property.

She did not answer his question. Instead she leaned closer to him and put a kiss on his lips.

Then her mother came outdoors. "Nicky, it's Agee on the phone. He wants to play tennis with you."

Caroline got up. "Tell him you will, Nicky."

"I'm too tired."

"You aren't really too tired."

Not really, he thought. Who knew what "really" meant? He did. It was lying in a place which was not home and wishing you were not as you were and being so lonely with so many people around you.

"No," he said. "I don't want to."

"This is what I mean, Nicky," she pleaded. "You've got to come back to us."

In the end he had agreed to play.

The first time was over. Nicky zipped the cover over his racquet.

"You can see the shape of the old self," Agee said, coming over.

"Nearly invisible," Nicky said.

He sensed Agee's hesitance to walk with him. They headed for the clubhouse.

"Later in the summer we'll play tournaments again," Agee said.

Nicky remembered the days when they had travelled the state like circus sideshow performers, playing before the crowds. The crowds were never quiet. They cheered losing shots, and always expected the favorite to win.

"No tournaments," Nicky said. "That's over."

Nicky stopped on the lawn. Caroline came down from the clubhouse toward them. She looked bright, her blond hair against the green of the trees. She twirled a daisy nervously in her hands.

Everything at the club looked perfect—the spacious lawn, the trees, the big clubhouse—while the rest of the world had to make do.

"I watched," she said cheerfully. "You both played very well."

He had looked for her car before they had gone out on the court. She must have come later. "Hello," he said, taking her hand.

Her blond hair fell to the sides of her face. She turned to Agee. "He'll soon be playing just as well as ever, won't he?"

She said he would be, he thought, precisely because that was what she was least certain about. He felt like an invalid who had to be walked and talked.

They said to him, "Nicky, look at the light."

He looked at the light. He was sure he had looked at the light. It was a small point. The voices came from their skulls, not from their mouths, as though they were in a cavern.

"Nicky, look at the light."

He was sure he looked at the light, but they kept repeating it.

Caroline looked at home in the clubhouse. "I've ordered lunch," she said.

They went in. Nicky looked around at the glass. It was an airconditioned room and it felt cold. There seemed to be glass everywhere.

On a table he saw a stack of magazines. That was what had done it before, and seeing them startled him. Before, he had stopped reading newspapers and watching television and looking at magazines.

Mr. Davidson, the club chairman, came over to shake hands. "Good to see you back, Nicky," he said.

Nicky nodded. It was as though he were back from the war, except that if he had come back from the war, their enthusiasm would not have been guarded.

"Looked pretty good out there, I must say."

"Look at the light."

The light came from a point in the flash light.

"That's fine, Nicky."

In the beginning he had seen the light, but then, as they said "Fine," he had not. He did not feel himself move.

"Look at the light again. Over here."

He did not move.

"That's very good, Nicky. You're getting much better."

Mr. Davidson held onto his hand like an old uncle.

"I wish it felt good out there," Nicky said.

Caroline moved off with Agee.

"Nicky," Mr. Davidson said, "I have a favor."

Caroline and Agee had gone off to leave the two of them alone.

"Maybe it will help you out, too," Mr. Davidson went on. "Damon, the club pro, can't take his lessons in July. He has that clinic in Jennings, and we need someone to take over for him for a while."

Caroline was sitting down at a table, looking at him. He could see that she knew what their conversation was about. He saw her mouth moving in pantomime, "Say yes."

"Look at the light, now, Nicky," they had said.

"Looks different now," Nicky had answered.

It was still that point of light, but now he could smile when he saw it. It looked very clear.

"You're going to be home pretty soon."

"I know."

"Have you made any plans?"

"Not really. I thought I would stay around home for a while."

"What about tennis?"

"Maybe play a little tennis again and think about what's ahead."

"It would mean ten dollars an hour plus the pro shop," Mr. Davidson said.

"I haven't played at all," Nicky said.

"You haven't forgotten," Mr. Davidson said, smiling.

"It's like riding a bicycle," Nicky said, "but it's rusty."

"Well, it's only lessons. It won't be hard for you." He saw Caroline at the table.

Tennis used to be just young days running in the sun. Now it was not.

"I'm sort of at loose ends," Nicky said. "It would help me out." He looked at Caroline.

"Good," Mr. Davidson said. "Then we're all set."

At eight every morning in July he was on the court in sneakers, white shorts, and white shirt. The sun burned him. In slow motion he demonstrated the strokes of the game to children and ladies: forehands with the handshake grip, reaching toward the net on the follow-through; backhands with the elbow locked at the moment of impact; serves like throwing the racquet over the net without letting go. He watched the awkward movements of the women, the uncontrolled hitting of the children; he listened to them laugh.

From the moment he had agreed to teach, Nicky began something new with the people around him. He had given in to telling people what they wanted to hear. Of course in the details of the senses he was scrupulously honest. He did not charge people too much on their lessons or say that shots were in which were truly out. He just did not tell them everything. He did not tell people what would hurt them. It was easier to omit.

"I don't mind the work," he said to Caroline.

"Really, Nicky?"

He did not mind the work. It was the feeling that he got from it that he could not stand.

Sometimes Caroline came out to meet him for lunch. They sat in the snack room where instants of his former life were hung on the walls: his arm around Agee after the state finals; another of the sectionals. He looked at his own tedious smiles.

"You ought to try another tournament," she said once. "Just for your confidence."

"Maybe I will," he said. He knew he could not.

At two he met a class of young boys. Caroline loved to watch the children. She sat beyond the fence on a green bench, laughing as the boys ran wildly over the courts. Nicky knew a few would become good if they played. But he could not wait that long. Ball after ball he hit to weak backhands, making sure the ball bounced to the perfect spot. "Watch the ball," he repeated over and over. "Racquet back sooner. It's too late when the ball is already there."

Caroline was the only respite, and yet he knew it was she he could never come back to. He spent most evenings with her, sitting and talking idly. He did not tell her he loved her. She believed he loved her without words, and he let her believe. He decided that at times he did love her, but since it was only at times, he knew he did not.

Sometimes they made love. Those were the times that all else faded from his mind, even the terrible light. He knew she wanted no other than him, and he tried to make her see that he had no other than her. He held her, knowing that for him there was no other chance.

He could feel that the sheets were clean. They looked tan behind her hair. Though Caroline was there in the darkness under him, he did not think of her. He knew that what he did was the worst thing he could do. Yet it was all he had, all he could do.

He knew it was not so much her, not so much being inside her body. It was being simply inside, lost within someone else, all thought concentrated outward. It was the end of having to think. It was terrible to have it not last forever, to awake and find the world more pale and less tenable than ever.

Always the next day he was back on the court with the children. He tried to vary his method, but it was not his method which lacked. Sometimes his mind wandered to the hospital where he had been tucked away from all of them, beyond the vision of all else, the all-else unknowing that it was to blame.

His mother used to say to him, "Nicky, are you well? You don't look well."

"No, I'm not."

"You don't look at all well."

"What do looks have to do with it?"

He would go down to the photography store to freeze those smiles. He knew that his was the equal of any of those terrible expressions. He went on from day to day, as if on a tightrope, the fear of falling increasing as the tightrope became looser and looser: the cars taxes directions space flights schedules discussions airplanes motels counters colors money neon swimming pools success government medicines advertisements driving him on and on over the loose rope.

He stood in one spot on the court, leaning over his basket of tennis balls, throwing hitting talking, "Careful, watch. Now follow through."

The long summer seemed to be made of the same weather, always hot air and blue sky. The sky seemed to open outward and beyond. Nicky baked to a deep brown; his hair lightened.

Damon did not come back to take over his teaching in August, but it did not matter then. When Mr. Davidson asked Nicky whether he would stay on, Nicky accepted. "I'll be glad to," he said.

Nicky never began to believe himself what he knew everyone else inferred from what he said. He was too removed and watched himself too closely. He did not make his world over into happiness. He drifted, not bothering to explain.

Toward the end of August, he began to live through the days. It seemed to him like a great eternity, each day adding to the others to make a dark pall, like velvet.

Each day he thought he would fall. But Caroline said, "You look so much healthier being out in the sun. You're much more like your old self, Nicky."

"I am myself," he said.

"Look at the light."

He could see the point of light, but he could not move.

"Do you think you might try a tournament? Just a small one?"

"I think I might," Nicky said. "We'll wait and see when one comes up."

He often told Caroline that he would be delayed at the club and that he could not come over to her place until later. This was true, but not for the reason he knew she would believe. She would think that he had a late lesson, or that the accounting of the shop had to be checked. But it was not for those reasons, or for any other that he imagined she would see.

It was only that he wanted to be alone after the club was empty.

The club was a perfect place. In the evening the courts were no longer sprayed with tennis balls; he did not have to watch shouting children as they raced after the balls; he did not have to say anything to anyone.

The club grounds were so peaceful in dark green. The air was filled with the sounds of crickets and breezes. Dusk came slowly.

One evening in late August, he stayed after lessons. He lay stretched out on the grass beside the courts. He stared through the sky, watching the light blue shade darken toward violet. The trees above him wavered and turned slowly to darkness. Stars began.

He loved watching the sky, imagining how deep it was and how it was filled up with space. His loose rope hung over that space. It seemed to him then that it would be peaceful, that fall, going through the space of the sky.

The world moved through several hours.

In this peace a motor sounded somewhere far down the gravel drive. The headlights of the car struck the leaves over his head, breaking the trees into shadows as the car moved down toward the clubhouse. He sat up. As the car turned into the parking lot, the beams moved across his white tennis clothes. He recognized the car as Caroline's.

The door slammed, and he lay back. Her footsteps across the grass drowned all the other sounds.

"What are you still doing here?" she asked. "I thought you had to go home tonight."

"I told you my mother asked me to come."

"But you didn't go?"

"No."

"I just called there and your mother said they hadn't seen you. We thought something might have happened."

She sat down on the grass beside him, folding her dress under her.

"You didn't come to me either."

"I've been here lying on the grass," Nicky said.

He nearly started to tell her how the sky seemed to go on forever, not in imaginable time, but in a way he could not even imagine, just deep and deeper.

Instead he said, "I would have come by to see you later."

"When you weren't home I was worried," Caroline said. "I had to see you."

He could not see her eyes. He thought that whenever it was important to see her eyes, they were sitting in the dark.

Something new was in her voice. Nicky turned on his side toward her. The sun from the day still swarmed in his skin. His legs felt numb and heavy. He didn't want to think about what it might be that she had to tell him. He started to reach out and touch her.

"Agee called and said I should talk to you about the tournament coming up," she said. "He thinks it might bring you back."

He knew it was not what she had come to say.

"What about my lessons?"

"It's just a tournament in the city. A small one."

"I mean, my lessons were supposed to bring me back, too," Nicky said.

"You are back, Nicky. But you don't want to go on giving lessons forever. You're a top player. Lessons aren't in you, but this is. Nicky, please."

All he could think of was falling through that endless dark space.

"Okay," he said.

That space. He reached for her and began stroking her bare arm. He heard her breath start, and he moved over closer to her. He did not want to hear what she had to tell him.

Nicky began hitting with Agee for an hour and a half every day. Caroline had signed up for an hour lesson right before lunch and gave up her time for their practice. Nicky took a half hour of his own.

Agee was good to him. Nicky started off riveted to the same spot on the court, as though it were a lesson. He could not adjust to Agee's hard shots.

"I can't," Nicky whispered over and over.

He made countless mistakes. He no longer watched the ball, but instead hit out of forgotten skill. He did just what he belabored in lessons to his students. Agee encouraged him and took it all.

After two weeks of practice, Nicky began to see the signs. His legs felt more elastic. His instincts improved; he knew where the ball would come. He started following his serve to the net with a series of quick little steps. The serve itself he whittled deeper into the service court, a little closer to the corners.

Caroline also came to watch.

"You must see the improvement from day to day," she said, when they had come from the court.

"*I* see the improvement," Agee joined in, wiping the sweat from his face. "I don't think the lessons have hurt you. You were only lazy."

Nicky smiled. He knew it was coming back. He felt the solid stroke of the racquet when he hit. He was trying shots that had been dormant for a year and a half: short topspin cross-courts, drop-shots, backhand volleys to the deep corners. They had begun to fall.

Even his mood during lessons picked up. He was less bored, and more enthusiastic about the game. "Weight always forward," he urged. "Step into the ball. Never backward."

Only one thing held him back: Caroline.

Every day she was there, not pressing him in any way, but there. She seemed to hang close to him, always at his side, and yet she did not have the same cheer in her. She seemed wary of everything he said.

"Tell me the truth, now, Nicky," she said. "What are you doing tonight?"

"I *am* telling the truth," he said.

"You're not planning anything?"

"No. Why are you like that? Because of the other night?"

He had thought about his omissions.

"No," she said.

"Look, I only wanted to isolate myself to think," he said. "I had to be alone because then I'm not lying to anybody."

"You don't have to explain anything," she said. "I understand."

"You don't understand. It wasn't only you."

"Now look here at the light, Nicky. Over here."

The point of light seemed very far away. The voices came from space. He tried to move.

"So you're back, Nicky. What happened out there? Look at the light."

"And now you think your life has purpose again?" Caroline looked at him closely.

He could see that her eyes were ready to cry.

"You said yourself that I had to start somewhere with one thing."

He knew tennis was not it.

Then the tears came. Nicky could see no reason, but he knew that reasons were not often seen. She rushed up to him and put her arms around him and held. It was the way he often held her, except that he could never cry.

Before every tournament match in the old days Nicky had had a ritual. He would sit by himself for half an hour in some quiet place and concentrate. He would hold his fists tightly closed for a minute at a time, pounding them slowly and sound-lessly against his knees. He would tell himself to watch the ball and to hit hard without being nervous. He tried to relax. And he told himself that, if he got behind, he should change his strategy. Before each serve he had to bounce the ball three times for luck. And if he were winning, he should never think he had won until the last point was played.

The hour before this tournament, Nicky knew that he was not in the old days. As before he went off by himself, but he did not think about relaxing or about any of the other things.

He had been with Caroline the night before. She had been quiet, sitting there on the swing. From the step where he sat, he could look down the pathway. He listened to the crickets.

"Come sit with me," she had said.

He had not moved. He could sense in her voice that it was finally coming. "What do you have to tell me?" he asked.

In a suddenness he had not expected, the words broke from her—a child, Nicky, a child—and for a long time he sat listen-ing to the darkness. He saw himself growing dimmer and dim-mer like the fireflies far away on the lawn, and he had gotten up and started walking out toward the dark trees.

Later, sometime during their lovemaking, he had told her that he loved her. It was not any kind of omission. He knew he had had to say it. He could not stand the dishonesty, but there was no chance anymore to come back.

"Look at the light now, Nicky."

He did not see a light.

"What was it, Nicky?"

He could not feel himself move.

"The light is over here. What was it?"

He could not speak. The space seemed to close around him.

"Was it the lies, Nicky?"

He did not see anything.

He took his racquets out to the court. In the warmup he hit the ball as if he were concentrating. He knew his opponent from years before and Nicky was certain to win easily. He moved mechanically around the court, reacting without thinking.

Nicky took eight practice serves. Then he stepped up to the line and bounced the ball three times. It was his old lucky way. Then he leaned back and pointed his racquet toward the net.

A simple motion from the shoulder. The left hand, holding the ball, came to the left knee and, as the weight of his body shifted forward over the baseline, Nicky's arm swung upward in an arc. Suddenly the tennis ball appeared against the sky, like a moon rising. Years of practice and countless tosses had taught him, but now the ball seemed to disappear before his eyes, and all he saw was the wide, deep expanse of space.

A Fairly Regular Four

FREDERIC RAPHAEL

It began, like modern history, in the mid-1960s. At first I used only to observe them enviously. Ronnie Trafford and his friends were often next on court after I had finished my lesson with old Ralph. Ralph had been a Davis Cup player, for England. Immediately after his doubles match, he'd been given the elbow. By the time I became his pupil at Abacus Road, on one of the few covered courts then available in London, he was bent at the waist like some antique butler, warped by deference. On the high-roofed court, he called you "sir" in a tone which promised no further concessions.

After I had done my stint of properly constructed forehand drives, he would propose that I advance to the net. The volley, Ralph insisted, was the simplest of shots: "You are a carpenter," he would remind me, "tapping in a nail."

If my volleying happened to induce a measure of complacency, Ralph had a trick to trump my vanity. He could, it seemed, procure a net-cord pretty well at will. The ball, delivered from the baseline, would strike the tape and hop over my outstretched "wand," as Ralph termed the solid wooden weapon. "Pity!" Ralph said. "Pity!" was my cue to thank him for my helpful humiliation.

There was a spectators' gallery along one side of Ralph's court, high under the wired glass roof. At the end of my hour, Ronnie Trafford would appear, doubly-sweatered like a fast bowler in the deep field. He watched the clock jerk towards the end of my lease.

Ronnie detested being kept waiting by any of those who made up what he called his "syndicate."

One day, as Ralph allowed one of my smashes to be too good for him and murmured, "On that note, I think we should stop," Ronnie Trafford called down that he had a problem. "Franco's mother appears to be poorly. We're one class-player short. Ralph, would you make us up?"

Ralph was nudging several dozen balls towards the corner where he caged them in a plastic waste-paper basket. "Short notice," he said.

"Come on, Ralph. You can relive past glories."

"Doubt it. What about my partner here?"

"He's tired," Ronnie said, with brutal consideration.

"He's young," Ralph replied.

Ronnie Trafford looked at me as if he doubted it. I doubted it myself—"I've got a programme to write," I said.

"I say," Ronnie said, with a little more warmth, "I've seen you on the television, haven't I?"

As I went to the dressing room, Ronnie was on his way down from the gallery, hand outstretched. "Just a friendly four," he said. "Do make us up."

During the next few weeks, as I progressed from raw re-
cruit to not infrequent participant, I learned that daggers were
regularly drawn. Hostilities began with the twiddling ritual of
rackets to decide who should partner whom. Normally, smooth
played with smooth, rough with rough, but if there was one
outstanding competent guest, Ronnie would preempt the honour. After all, it was he who had secured the privileged hour of
our session. It was his secretary, the invaluable Miss Pomfret,
who circularised the syndicate for their availability—before
informing them in terse style who had been chosen by Ronnie's
one-man selection committee for the following month. Anyone late on parade tended to find himself relegated to stand-by.

Ronnie had begun in modest circumstances, but he was determined to rise above them. The Jag was already in the driveway and the driveway was in Ealing, like the estate agency
founded by his late father. It had been a small local firm when
Ronnie returned from decorated service in the Kosbies. The
army had been his travel scholarship, the officers' mess his university. The M. C. was his unarguable ace of trumps. And he
played it as often as it was needed.

Good form, I soon discovered, was important to him. He
glared at Milstein's terrible socks (black, with red lozenges)
when he had to wear them on court. He was appalled when Milstein then went on to his office in the same sweaty pair. Ronnie carried his business suit into the changing room in a plastic
sack. His toiletries were arranged on the cracked glass shelf in
the showers. He didn't snap the regimental cufflinks until he
was as powdered as Turkish Delight. Having been an officer,
he had every intention of being a gentleman.

If Ronnie had a fault, it was that he very much liked to win. I should confess, before others accuse me, that I myself can get quite sulky over tiddlywinks. Ronnie showed none of my sullen signs of bad breeding, but he did take an elastic view of the baseline. When Oliver Randell and I were deemed to have a crucial point, after my partner's smash had clearly whitened the tape at Ronnie's end, it required something between a shrug and a smirk from Oliver to ensure that my congratulations were effusive enough to keep me in the syndicate.

As the sixties swung by, I became more and more of a fixture. Some people dropped out; new ones dropped in. A *film star,* courting Ronnie's ravishing daughter, aced us handsomely before decamping to shoot it out on a TV series in Arizona leaving Flora briefly flat. *Juan-Carlos O'Higgins,* from the Chilean embassy, was rather too good for us, especially after being appropriated as a C.D.-plated partner by Ronnie. When *Jolyon Taggart* and I had gone down 6-0, 6-0, 6-0, it was hard to sustain the illusion of a close-run thing.

The syndicate soldiered on, in good fours and in bad. Ronnie prospered in all political climates. His son married well; the resuscitated Flora even better. Ronnie and his wife moved from Ealing to Chiswick Mall. His West End office boomed; the one in Cannes had to be expanded. The old Jag yielded to the new Roller.

The quartet celebrated anniversaries with what seemed like accelerating regularity. Waistlines thickened; hair thinned; teeth lengthened. The game went on. Did friendships ripen?

We saw each other only on court. Under those freezing or scalding Abacus Road showers, we discussed public scandal, but rarely personal matters. One startling morning, however, Jolyon Taggart's soapy back was seen to be covered with a scrawl of red lacerations, the raw advertisement of an improbable passion.

Ronnie and I looked at each other simultaneously, with amused straight faces. It was a strange, inconsequential bond between us.

Jolyon dried himself, oblivious of the script we read on his back. Shortly afterwards, he announced that he had got married. We wished him luck, but only Ronnie was surprised not to have been invited to add a little class to the occasion. For the rest of us, tennis was tennis. Life was on another court.

By the early 1970s, Ronnie had the country place (Wiltshire) and the Riviera hideaway, which—he promised me—more than paid for itself. He took the family to Gstaad immediately after Christmas and in summer they sailed out of Bodrum under the canny captaincy of good old Osman. During these absences, the syndicate discovered what *Hamlet* was like without the player-king. Fewer balls that landed plumb on the line were called out; fewer aces were deemed just to have nicked the net. On the down-side—Milstein was not so punctual as when Ronnie was time-keeping. If there was less bull, there was also less fun. When Ronnie returned from the slopes or the beaches, we smiled at his tanned shoulders and suet-pudding behind, but we rejoiced to have our winners called out and punctuality re-imposed by our manifest president.

It was against all precedent when, one winter morning, Jolyon Taggart failed to turn up. "He'll be here," Oliver said as ten o'clock came and went, but he was wrong. At twenty past, the telephone rang in Ralph's back room, where he sipped Scotch Broth direct from a tin which, we guessed, often contained more scotch than broth. Jolyon was terribly sorry, but he had a crisis. He couldn't make it that week. Ronnie tried to cajole Ralph into the arena, but he pleaded age, convincingly. We played one of those unsatisfactory threesomes which everyone always pretends have been surprisingly good fun.

Ronnie had a word with Jolyon, who swore that everything was now under control. The following week, Oliver was there ahead of time, and so was I. Ronnie's clothes preceded him into the dressing room in the hands of Trump, the chauffeur. Exit Trump to polish RBT 1, the eponymous Roller. The hour struck and we were still only three. "Really!" Ronnie said. "Parade's parade!" Jolyon arrived, on the double, ten minutes after we began a protracted knock-up. I greeted him affably from the far end, where Oliver and I were giving Ronnie the honour of hitting every ball, as he had assumed we would. "You may as well play with me, young man," Ronnie said, as Jolyon shucked his track-suit.

"You're the boss," Jolyon said.

He was usually a resourceful and steady partner. You would not have guessed it that day. Even Ronnie's creative linesmanship could not stop Oliver and me from winning one game after another. Ronnie grew baleful. We trooped into the showers without any of the usual *badinage.* All might have been well, or at least endurable, if Ronnie had not said, "I hope this isn't going to be a regular occurrence, young Jolyon, you keeping us waiting on the start-line."

Jolyon had always struck me as phlegmatic. If he was capable of passion, one could never imagine him bursting into tears. That is exactly what he now did. Naked, he cried like a baby. No, worse, he cried like a man: pain convulsed him. She'd left him. Taken the kid. What was he going to do? Did we have any idea what she meant to him?

We sighed. We bit our lips. We were truly very sorry. Ronnie powdered and anointed himself and tied his kipper-tie with chin-up concentration. Jolyon stumbled into his clothes, scarcely dry from the shower, snorting his way to self-control. Ronnie took the trees from his hand-stitched shoes, adjusted his sock-suspenders, and cleared his throat. "May I ask whether there is likely to be a repeat performance?"

"My wife's walked out on me, you bastard."

"And is that likely to have permanent consequences on your punctuality?"

"Who exactly do you think you are?"

"Call me Muggins, if you must," Ronnie said. "Otherwise known as him what makes the arrangements. Who did you think I was?"

"Has anyone ever told you . . ."

"Jolyon . . ." I tried to blow the whistle before the foul.

". . . what a ludicrous old cheat you are? What a stupid, pretentious, flagrant old oik you bloody well are?"

Ronnie put his shoe-trees into the pouch of his Florentine leather sack. He filed his Pour Homme toiletries in their plasticated sheaths. "Do I take it," he said, "that Master Taggart will not be here next week?"

"If you only knew how enjoyable it is when *you're* not here to call the ball out when it's miles in—"

"Or any week?" Ronnie said.

"You may have been an officer, but you'll never be a gentleman, never mind what bankrupt aristocrat your precious Floradora has managed to marry. You're a jumped-up poop. And why would anyone ever want to play tennis with you anyway?"

Ronnie took his belongings and his combination-locked briefcase and looked at me. I was ashamed. How often we had laughed at the Sultan behind his back! I waited for him to draw his snicker-snee and strike the infidel dead. His brave blue eyes were brimming with tears he willed himself not to shed. I realised that he could not trust himself to speak. He walked out of the dressing room.

The month ended without the usual roneoed form arriving from Miss Pomfret. I telephoned Ronnie's office to curse the Post Office and check that I was on the team-sheet. Miss Pomfret's voice was December itself. "Mr. Trafford is not in the office," she said, "and we're not expecting him. There are no plans for further tennis in the foreseeable future."

I telephoned Ralph, in the hope of a keep-fit session. There was no reply. I drove to Abacus Road a day later. The place was locked. A board announced that the premises were "Under Offer." Ronald B. Trafford and Associates were handling the sale.

I discovered Jolyon's number and, when the daffodils pushed through, we played a few times, with Milstein and Oliver Randell, on a common-or-garden court by the Royal Hospital. No one called the ball out when it was in; no ace was retrospectively demoted to a net-cord. Milstein's scarlet socks hardly seemed to matter. We were spared advice on property investment and no famous names were dropped. No one glared if you missed an easy one or took it for granted that you preferred serving into the sun. Yet somehow the game lacked magic.

Ronnie made a bomb out of the Abacus Road site, so a satirical magazine reported. I suspected that Jolyon had passed the word. Certainly Ronnie could afford a whacking contribution to Tory Party funds just as the new broom swept into Number Ten. Might a peerage be his eventual reward? I can imagine how he will have his racket covers emblazoned with his coat-of-arms. Jolyon was quite right about him, of course, in a way, but I look back with nostalgia on the covered court in Abacus Road, where the eighteen-storey headquarters of International Pharmaceuticals is said to appal the Prince of Wales. When I drive past, I seem to hear the ghost of Ralph, now gone, as Ronnie would say, to join the Great Umpire in the Sky, as it murmurs, "Pity!"

Mixed Doubles

IRWIN SHAW

As Jane Collins walked out onto the court behind her husband, she felt once more the private, strong thrill of pride that had moved her again and again in the time she had known him. Jane and Stewart had been married six years, but even so, as she watched him stride before her in that curious upright, individual, half-proud, half-comic walk, like a Prussian drill sergeant on his Sunday off, Jane felt the same mixture of amusement and delight in him that had touched her so strongly when they first met. Stewart was tall and broad and his face was moody and good-humored and original, and Jane felt that even at a distance of five hundred yards and surrounded by a crowd of people, she could pick him out unerringly. Now, in well-cut white trousers and a long-sleeved Oxford shirt, he seemed elegant and a little old-fashioned among the other players, and he looked graceful and debonair as he hit the first few shots in the preliminary rallying.

Jane was sensibly dressed, in shorts and tennis shirt, and her hair was imprisoned in a bandanna, so that it wouldn't get into her eyes. She knew that the shorts made her look a little dumpy and that the handkerchief around her head gave her a rather skinned and severe appearance, and she had a slight twinge of female regret when she looked across the net and saw Eleanor Burns soft and attractive in a prettily cut tennis dress and with a red ribbon in her hair, but she fought it down and concentrated on keeping her eye on the ball as Mr. Croker, Eleanor's partner, sliced it back methodically at her.

Mr. Croker, a vague, round, serious little man, was a neighbor of the Collinses' hosts. His shorts were too tight for him, and Jane knew, from having watched him on previous occasions, that his face would get more serious and more purple as the afternoon wore on, but he played a steady, dependable game and he was useful when other guests were too lazy or had drunk too much at lunch to play in the afternoon.

Two large oak trees shaded part of the court, and the balls flashed back and forth, in light and shadow, making guitarlike chords as they hit the rackets, and on the small terrace above the court, where the other guests were lounging, there was the watery music of ice in glasses and the bright flash of summer colors as people moved about.

How pleasant this was, Jane thought—to get away from the city on a weekend, to this cool, tree-shaded spot, to slip all the stiff bonds of business and city living and run swiftly on the springy surface of the court, feeling the country wind against her bare skin, feeling youth in her legs, feeling, for this short Sunday hour at least, free of desks and doors and weekday concrete.

Stewart hit a tremendous overhead smash, whipping all the strength of his long body into it, and the ball struck the ground at Eleanor's feet and slammed high in the air. He grinned. "I'm ready," he said.

"You're not going to do that to me in the game, are you?" Eleanor asked.

"I certainly am," Stewart said. "No mercy for women. The ancient motto of the Collins family."

They tossed for service, and Stewart won. He served and aced Eleanor with a twisting, ferocious shot that spun off at a sharp angle.

"Jane, darling," he said, grinning, as he walked to the other side, "we're going to be sensational today."

They won the first set with no trouble. Stewart played very well. He moved around the court swiftly and easily, hitting the ball hard in loose, well-coached strokes, with an almost exaggerated grace. Again and again, the people watching applauded or called out after one of his shots, and he waved his racket, smiling at them, and said, "Oh, we're murderous today." He kept humming between shots—a tuneless, happy composition of his own—like a little boy who is completely satisfied with himself, and Jane couldn't help smiling and adoring him as he lightheartedly dominated the game and the spectators and the afternoon, brown and dashing and handsome in his white clothes, with the sun flooding around him like a spotlight on an actor in the middle of the stage.

Occasionally, when Stewart missed a shot, he would stand, betrayed and tragic, and stare up at the sky and ask with mock despair, "Collins, why don't you just go home?" And then he would turn to Jane and say, "Janie, darling, forgive me. Your husband's just no good."

And even as she smiled at him and said, "You're so right," she could sense the other women, up on the terrace, looking down at him, their eyes speculative and veiled and lit with invitation as they watched.

Jane played her usual game, steady, unheroic, getting almost everything back quite sharply, keeping the ball in play until Stewart could get his racket on it and kill it. They were a good team. Jane let Stewart poach on her territory for spectacular kills, and twice Stewart patted her approvingly on the behind after she had made difficult saves, and there were appreciative chuckles from the spectators at the small domestic vulgarity.

Stewart made the last point of the set on a slamming deep backhand that passed Eleanor at the net. Eleanor shook her head and said, "Collins, you're an impossible man," and Croker said stolidly, "Splendid. Splendid," and Stewart said, grinning, "Something I've been saving for this point, old man."

They walked off and sat down on a bench in the shade between sets, and Croker and Jane had to wipe their faces with towels and Croker's alarming purple died a little from his cheeks.

"That overhead!" Eleanor said to Stewart. "It's absolutely frightening. When I see you winding up, I'm just tempted to throw away my poor little racket and run for my life."

Jane lifted her head and glanced swiftly at Stewart to see how he was taking it. He was taking it badly, smiling a little too widely at Eleanor, being boyish and charming. "It's nothing," he said. "Something I picked up on Omaha Beach."

That, too, Jane thought bitterly. Foxhole time, too. She ducked her head into her towel to keep from saying something wifely. This is the last time, she thought, feeling the towel sticky against her sweaty forehead, the last time I am coming to any of these weekend things, always loaded with unattached or semi-attached, man-hungry, half-naked, boney-mouthed girls. She composed her face, so that when she looked up from the towel she would look like a nice, serene woman who merely was interested in the next set of tennis.

Eleanor, who had wide green eyes, was staring soberly and unambiguously over the head of her racket at Stewart, and Stewart, fascinated, as always, and a little embarrassed, was staring back. Oh, God, Jane thought, the long stare, too.

"Well," she said briskly, "I'm ready for one more set."

"What do you say," Stewart asked, "we divide up differently this time? Might make it more even. Croker and you, Jane, and the young lady and me."

"Oh," said Eleanor, "I'd be a terrible drag to you, Stewart. And besides, I'm sure your wife loves playing on your side."

"Not at all," Jane said stiffly. The young lady! How obvious could a man be?

"No," said Croker surprisingly. "Let's stay the way we are." Jane wanted to kiss the round purple face, a bleak, thankful kiss. "I think we'll do better this time. I've been sort of figuring out what to do with you, Collins."

Stewart looked at him briefly and unpleasantly, then smiled charmingly. "Anything you say, old man. I just thought . . ."

"I'm sure we'll do better," Croker said firmly. He stood up. "Come on, Eleanor."

Eleanor stood up, lithe and graceful in her short dress, which whipped around her brown legs in the summer wind. Never again, Jane thought, will I wear shorts. Dresses like that, even if they cost fifty dollars apiece, and soft false bosoms to put in them, too, and no bandanna, even if I'm blinded on each shot.

Stewart watched Eleanor follow Croker onto the court, and Jane could have brained him for the buried, measuring glint in his eye.

"Let's go," Stewart said, and under his breath, as they walked to their positions on the base line. He added, "Let's really show the old idiot this time, Jane."

"Yes, dear," Jane said, and pulled her bandanna straight and tight around her hair.

The first three games were ludicrously one-sided. Stewart stormed the net, made sizzling, malicious shots to Croker's feet, and purposely made him run, so that he panted pitifully and grew more purple than ever, and from time to time muttered to Jane, "Ridiculous old windbag," and "I thought he had me figured out," and "Don't let up, Janie, don't let up."

Jane played as usual, steady, undeviating, as predictably and sensibly as she always played. She was serving in the fourth game and was at 40-15 when Stewart dropped a shot just over the net, grinning as Croker galloped heavily in and barely got his racket on it. Croker's return wobbled over Stewart's head and landed three inches beyond the base line.

"Nice shot," she heard Stewart say. "Just in."

She looked at him in surprise. He was nodding his head emphatically at Croker.

Eleanor was at the net on the other side, looking at Stewart. "It looked out to me," she said.

"Not at all," Stewart said. "Beautiful shot. Serve them up, Janie."

Oh, Lord, Jane thought, now he's being sporting.

Jane made an error on the next point and Croker made a placement for advantage and Stewart hit into the net for the last point, and it was Croker's and Eleanor's game. Stewart came back to receive the service, not humming any more, his face irritable and dark.

Croker suddenly began to play very well, making sharp, sliding, slicing shots that again and again forced Stewart and Jane into errors. As they played, even as she swung at the ball, Jane kept remembering the shot that Stewart had called in, that had become the turning point of the set. He had not been able to resist the gallant gesture, especially when Eleanor had been standing so close, watching it all. It was just like Stewart. Jane shook her head determinedly, trying to concentrate on the game. This was no time to start dissecting her husband. They had had a lovely weekend till now and Stewart had been wonderful, gay and funny and loving, and criticism could at least be reserved for weekdays, when everything else was dreary, too. But it *was* just like Stewart. It was awful how everything he did was all of a piece. His whole life was crowded with gestures. Hitting his boss that time in the boss's own office with three secretaries watching, because the boss had bawled him out. Giving up his R.O.T.C. commission and going into the Army as a private, in 1942. Giving five thousand dollars, just about the last of their savings, to Harry Mather, for Mather's business, just because they had gone to school together, when everyone knew Mather had become a hopeless drunk and none of his other friends would chip in. To an outsider, all these might seem the acts of a generous and rather noble character, but to a wife, caught in the consequences . . .

"Damn these pants," Stewart was muttering after hitting a ball into the net. "I keep tripping over them all the time."

"You ought to wear shorts, like everyone else," Jane said.

"I will. Buy me some this week," Stewart said, taking time out and rolling his cuffs up slowly and obviously. Jane had bought him three pairs of shorts a month before, but he always pretended he couldn't find them, and wore the long trousers. His legs are surprisingly skinny, Jane thought, hating herself for thinking it, and they're hairy, and his vanity won't let him. . . . She started to go for a ball, then stopped when she saw Stewart going for it.

He hit it out to the backstop. "Janie, darling," he said, "at least stay out of my way."

"Sorry," she said. Stewie, darling, she thought, Stewie, be careful. Don't lay it on. You're not really like this. I know you're not. Even for a moment, don't make it look as though you are.

Stewart ended the next rally by hitting the ball into the net. He stared unhappily at the ground. "The least they might do," he said in a low voice to Jane, "is roll the court if they invite people to play on it."

Please, Stewie, Jane begged within herself, don't do it. The alibis. The time he forgot to sign the lease for the apartment and they were put out and he blamed it on the lawyer, and the time he lost the job in Chicago and it was because he had gone to the wrong college, and the time . . . By a rigorous act of will,

Jane froze her eyes on the ball, kept her mind blank as she hit it back methodically again and again.

Eleanor and Croker kept winning points. Croker had begun to chop every ball, spinning soft, deceptive shots that landed in midcourt and hardly bounced before they fell a second time. The only way that Jane could return them was to hit them carefully, softly, just getting them back. But Stewart kept going in on them furiously, taking his full, beautiful swing, sending the ball whistling into the net or over the court into the backstop. He looked as pretty and expert as ever as he played, but he lost point after point.

"What a way to play tennis," he grumbled, with his back to his opponents. "Why doesn't he play Ping-Pong or jacks?"

"You can't slam those dinky little shots like that," Janie said. "You have to get them back soft."

"You play your game," Stewart said, "and I'll play mine."

"Sorry," Jane said. Oh, Stewart, she mourned within her.

Stewart went after two more of Croker's soft chops, each time whipping his backhand around in his usual, slightly exaggerated, beautiful stroke, and each time knocking the ball into the net.

He can't help it, Jane thought. That is the way he is. Form above everything. If he were hanging over a cliff, he'd let himself fall to the rocks below rather than risk being ungraceful climbing to safety to save his life. He always has to pick up the check in bars and restaurants, no matter whom he is with or how many guests there are at the table, always with the same lordly, laughing, slightly derisive manner, even if we are down to our last fifty dollars. And when they had people in to dinner, there had to be two maids to wait on table, and French wines, and there always had to be those special bottles of brandy that cost as much as a vacation in the country. And he became so cold and remote when Jane argued with him about it, reminding him they were not rich and there was no sense in pretending they were. And his shoes. She blinked her eyes painfully, getting a sudden vision, there in the sun and shadow, of the long row of exquisite shoes, at seventy dollars a pair, that he insisted upon having made to his order. How ridiculous, she thought, to allow yourself to be unnerved at your husband's taste in shoes, and she loyally reminded herself how much a part of his attraction it had been in the beginning that he was always so beautifully dressed and so easy and graceful and careless of money.

The score was 4-3 in favor of Eleanor and Croker. Stewart's shots suddenly began to work again, and he and Jane took the next game with ease. Stewart's grin came back then, and he cheerfully reassured Jane, "Now we're going to take them." But after winning the first two points of the next game he had a wild streak and missed the base line by a few inches three times in a row, and they eventually lost the game.

I will make no deductions from this, Jane told herself stonily as she went up to the net for Stewart's serve. Anybody is liable to miss a few shots like that—anybody. And yet, how like Stewart! Just when it was most important to be steady and dependable... The time she'd been so sick and the maid had quit, and Jane lay, broken and miserable, in bed for three weeks, with no one to take care of her except Stewart... He had been charming and thoughtful for the first week, fixing her meals, reading to her, sitting at her side for hours on end, cheerful and obliging, making her illness gently tolerable. And then he had suddenly grown nervous and abrupt, made vague excuses to leave her alone, and vanished for hours at a time, only to come back and hastily attend her for a few moments and vanish again, leaving her there in the rumpled bed, staring, lonely and shaken, at the ceiling as dusk faded into night and night into morning. She had been sure there was another girl then and she had resolved that when she was well and able to move around again, she would come to some decision with him, but as unpredictably as his absences had begun, they stopped. Once more he was tender and helpful, once more he sat at her side and nursed her and cheered her, and out of gratitude and love she had remained quiet and pushed her doubts deep to the back of her mind. And here they were again, in the middle of a holiday afternoon, foolishly, in this most unlikely place, during this mild, pointless game, with half a dozen people lazily watching, laughing and friendly, over their drinks.

She looked at him a few moments later, handsome and dear and familiar at her side, and he grinned back at her, and she was ashamed of herself for the thoughts that had been flooding through her brain. It was that silly girl on the other side of the net who had started it all, she thought. That practiced, obvious, almost automatic technique of flattering the male sex. That meaningless, rather pitiful flirtatiousness. It was foolish to allow it to throw her into the bitter waters of reflection. Marriage, after all, was an up-and-down affair and in many ways a fragile and devious thing, and was not to be examined too closely. Marriage was not a bank statement or a foreign policy or an X-ray photograph in a doctor's hand. You took it and lived through it, and maybe, a long time later— perhaps the day before you died—you totalled up the accounts, if you were of that turn of mind, but not before. And if you were a reasonable, sensible, mature woman, you certainly didn't do your additions and subtractions on a tennis court every time your husband hit a ball into the net. Jane smiled at herself and shook her head.

"Nice shot," she said warmly to Stewart as he swept a forehand across court, past Croker, for a point.

But it was still set point. Croker placed himself to receive Stewart's service, tense and determined and a little funny-looking, with his purple face and his serious round body a little too tight under his clothes. The spectators had fallen silent, and the wind had died, and there was a sense of stillness and expectancy as Stewart reared up and served.

Jane was at the net and she heard the sharp twang of Stewart's racket hitting the ball behind her and the riflelike report as it hit the tape and fell away. He had just missed his first service.

Jane didn't dare look around. She could feel Stewart walking into place, in that stiff-backed, pleasant way of his, and feel him shuffling around nervously, and she couldn't look back. Please, she thought, please get this one in. Helplessly, she thought of all the times when, just at the crucial moment, he had failed. Oh, God, this is silly, she thought. I mustn't do this. The time he had old man Sawyer's account practically in his hands and he got drunk. On the sporting pages, they called it coming through in the clutch. There were some players who did and some players who didn't, and after a while you got to know which was which. If you looked at it coldly, you had to admit that until now Stewart had been one of those who didn't. The time her father died, just after her sister had run off with the vocalist in that band, and if there had been a man around, taking hold of things, her father's partner wouldn't've been able to get away with most of the estate the way he did, and the vocalist could have been frightened off. One day's strength and determination, one day of making the right move at the right time . . . But after the funeral, Stewart had pulled out and gone to Seattle on what he had said was absolutely imperative business, but that had never amounted to anything anyway, and Jane's mother and sister, and Jane, too, were still paying for that day of failure.

She could sense Stewart winding up for his service behind her back. Somewhere in her spine she felt a sense of disaster. It was going to be a double fault. She knew it. No, she thought, I mustn't. He isn't really like that. He's so intelligent and talented and good, he can go so far. She must not make this terrible judgment on her husband just because of the way he played tennis. And yet, his tennis was so much like his life. Gifted, graceful, powerful, showy, flawed, erratic . . .

Please, she thought, make this one good. Childishly, she felt, If this one is good it will be a turning point, a symbol, his whole life will be different. She hated herself for her thoughts and stared blankly at Eleanor, self-consciously alert and desirable in her pretty dress.

Why the hell did she have to come here this Sunday? Jane thought despairingly.

She heard the crack of the racket behind her. The ball whistled past her, hit the tape, rolled undecidedly on top of the net for a moment, then fell back at her feet for a double fault and the set.

"Too bad." She turned and smiled at Stewart, helplessly feeling herself beginning to wonder how she would manage to find the six weeks it would take in Reno. She shook her head, knowing that she wasn't going to Reno, but knowing, too, that the word would pass through her thoughts again and again, more and more frequently, with growing insistence, as the days went by.

She walked off the court with Stewart, holding his hand.

"The shadows," Stewart was saying. "Late in the afternoon, like this. It's impossible to see the service line."

"Yes, dear," Jane said.

The Blacktop Champion of Ickey Honey

ROBERT T. SORRELLS

I try hard to be optimistic about life, but when Hoke Warble came to me and told me he had agreed to a $1000 grudge match with Newton Slock, I said, "Hoke, why don't you just go on and give Newton his money right now and save yourself and all of us, your friends, the embarrassment of having to sit out there on those splintery bleachers at the Ickey Honey Country Club under what will no doubt be a broiling August sun and watch you get your ass whipped?"

Or words to that effect.

But first, *Ickey Honey*. It's a hamlet in Punkin County, South Carolina, and though now called the Gateway to the Blue Ridge, it is not quite far enough up in the mountains to get more than one snow every four or five years that doesn't melt by noon. It's really more "out from" than "up toward."

Too—contrary to whatever those slack-jawed kids over in the college town of Clemson might say about it—the name is not what you might think. *Honey,* for instance, is a corruption of an old Indian word, Honea, which in the Cherokee means *Path.* The *Ickey* is another corruption from the Cherokee, *Ike-owaywa,* which, imperfectly translated, means *The Place From*

Which One Leaps Out. So those Clemson people delighted in telling each other that Ickey Honey was the jumping-off place, the end of the earth. In fact, however, to the Cherokees Honea Ikeowaywa was the Point of Beginning, the place from which the hunters went to hunt, the warriors to make war, and so on, with the implication that they were the actual center of things, the place where all paths come together. Something like Rome, I gather.

But what can you expect from a corrupt people if not a corruption of language?

However, the old-line natives retained the history, after a fashion, and that is why our high school athletic teams call themselves the Warpathers. We kept our high school, by the way, because when all that consolidation got started about 20 years ago, we fell off the county superintendent's list. So by being lost we managed to keep our integrity, unlike most of those new schools which ended up in the middle of some junky hunk of land without even a dusting of topsoil: schools juxtaposed to nowhere and neighbored by nothing but parking lots for the buses.

In Ickey Honey, at least, you had to walk past the school every day of your life, and you knew it was where you had to put in your time, like it or not, and you knew it was a part of the whole Ickey Honey scene—just like the church you had to go to. I am not saying that everyone liked it. I am simply saying that it was there and so were you, and the result was you grew up with a very personal one-to-one relationship with things.

As to Hoke Warble, he was less what you'd call a friend than a part of me. Neither "Friend" nor "Enemy." Just always

Hoke, the derivation of whose name I will spare you the complex though fascinating details. Hoke was as native to Ickey Honey as cones to our pines or red to our earth or shotguns to our weddings.

At the same time, though, it must be admitted that Hoke had certain desires in this world, one of which was To Rise. Hoke even wanted to excel. Now you must also understand this: coming from a place like Ickey Honey can do things to you as well as for you. If we grew up rich in deep and abiding relationships to our buildings and our people, we grew up poor in vocational models. A few gas station attendants, some feed store people, a grocer or so, and the preachers twice a week. That was it. When I was growing up we didn't even have any rednecks in town on Saturdays. We were the rednecks, and every Saturday you'd find most of Ickey Honey hunkered down chewing and whittling and staring bug-eyed on the sidewalks of such big towns as Six Mile and Ninety-Six.

So either you praised the virtues of living crimeless in Ickey Honey, or the minute you set eyes on a real town you started plotting your escape. But if you were Hoke, you dreamed on a grander scale. Where most of us decided to stay or leave for the wider world, Hoke decided he could both stay and leave by bringing the Wider World into Ickey Honey. After finding out that other places were far brighter and more inviting, and after dutifully toting his slide rule around Clemson for four years, Hoke wanted Ickey Honey to be worthier of him than he figured it was. He wanted Ickey Honey to improve.

So he established, subscribed, and built the Ickey Honey Country Club, the first step on Ickey Honey's forced march into Growth and Development. A disinterested observer, however, might have concluded that the Country Club was really something else. A city park, say, with an imposing gateway arch to belie what was on the other side: a pool, covered over after six drownings (though no people), a memorial plaque to Hoke, two outdoor basketball goals, their metal nets missing, and the tennis court.

The tennis court. Hoke built it 15 years ago, long before tennis, like golf in its time, had become a game of the masses. Hoke, some said, had always been a man of vision. As a matter of fact the last time I heard that said was the day Hoke came in to talk to me about the Best Two Out of Three Set Grudge Match. As another matter of fact, he said it himself.

"What do you mean, 'Get my ass whipped'?" He extended his head as far as he could from his neck and glared up at me. I am five feet ten.

"Of course I will beat him," he demanded, and swabbed his sweating face with a huge handkerchief. It was late June, but summer had come early.

"Huh!" he bullied further, a forefinger jabbing right between my eyes. "I will destroy him. Newton Slock. Yech! That's not even a name. What kind of name is that? You know all about weird things."

The implications of his questions fanned the fires of his own inventiveness.

"I'll tell you about weird. Newton Slock. *That's* weird. Do you know how big a freak he is? Let me tell you about Newton Slock . . ."

"No, Hoke," I interrupted. "You don't need to tell me about Newton Slock. I know about Newton Slock. Newton Slock attended Presbyterian College for Gentle Men, and in his four years there he was President or Editor of everything from the Minor Sports Club to their yearbook *The Guiding Light.*"

"Huh!" Hoke said, his red face cracked by a sour smile. "Huh! It's easy to see you've been around him for a minute and a half. I'll destroy him," he said by way of getting back to basics, and he wadded his handkerchief down into a pocket of his blue shorts.

"Listen, DB," I said. DB stood for *Drag Butt,* a nickname Hoke hadn't much cottoned to, but which stuck anyway because Hoke was built like . . . well, like a toad, maybe. Or a fireplug. A sack of corncobs?

"DB," I said, "first off, Newton Slock is your friend. You got him here to help 'improve' the town by making it into a subdivision for which I don't much love either of you. And he has helped you make a passel doing it.

"Also," I went on quickly before he could stick his finger back between my eyes like the barrel of a Saturday-night special, "Newton Slock is a very competent tennis player who was captain of his team in college and who has played a lot of tennis since.

"And who," I hurried right on, "has not spent nearly so much of his leisure time as you sitting and *watching* tube tennis whilst drinking cases of beer and consuming plastic snack-slops by the crate."

"You don't understand a thing," Hoke said. I had run out of breath. "There is no way that weirdo can beat me."

"How about by playing better tennis?" Forthrightness compelled me at least to put it forward as a possibility.

"And he can't because first off," he shoved that salami-shaped thumb up at me, "he is a *Freak!* Second off," and he pulled his index finger up from his fist, "he is *wrong.* Third of all ..."

Now it looked like a salami and two Vienna sausages. I wondered how he ever managed to hold a racket with a hand like that.

"... I'm right."

His hand stayed bunched near my chin; so I had a chance to look at his fingers for a minute before I answered.

"Hoke, it occurs to me that all the Right in the world will not make you as good a tennis player as Newton Slock."

He looked crushed, not because it occurred to him my judgment might be sound, but because he must have suffered a sense of betrayal.

"Lookee," he said to me.

I looked at his hand. So did he. He even started to point at it before quickly stuffing it into his shorts pocket.

"You don't even know what he's done. How can you talk like that and not even know what he's done?"

I had wondered what had happened, but I knew Hoke well enough to know he would never answer a direct question.

"He cheated you," I said and turned as if to walk away.

He grabbed my arm.

"You're gonna hold the stakes," he said.

"Fine," I answered real quick, figuring I'd gotten off pretty light if that's all there was to it. But I smelled the rat when I looked at him.

"You're also gonna get me in shape," he said with what I took to be a leer.

"No way."

"Lotsa ways."

"Hoke, you idiot. I don't know a durned thing in the world about tennis or how to get in shape for playing the fool game."

"I'll teach you. There's nothing to it. Honest. All you have to do is keep your eye on the ball and return their shots. Let them wear themselves out. Simple."

"I'll tell you what's simple," I said. "What's simple is that I can't even be out in the field as a county agent nearly as much as I'd like because I got no knees, what with arthritis from old Warpathers football days. And that means I have to ply much of my trade in an office which doesn't keep me very even-tempered, which means in addition that there is no way I *can* go hoppitying around a macadam tennis court like some twenty-year-old. And neither can you because you'd drop dead from cardiac arrest and heat prostration—especially in this kind of weather."

"One more thing," he said, just like I'd never opened my mouth. "You're going to referee, too, so you might as well start boning up on the rules."

I did not respond. He knew I could be as hard-headed as anyone including himself—and that when I clammed up he'd better talk fast because I never bothered to spend much time arguing cases. You get so you mean it or you don't in this world, and there's no point standing around jawing. Now Hoke, being what he called an entrepreneur, was nothing but a sack full of arguments.

"All right," he said. "I thought you were a friend. All right."

He looked like he always does when he busied his mouth to work his brain. I still wasn't going to ask him what all this mess was about.

"Then I'll tell you," he said. "Tell you short and sweet."

"All right," I said.

"It's really very simple," he said, giving all the appearance of being calm and in control under intense emotional pressure.

I gestured for him to please go on.

"He's a cheat."

"A cheat?" I said.

He looked confused. Then, "Land," he nearly whispered. "Land is the wealth of a nation."

I said nothing.

"He has been robbing me blind and I intend to beat the bastard at his own game, Lodi. Then I'm going to kill him."

It was the first time all day he had called me by my name.

As for myself, I'm a County Agent. An entomologist, really, who got into county agenting so I could eat regularly. Too, the job let me stay in or near home, which suited me just fine.

Lodi Poidle. I was drafted to fight the Korean War, but ended up in Austria, realized that *Poidle* was a corruption of *Peutl*, and that it was from Austria we came some hundred and fifty years ago. But that was through my father. Through my mother, a Scot, we have been here God only knows how long. Also through my mother we have been here more or less forever, since she was part Cherokee. When I was a child and asked which part, she only laughed, but when my father asserted at the dinner table that he knew which part was Indian, she would just smile sweetly and say, "The Princess part."

So in Salzburg, Austria, I learned to skate and ski, to speak a little German, and to be dissatisfied forever with American bread and beer. Then back home to finish school, take the county agenting job, marry, and accept my place as a stable member of the Ickey Honey community. And all because of bugs.

When I was little, I remember, I loved the pines: loblolly, slash, white. I remember sitting in a plantation of them once, listening.

Crunch, crunch.

I finally asked my father what it was I kept hearing. He sat down beside me, listened carefully, and said, "Pine borers. They are eating the trees. Look," and he showed me their holes, even got his knife and dug out a few of the varmints.

I said, "They are eating up all the trees?" He said, "Yes, Lodi." I wept, then spent years hating the pine borers with all the passion of my youth, determined to learn how to save the world from them. That's why I went to college in the first place. But there I learned to love bugs. The fruit fly, for instance. You have to admire him after a while. And nits and newts and mites and all the rest . . .

"Buggy!"

It was Hoke shouting at me. I rested my racket on my toes. He was unhappy with my play.

"Damn, Lodi. You got to go after the ball. You got to chase it to hit it back. Isn't anyone going to hit it right to your forehand every time. You're not giving me the first sign of a sweat."

"Sweat! All I have to do is stand here and I sweat."

"Well if you'd wear shorts and a T-shirt instead of those khaki trousers and shirts you wouldn't get so hot."

I pointed the racket at him. "Hoke, you're stupider than you look if you think I'm going to walk around this town in short pants that look like underwear."

"Get ready for another serve, Lodi. If I can get my power up for the serves I can take him."

"Hoke, if there's anything Newton can do it's return serves."

Hoke glared across the net at me. "Oh yeah? Well if there's anything else he can do it's foot fault." His face was a ball of red, wet hatred. "You got to watch him careful on that or he'll foot fault on me all day long if you don't catch him and call him on it."

I walked off the court toward the bench and started to button up my shirt.

"Hey!" Hoke yelled, racing around the net. "Where you going? You promised me two hours this morning. We only been out here thirty minutes."

"I think it probably isn't right for me to train you if I'm going to have to referee the match, Hoke, because I'll have to call your foot faults, too."

"I don't foot fault."

"You do."

"I don't."

"Do."

"Don't," he hollered.

I stood quietly and stared him down.

"Much?" he asked.

"Every time," I answered.

"Well hell, Lodi. You mean you'd call something like that on me after what he's done? Would you?"

I finished tucking in my shirt.

"Lodi?" he whined. "Man, I *need* you. You got to *help* me. You got to tell me things like how does he serve? And, how does he play the net? And stuff like that. Lodi?"

I faced him. "Hoke, how many years have you been playing tennis with Newton Slock?"

He shrugged. "Ten, maybe. Why?"

I could only shake my head. This was beginning to surpass wonder.

"Then you have probably played two thousand games with Newton Slock, since for the first five of those years he was the only other person in town who knew how to play."

"So?" he shrugged. "What's that got to do with foot faults?"

Even I was stunned. "It means I'm going to call them," I mumbled.

"Good!" he shouted, beaming at me like he meant it. "I just had to make sure you were still Mr. Incorruptible. Get your racket and let's go."

I did, too. I was a good example of how Hoke Warble—slide rule dangling jauntily from his hip, wearing his civil engineering degree on his sleeve like some wear their hearts—was able to borrow money enough to buy land, hire surveyors, rent bulldozers, and, by whispering the sweetest of honey into the ears of conservative builders, turn them into daring speculation contractors. He could talk people into things. Part wheedle, part bully, but mostly a playing on your own greed or whatever strength he knew he could grab you by and turn you with. And to give credit, the minute he knew that Clemson Agricultural College was going to stop being a military academy and start being a University with coeds, was the minute he understood the power of wide roads leading from Clemson direct to where the town I grew up in stood. No need to guess who owned the best rights of way when it all got started.

That was Hoke, but it was almost worth it to watch him play tennis. His serve, for instance, wasn't what you could call good, but it was hard to return. He held his racket in what at first appeared to be the ordinary way, only because his hands were so small, he had to chisel the grip down and then hold it about three inches up from the end. Also, he couldn't hold but one ball at a time in the other hand. But since all the pros had three balls, he did too—in his pockets. I mean you to understand he kept two or three balls in *each* pocket. As I have suggested, Hoke already filled out his clothes. So to stuff all those balls into the side pockets gave him the appearance of a hog with great wens on each hip.

Then he would peer steadfastly across the net at his opponent. With the ball held right up against the bottom of his racket, he would begin to rock his entire body forward and backward while at the same time he shoved his arms back and forth so you weren't sure what to watch. When he had gotten himself all wound up, he would lean way over toward the net, bring his racket to the ground in front of his left toes, rear back, and with a quick jerk and grunt serve the ball.

As a rule, he served three times. The first went into the net. The second ticked the top of the net. And the third he just pooped the ball into play. When the time came for you to do something, you were either worn out watching all that business or just exactly bored enough to be out of the notion to play.

But play we did: I would serve and serve so he could practice his returns. Then he would serve and serve while I shagged balls for him. It was wearing work, but Hoke went at it like a pro. Hours and hours and hours of it.

I thought once that he might lose 50 pounds working like he did with out-and-out hot weather already settled in like it was. But every time he finished sweating off eight pounds (he weighed in before and after each session) he'd drink about a quart of beer with his sandwiches and snack-slops. Plus his regular meals. So he ended up eating more than usual. And the more he trained, the bigger he got.

"But stronger, Lodi," he'd insist. "And quicker."

Which brings me to Newton Slock.

Newton wasn't a native. Newton was from what is called the Low Country, a section of our fair state thick with history, plague, cotton, a language called Gullah, and rich people who still can't stand the sight of someone from Up Country who can afford to drive his own car to work.

Now there are two ways for people like me to approach an outsider like Newton. One is to say that at least he has seen the light and come to where God intended people instead of sand fleas and red bugs to live. The other is to remain always suspicious. Since he was a good friend of Hoke's, I was at least somewhat predisposed toward the latter, but being me, I was also prepared for the former.

All of Newton's activities in Presbyterian College for Gentle Men were nothing but preparation for the Life of the Real World, as he phrased it. Committees, activities, meetings, clubs, organizations, Service to the Community . . . Lord, there was no end to it. He was Hoke's P. R. man, in short, and the volume of leaflets, letters, flyers, pamphlets, and advertisements he flooded into the mails was worthy of any government bureaucrat. Not to mention the number of dinners eaten or rounds of golf played with university deans, textile mill executives, and editorial writers for the local newspapers—all to help turn Ickey Honey into a subdivision worthy of Hoke Warble.

"Not a subdivision," Newton gently said one day years ago. "What we are creating here is a Residential Community, Lodi," and he looked at me with those Gentle Man's sincere eyes.

"I see," I said back. "But what's it going to *do?*"

"Do, Lodi?" He never broke stride. "Why, it won't have to *do* anything. It will provide a restful place for people to live in. It will be a retreat where people can reintegrate themselves and so face the next day's challenges."

"It seems to me," I tried, "that people are already integrated if they live more or less where they work."

"Ah, Lodi," he smiled.

"It seems to me, Newton, that when you make a person live away from his work, or when you make him do work he hates so much that he feels he has to live away from it, then you have separated him out from himself so that he has to reintegrate. My father never needed any reintegrating because, being a forester and a farmer, he lived where the fruit of his labor was."

"Your father lived in another time, Lodi."

"Newton, I live right here in Ickey Honey where my work is."

"Hmmm," he said wisely. "Bugs are ubiquitous, yes, but not all of us in this modern world of today are able to do that. This nation isn't agricultural anymore, Lodi."

He said that very archly as though I probably hadn't heard the news yet. I was going to tell him that people had always lived in towns, and that in lots of places they lived happily and well-integrated right above their shops. But I figured it wouldn't help.

Besides, Newton was a nice enough person. He was not mean. He was not a beast. It's just that I didn't understand how someone who was supposed to be so smart could really believe the things he kept saying.

So we practiced, Hoke and I. We practiced the forehand return, the backhand return, lobs, serves, the serve return, the two-hand grip. He practiced doing like Arthur Ashe, or Jimmy Connors, or Ilie Nastase, or ...

But through it all, Hoke remained largely his own man. When I had told him earlier that I couldn't go hoppitying around the court it was because Hoke was about the only player I had ever seen, and hop was what he did most. He always seemed to go up and down more than back and forth. That never changed much, either, though I must admit that as the match drew nearer Hoke was able to make his upping and downing more useful. And just a week before the match itself, he had a long and serious talk with me before our practice session.

"Lodi," he said, the sincerity nearly choking him. "You'll never know how much I appreciate your helping me this way."

I shrugged. "I've actually come to enjoy it, Hoke," I said. "I didn't think I would, but I have actually come to like the game. Sort of."

"I will tell you something," he went on. "I am going to beat him."

I waited for more, but there was silence. I looked up and damned if there weren't tears in his eyes.

"Well," I said. "Well, Hoke. I never thought you had a chance four weeks ago. But durned if I don't think you can give him a real run for his money now."

At that, the tears disappeared, and so, too, I think, did the era of good feeling that we had been sharing.

"Money!" he snorted, and it did not take a genius to gather he was not alluding to the $1000 bet. Had Newton been cheating him? I still couldn't believe it, couldn't believe, at any rate, that there was something illegal involved. I kept my own counsel and waited for Hoke to reveal himself.

He gave me a man-to-man stare and a professional little pat on my bottom as he said, "Let's hit it, Lodi," his voice quiet but firm with the sureness of a man who knows his destiny is soon to be fulfilled.

As for my own destiny, it was bouncing along innocently enough until the day I was driving back to my office after a visit to look at a garden club president's scaly azaleas. A sporty little Audi had nipped in front of me and on the left side of its bumper was a sticker. It pictured a hand clenched tightly around a tennis racket being held on high. The inscription read: TENNIS NOW! On the other side of the bumper was another sticker. It read: ALL POWER TO THE COURTS. Dawn glimmered slowly in my gut where a voice rumbled lowly unto me saying, *Lodi, Old Bean, someone has been very busy promoting this thing while you were out training Hoke.*

They came in from all around, the Natives did. They came in from places that hadn't even been crossroads for 30 years. They came in in their pickups and on their baled-together flatbeds. They came in with NeHis, R.C.s, little packets of salted goobers, peanut butter crackers, Cheez-Its, and dangerous-looking sacks worn soft from constant reusing. They came in in overalls, ankle boots, their sides sliced to give bunions ease, their little children barefoot and knobbly-ankled, their teenaged daughters slumpshouldered against maturity, their boys ballsy but stiff-necked against the alien feel of a town grown smooth and untouchable to the rough clutch of their snag-nailed hands; their sense of being forever excluded, as heavy and real to them as the heat that had hunkered down on us all for the past week.

They found places for their vehicles near the Ickey Honey Country Club, parked, and made their way to the tennis court. There were stands on both sides of the court, and for no reason other than that he had parked nearest it, the first arrival had stepped warily up on the closest set of plank bleachers; followed, then, by the others as they clanked and chugged into town and in their own turns parked near the vehicles they knew, the ones they understood to be like their own and thus peopled by their own kind. They climbed the seats, sat, looked around with care, not wanting to move fast enough to draw attention to themselves.

Across the way another crowd was taking its place: white trousers and shorts with deck shoes for sailing on the lake, smoothly tanned all over, lounging, at ease, relaxed and chatting with one another.

Yet they sedulously avoided eye contact with the people on my side. Except, that is, by flicking, darting little side glances. Their heads stayed averted. They were the Residents.

After not too long the principals arrived. From the Residents there came a polite pat-a-pat-a-pat of applause. From the others . . .

I would like to say that I heard groans when Hoke and Newton made their appearances. I would like to say they gasped . . . or snickered . . . or did something outrageous. But they didn't, and I loved them for holding their collective judgment in abeyance. And yet . . .

. . . and yet something went through them when they saw the two men, when they saw that *those* were to be the contestants they had lurched into town to see, were willing to sit on splintery planks under an already roasting sun to watch as the ancient rituals of man's pride in self and family and place were satisfied.

. . . something of wonder crossed their faces.

To their right was Newton Slock: six feet two inches, trim,

darkhaired, fit looking; his tennis shoes were Adidas, a solid suede, a no-nonsense shade of blue with socks to match; his tennis shorts were lighter in color, more what you might call Bonnie Blue; his shirt—its rolled collar very precisely casual—was color-coordinated with the shorts and sneakers, a thin rim of maroon piping around the sleeves of the shirt and down the sides of the shorts. On his wrists were light blue sweatbands. Topping it off was a visor, blue on the underside, a rich, creamy off-white above. A take-charge guy, you could tell right off.

And to their left was Hoke. He too had chosen Adidas, but they were white trimmed in gold. His socks matched, as did his shorts and shirt, with its little alligator emblazoned over his heart. Not only did he have sweatbands on his wrists—bright gold ones—but a sweatband encircled his head as well, like a tight halo.

They were a sight indeed. Hoke did squat bends while Newton went through a complex routine of circular arm movements. Apparently they were not going to give each other any warm-ups like every other tennis player in the world does before a match; so the next move was mine. I stepped toward the net, careful not to get onto either side of the court lest one of them accuse me of favoring the other. I motioned them to come to me.

"Well," I began.

They glared at each other.

"Well, here we are. I reckon it's time to start."

Newton kept up his arm swinging while Hoke bounced up and down on his toes. They looked like two boxers.

"Hoke, Newton, this is a grudge match for one thousand dollars winner take all, best two out of three sets. The first two can be won on tie-breakers, but if it should go to the third, we play Old Rules and you have to win by two games. Right?"

"That's what we agreed to, Lodi," Newton said, and you could have slid to Heaven on the oil in his voice.

"All right, then," I said. "Newton, since you have been challenged, you serve first. Hoke, where are you going to start off?" He nodded to where he had been warming up. "All right, then . . ." I was about to tell them to shake hands now and come out fighting, but they had turned away and were heading to their respective positions.

What shall I say of that match? Newton served and scored. Served and scored. Served and scored. Served and won the first game. They swapped courts.

Then it was for Hoke to serve. He did, and the ball smashed into the net. He served again, and it bounced off the top of the net to land in the service area. He served once more, pooping the ball over the net toward Newton who returned it with a forehand smash that ripped by Hoke just as he was on a bounce up and thus unable to give chase.

His other three serves met much the same fate. Newton whapped them all back so hard poor Hoke could hardly see them coming, and I wondered why, after he served the ball, he didn't move instead of obstinately bouncing straight up and down where he was. Newton returned every single serve clear across the court from Hoke, who didn't seem to catch on to what was clear even to a gravelly voiced little native son behind me. "Poppa," he asked the puff-eyed, nine-fingered, frighty-looking man directly behind me, "oughten that there fat one to do something else?"

And that was pretty much the story of the first set—except for the two games Newton lost or gave away by playing left-handed. I breathed a little sigh of relief: at that rate it couldn't take too long.

However, I hadn't counted on temper. After Newton won the third game of the second set and was starting around to wipe his face at the net before going to the other court, Hoke flung his racket against the fencing behind him and loosed a terrible flow of invective. I was startled, but Newton was stopped in his tracks, and the crowd on my side loved it. A small but hearty bit of laughter riffled through them to make its impact on Hoke, who by then had stalked to the fence to retrieve his Wilson T 4000 "Pro" Frame with Sensor Dome to Reduce Vibration from Contact. He stared hard at it as though to make certain it had withstood the throwing it presumably was made to withstand. Newton wiped his face and I noticed him looking across at Hoke who swigged mightily several times from a tennis-ball can filled with Crocodile Juice or some such business. It was a green, mostly sweet liquid that Hoke seemed to think would see him through life. I drank some once when I was getting him in shape, but it tasted like Kool-Aid to me.

He drank mightily, I say, and glared unadulterated hate back at Newton. They each finished their refreshments and ablutions and took up their positions once more. It was Hoke's turn to serve, his last serve having been broken, as they say in tennis circles, by Newton.

Hoke may some day in his life be out, but he will never be down. I think we'll have to bury him standing up. I not only had not counted on bad temper, I had not counted on Hoke's basic, well, sneakiness. He quick-served.

Instead of going through his usual folderol of a wind-up, he took his preliminary stance but flipped the ball quickly and popped it over the net. Newton stared at it as it bounced once, then twice, then even a third time before his brain responded to what his eyes so clearly saw.

"What was that?" Newton yelled.

"That was fifteen-love, Dummy," Hoke yelled back.

Newton straightened. Still in disbelief, he looked over at me. Then I realized he wanted a ruling. There hadn't been anything for me to do once the game got underway, and I had almost forgotten I was supposed to referee. But what did I know? Newton had been ready. Hoke had been ready. They had both been where they were supposed to be.

"Fifteen-love, Newton," I called back, and held my hands out to let him know there was nothing personal in it from me.

"Serve it up like that again, DB," Newton dared. "Serve it like that again." He looked ready for tigers.

Hoke was craftier than that, though, and what he did was to throw the ball up in the air. Then he gripped his weapon with both hands, and as the ball descended, he took aim on it like a batter would on a hugely arcing, slow Ephus pitch. The ball hung high in the air hardly rotating enough to have any kind of spin on it at all, floated so slowly you could count the puce hairs on its hide. Then at just the right moment, he slashed as viciously as ever any medieval knight slashed at the juncture of an enemy's neck and shoulder. It cleared the net by a fraction, hit just in the service area, and spun off the side of the court so hard and fast that even if Newton had been ready for it there was no way he could have gotten to it.

Hoke cackled, positively jumping up and down at the spectacle of Newton standing bug-eyed.

"That's thirty-love in case you were going to ask." He whickered and fairly danced into position for the next serve ...

... which Newton returned out of bounds, losing for the moment the cool which was his hallmark in the tennis world of Ickey Honey.

So that for the next serve, Hoke was in a position to win his very first game of set two. He readied himself as Newton gripped and regripped the handle of his nylon-stringed, high-tensile, steel Wilson T 2000. Around came Hoke for the serve. Smash! into the net ... *Pop!* off the top ... and while Newton eased up to blitz the *Poop* that had to follow, Hoke himself, after pooping, rushed the net with a scream and a whoop that caught Newton unaware just enough for his return not to have very much on it. Hoke caught it on the run and blasted it with a leaping two-handed Splat! that sent it careening not only off the court but over the restraining fence behind Newton as well.

"No!" screamed Newton Slock, looking now again to me for official confirmation of his protest. "No fair. Foul. You can't scream like that."

I hadn't read that you couldn't scream like that. As a matter of fact as an old Warpather I had thought the scream pretty good, reminiscent of the times Hoke, a terrifying-looking but otherwise ineffectual linebacker, would leap feet first across the line of scrimmage warcrying all the way. It often got him kicked out of the game, but by that time it would have worked its purposes of scaring the opposition and getting him kicked out so he wouldn't have to play any more that afternoon.

"No fair," Newton kept insisting. "You're not allowed to distract your opponent that-a-way. It isn't cricket." His normally dulcet tones had become peculiarly shrill.

All the while Hoke cackled to himself and strutted up and down the backline of the court. He wiped a trickle of Crocodile Juice from his chin.

"Come off it, Newton Shlock," he called. "You're still ahead three games to my puny one. Can't you stand that? Heh heh heh," he finished. "Heh heh."

That seemed to calm Newton down a bit as he took up his position. He looked ready to serve, but then turned and walked away a few steps talking to himself.

Come on, baby, we could all hear him mutter. *Let's put this joker down and get on back home.*

He apparently did himself some good, because he got back to the line and served one of the most bully fast serves I ever saw.

The crowd on both sides *oozed* at it, but Hoke stood there calm as pie.

"Out," he said very politely and very softly.

"What? What do you mean out? That serve was fair by six inches." Newton looked over to me.

I was in for it.

"I didn't see it," I said, hoping it was loud enough for them to hear without being so loud as to let everybody know I hadn't watched where it hit.

"Better play it over," Hoke mewed.

"Play it over, hell!" Newton bellowed. "It was in."

"Rule says," Hoke went on calm as a sleeping cat, "you got to play it over if it is contested and the judge can't make a call. Heh heh heh."

It was, and I couldn't. I shrugged to say I was sorry. Newton talked to himself again for a little, then went back to the line, but Hoke had gotten to him and he double-faulted. Love-fifteen.

Newton started putting himself into it now. He wiped the sweat from his brow, blinked twice, and served again. Hoke held his racket out and let the ball return itself. Newton either hadn't expected him to be able to return that hard a serve, or was starting to wear down mentally a little, because he never tried to make a play on it.

Love-thirty.

With the next serve, he heaved mightily once more and got off another blistering serve, but just as last time Hoke got the racket out to it and let the ball return itself. Newton managed to return that return, but Hoke fed him a high, deep lob that Newton had to run back for. The sun was high by then and the sweat was rolling fast off everybody, so Newton didn't get as much string on the ball as he should have. It got back over the net, but Hoke pounced on it and placed it out of reach.

Love-forty.

Newton's first serve was laid in with great strength, but it caught the net for a fault. The second serve was milder. Hoke got to it and lobbed it high and deep again. Newton ran back and smashed a return, but Hoke caught it at the net and made Newton run up fast to get it back over. Another deep lob, another pop over the net, another run by Newton, another deep lob, another hard run to the net where he smashed it past Hoke for the score.

Fifteen-forty, but Hoke had worked very little and Newton had worked a lot.

Even I had to admire Hoke at that point. He was playing what's called a very smart game, and I started to wonder if maybe he had a chance after all. I also started to wonder whether Newton didn't understand what was going on yet. He lost the next point and the game on exactly the same kind of *I'll-hit-it-while-you-run-after-it* play of the point before.

They swapped courts once again, pausing longer at their rest areas to drink deep and sponge off. It was hot. I heard cans getting popped in the stands behind me, and the deep, soft sounds of slurped foam came trailing on the sweet smell of hot beer.

Score, Set Two: three games to two, Mr. Slock.

The Natives had finally warmed up to the game as well as to the day. Though they were even more ignorant about it than I had been, they began to understand the basic points, though in truth the thing they liked best was the way the players urged themselves on.

Newton's favorite routine was to wheel around from the

net when he had made a particularly bad play and stalk away where he would set one hand on a hip and talk—actually to himself, though it looked like he was trying to reason with the fence. He would gesture and gesticulate, then shake his racket at it as if threatening to raise a lump on its mesh if it didn't start doing better.

But there were more violent moments, too. His standard form of mayhem was to stare across the net at Hoke after a goof, then swirl around and fling his racket at the fence. When he did that, a nicely large murmur of approval would well up from the stands on my side. Once, I heard someone whose voice came from very near where most of the beer popping came from holler out that he ought to have flang the racket at Hoke, heh-heh-heh. That brought even louder murmurs of approval from his friends, and I heard three cans pop nearly at once.

Hoke, on the other hand, was constantly in motion anyway, and his usual sign of disgust was to skim his racket across the court at the fence behind him. If that didn't do any good on the next point, he would take it in both hands and approach the post that held the net up, and there he would pop the strings on the top of the post as though not so much to see how really and truly well-built the Stratabow construction was (he had changed from his Wilson Sensor Dome to a Wilson Chris Evert), but more to let it understand that another bad miscue would bring it instant ruin. Beyond that, he would slam the flat of it against the top of the net, smash the edge of it into the fence behind him, or toss the whole thing up into the air as he walked away from whatever had disgusted him . . .

. . . Such that when Newton and Hoke both were going hot and heavy at themselves, it sounded less like a tennis match than the preliminary clash and rattle of muskets as advance scouts began feeling for enemy pickets to discover the whereabouts and strengths of an entrenched foe.

The heat was getting ferocious. Each serve took more time. Each return required more effort. The stops at the refreshment areas between court swappings lasted longer. The cans popped more often behind me, and the paper sacks were getting plopped down under the stands, empty now of their contents.

Once, even, play had to be stopped a minute as a fan—caught in the heat and believing as Newton had earlier on that the match couldn't last too long and having sucked more beer sooner than he might otherwise have, and having friendly nips from the soft sacks around—fell not only asleep, but down as well; fell from the top row of the bleachers to the ground beneath, much to the huge delight of his friends, whose thoroughgoing and hearty laughter disturbed Hoke right as he was about to serve. Though it bothered Hoke—who wasn't about to say anything to them about letting the players be the ones to scream and shout—it didn't seem to bother the fellow who had fallen. He grunted once when he hit, belched, and lay quietly the rest of the day, except for his snoring.

But as the play wore on, it became apparent that Hoke had put the hex sign on Newton, who just couldn't manage to get any sort of real lead again—Hoke had taken the second set seven-six. Newton was still winning his share of games, but he was taking longer and longer to do it, and it appeared to me that he hadn't planned on having to stay out in this August sunshine for as long as we all were. The number of deuce games and the number of deuces in those games was telling on him. How Hoke managed to stay on as long as he did, I don't know. Greed probably. And I suppose a certain amount of pride, too.

But it was not until Hoke tied the third set at six games that I really noticed how much slower on their feet they were. Newton was preparing for the first serve of the 13th game. It was one o'clock in the afternoon and they had been playing steadily since ten that morning. By now about four more people had dropped from the stands, each with a kind of soft thud and grunt. The ones who could stick it out with the beer, and with the air thick enough to chew, it seemed, grew more and more interested in the game, though their outbursts were reserved for the more spectacular plays.

Newton served right to Hoke who returned it—there had come to be a good bit of extended volleying by now rather than the attempts to dominate every point—and after a bit Hoke managed to put the ball out to where Newton had to make a little run for it. Earlier in the day it would have been nothing, but Newton never got to the ball. He had begun making chase and even had his racket extended, his arm and him leaning way out after it, but his legs hadn't been able to follow. It was like his body was outrunning his feet such that he simply fell down. I even wondered, I hate to admit it, how Hoke had gotten over there to weight Newton's shoes like that.

Then I glanced over at Hoke and noticed something about him, too. His fancy sneakers had long, ugly black streaks on them which at first I took for slits, but which I finally realized was tar. Then I looked at the court itself, and there I saw great ripples that hadn't been there at the start of the game. It was like looking at a relief map of Appalachia, great crinkles ridging up all over.

Then Hoke, reaching up high after charging the net, fell flat on his ass. His feet just purely slid out from under him. It was the court, I realized, even with the stands clapping and whistling happily behind me at Hoke's comic fall. They were playing on what was quickly becoming a lake of tar.

"Stop," I shouted, and jumped to my feet.

It was too sudden a move in the heat, I suppose, because the next thing I knew, Hoke was pouring that sticky Crocodile Juice all over me.

"You all right?" he asked.

"Yes, I think so."

He didn't even say *Good* or anything, but started right back out to the tar pit to resume the game.

"Wait," I shouted again. "Newton, Hoke, come over here."

"What for?" Newton panted.

"Because I'm the darned referee, Newton, Now get over here. Hoke, you too."

They approached and I said, "This can't go on. That tennis court of yours is melting, Hoke."

"What do you mean, 'That tennis court of yours'? What do you mean by that?"

"Hoke, you built the durned thing and it is melting. There is no proper way to finish this match today. Neither one of you can stand up." I tried to appeal to their softest spots. "Neither one of you can play up to your finest capabilities. It's all tied right now. Call it a draw and each of you keep your money, or finish it up tomorrow after the court has cooled."

"Tomorrow is Sunday, Lodi," Newton felt inclined to inform me.

"Sunday Schmundy," Hoke wrinkled up his nose at Newton. To me he said, "Lodi, durn it, you don't interrupt tennis matches. It ain't cricket, you know," and he laughed in a labored and wheezy kind of way.

"But if it rained we'd postpone it until there wasn't any more rain and until the court was dry, wouldn't we?"

"This ain't rain, Lodi. This here is nothing more than tennis weather."

Tennis weather? I thought.

"But Hoke . . . Newton . . ." I tried to plead for good sense, but the onlookers started stomping their feet, started shouting questions as to whether or not someone had won and weren't they going to get to see the rest of the thing.

Hoke, his Stratabow in one hand, opened his arms up toward the stands and said, "Lodi, you wouldn't want to disappoint them, would you?"

I looked back and saw the soft paper sacks getting softer and softer, and I saw fresh reserves of supplies being carried up from the local markets.

"All right," I said. "But it's dumb."

I sat back down, weary from trying to make fools act sensible. There I was sitting out in God only knew what kind of heat; there they were running around smacking puce and mint green and baby blue balls back and forth at each other for reasons that still remained obscure and suspicious to me; and across the way was a handful of soft gulls, anxious to believe people like Newton Slock, willing to be ashamed of little old hamlets like Ickey Honey that hadn't ever done them any harm by being there, delighted to know nothing of my town's past, perfectly programmed to accept that prior to Residential Communities there had been nothing but Chaos; while to my rear was a surly wad of retards and mean things waiting in a sad and desperate way for some blood to flow.

"Serve it up," I hollered. "Hell on it. Serve it up."

And as they resumed their stances, Poppa reached up from behind me and slapped my arm. I jumped.

"This thang gonna keep on a while?" he asked.

I nodded. "It looks it," I said.

"Then here," he said. "You look to need it," and he slipped a tall can of beer into my hand. I could have kissed him. Instead, I tilted my head back and drank that beer down in gulp after gulp after gulp. God, but it was good. I never took the rim from my lips until it was empty. Then I belched once and felt lots better.

The play went on without me, but I tried to follow what was happening just in case they were to make me decide an issue. The fact is, though, they had begun playing for real and they had too much to worry about just staying on the court without wasting a lot of energy being snippy with each other. In the meantime, I got madder and madder.

They could hardly move any more. Their shoes were clogged with tar; they slipped constantly; and the natty outfits they looked so prancy in earlier were beyond redemption. Talk about your Deep-Down Dirt, I'd like to see a washing machine get those duds clean. Ha! And there was another beer in my hand.

Soon I even noticed that their rackets were getting gummed up. And the balls would hardly bounce. And the more beer I drank, the angrier I got about it. But I did have to admit that it was funny. Once, Newton just plain could not lift a foot from the court. He was reaching and stretching, and—of course it could have been partly the beer by then—it seemed like slow motion as he fell the length of himself onto the court. The crowd appreciated that as did Hoke, who coughed and wheezed and managed to let out a little bleating laugh of his own.

But on the next play, Newton—not to be outdone or shown up without a fight—caught Hoke prancing slowly along the line of the net, delayed his swing by a fraction, and placed the volley with tremendous drive and accuracy right in Hoke's balls.

Down he went with a squawk like Daffy Duck winged in midflight. Oh how my Natives loved that. Poppa pounded me on the back.

"What happened?" he demanded, his face a terrible crimson.

"That air feeler he clipped him right in the balls, Poppa," his son answered, "and down he went. See there?"

Hoke was indeed holding himself near the afflicted area, but seemed to be all right, more or less.

"In the balls?" Poppa screamed. "In the balls?" His face cracked into something that must for him have approached a smile, but it was hard to say, because it gave way almost directly to a look of pain and loss.

"Goddamn," he said. "Goddamn. The only thing interesting to happen out there the whole day and I miss it. Goddam it, Boy, whyn't you tell me? Whyn't you *tell* me?" and I thought he was going to clip the boy across the mouth. Instead, he popped two more beers and gave me one.

"Durn," he muttered, by then too heartsore even to curse.

Hoke was back up on his feet ready to go. The games by then were eight and eight.

I think.

Yes, they must have been. Eight and eight with Newton about to serve yet once more. He took his time about it, even managing again to go back to his friend the fence and talk to it a while. Then it was back to the line.

I drank another can of beer. Entire.

It was just like the very first serve of the game. As a matter of fact, I was thinking it was the very first serve of the game, because Newton looked exactly as he had, except for the oil and tar he had dredged up from the macadam court, of course. But he wound up the same way, and I finally understood that he was out to win two games in a row so he could put all this madness behind us.

Good luck, Newton, I found myself saying as I chuckled into despair, knowing as I did that he would never be able to do it. This match, I had come to understand, was like the rock of Sisyphus: there was no end. No matter who got an advantage, it would be deuced the next time around. We were all damned. The world had come to an end the night before, only none of us understood it. For reasons unknown to us all, we were here for Eternity to watch Newton Slock and Hoke Warble battle each other in a tar pit with balls that bounced less and less, on feet that stuck more and more, under a pitiless sun that was to grow hotter and hotter with the passing of each millennium until our brains were seared and scorched beyond the redeeming power that any further harrowing could possibly bestow. Me and these careless nine-fingered folk and their children . . . and the beer would get foamier as the air got heavier . . .

Newton served.

. . . and we were all in it together for no reason under the sun except that we had planned our own destruction this way. We had all planned to be doing what we were doing, and the World was stopped right then and we were cursed and damned to keep it up until the very edge of Time itself . . .

Hoke got his racket out with just enough of a push behind it to get the ball back over the net.

. . . and if I had been doing what I was supposed to be doing when God placed his mighty finger on our little spinning ball and said, "Stop. It is enough," I would now be out in the pine groves listening to the cooling breezes soughing through my beloved trees. I would be noting with loving interest the progress of the borers and listening to their little *crunch-crunches* with both the sadness of the Tree Lover as well as the admiration and awe of a True Bug Man. Or I could have taken that trip back to Austria that I had wanted to take for so long, but for which there simply never had been the money or the time— or so I had kept telling myself . . .

Newton made a beautiful play on Hoke's return and drove it deep into the corner.

Instead, here I was with these people I did not love, though

I might have a grudging admiration for their ability to survive; instead, here I was having to watch that which I did not love, though again I had learned to have a modest admiration for it; instead, here I was exposed to all, having to judge that which I knew so little of . . .

But it was higher than he would have preferred, and with the increasing heaviness of the balls, it bounced stolidly up rather than skittishly off and out of reach.

Instead, I had not lived my life as we are admonished to do: as though each moment might be our last and that therefore each moment should be lived as the moment of greatest good, because if God wearied of watching us spin and spin and spin . . .

So Hoke got to make a play on it. He returned it. Newton had to make a run and answer with a high lob.

He could end it all at any time. Which it was more and more apparent He had already done. He was the Final Arbiter, the Last Word, the Judge . . .

But it went right to where Hoke was.

The Great Referee in the sky . . .

And he had it played perfectly.

The Great Referee can just say STOP! and it stops . . .

He timed it all, screwed his nerves and wind and Head PBI High Tensile Aluminum Framed racket all into a single piece of fury, brought his arm around in his most convincing swing of the afternoon, and smashed it into Newton's court. The ball was more a projectile hurtling with blind rage and savage speed, but Newton, knowing he had to take this point to keep himself going, was up to the moment; he was prepared; his arm was already drawn back to deliver a telling, highly controlled blow for superior competence, when the ball hit.

SLUUURCK!

The sound of it echoed, reverberated forward to Eternity and back into the fastnesses of Pre-history, and forward again to our own blink of Time. It was an answer to prayer. That's all I could think of at the time. An answer to prayer. And I remember wondering why God had deemed my charred soul worthy of salvaging for yet a little longer. The ball—charged though it was—went slurking directly into a thick, gooey tar bubble, tried to bounce up as is its nature, and though it managed to proceed some two inches on its destined course, remained, finally, where it was, like a fly foolishly buzzing into a spider's web, a captive like the rest of us; a thing caught forever in the wrong place at the wrong time.

Until—with the clarity of Vision we all hope Deity surely must have—I sprang to my feet, beer can clutched in each hand, arms spread in the benediction of salvation, and pronounced:

STOP! IT IS ENOUGH.

And with that, I collapsed giddily, face down, eyes wide, my lips spread in a sanctified smile, my brain purged forever of trivia, it now being heavy with the insight and inspiration of Deity; collapsed, I say, into the slick pool of Hoke Warble's rapidly melting tennis court.

My head almost started hurting all over again when I read the weekly paper and looked at that picture of Hoke Warble and Newton Slock grinning like jackanapes, shaking hands, holding out those thousand-dollar checks they were donating to the Ickey Honey Country Club and Recreation Center to have more tennis courts built so all those Residents and nine-fingered folk could come play tennis with each other and spend their hard-earned money in the Pro Shop on expensive rackets and sneakers and alligator shirts and warm-up togs and colored balls and . . .

I spread more goo across my flaking forehead to ease the sunburn which was still pretty uncomfortable, but I had been put to bed for heat stroke. That's what the doctor called it. I suppose he was right as far as he knew, but I'm not so sure that that's what really put me down. I think it was the knowledge that I had been taken in and that the entire Thousand-Dollar-Winner-Take-All-Grudge-Match was a put-up job from the start. To create some lively interest in the sport, is what the paper quoted Hoke as saying. And it was to become an annual thing, Mr. Warble had strongly hinted. It would attract visitors, he said. They would spend lotsa money, they did not quote him as saying. It would put us on the map, he did add. It would put us on the map.

It was enough to make a grown man sick.

My trouble, I'm sure, is that I try to be straightforward about things. So it seems to me that they could have gotten that interest by fixing up the court they already had and by getting the people who wanted to play to build a new one. But as I say, Hoke always was one to see things on a somewhat grander scale than the rest of us. He always needed a little drama in his life. As for me . . .

Well, I don't mind there being more tennis courts. And I don't mind there being a Club House. And I don't mind them taking the cover off the old swimming pool and fixing it up so it can be used again. That's all nice enough. I guess I don't mind things changing and growing, really. It's just that I like to see things grow where they will grow. Maybe I've been too favored by the natural flow of our small streams and the twists and turns of the gulleys and draws, the odd profile of a mountain face, or the startled explosion of a deer flushed from hiding when you weren't looking for it. I guess I like for streets to follow the natural bend of the land. I guess I still like towns that have kinks in them, kinks and little odd places that are there because there were some kinky and odd people around who put their marks on the place at one time and another. Kinks and odd corners: that's what lets people know they are in Ickey Honey—or anyplace else that is still somewhere. Kinks and odd corners on the maps of our hearts.

Balance His, Swing Yours

WALLACE STEGNER

The ping of tennis rackets was a warm, summer-afternoon sound in the air as Mr. Hart came up through the hedge. He stopped to survey the grounds, the red roof of the hotel, the fans of coco palms graceful beyond the white wall. Past the wall the coral rock broke off in ledges to the beach, and beyond the sand was the incredible peacock water of the Gulf.

February. It was hard to imagine, with that sun, the brown skins of the bathers between the palms, the ping of rackets. The whole place, to Mr. Hart's Colorado eyes, was fantastic—hibiscus and bougainvillea and night-blooming jasmine. He squirmed his shoulders against the itching warmth of his first sunburn, caught the previous afternoon, and ruminated on the hardly believable thought that to many people this summer-in-February paradise was a commonplace thing.

The sound of tennis led him past the shuffleboard courts and around a backstop cascading with scarlet bougainvillea. A girl was playing with the pro, and beyond the court, in lawn chairs, lay two of the three people Mr. Hart had so far met. His reaction was immediate. Good.

Good it was the two boys, not the impossible Englishman

who had descended on him at breakfast. He cut across the lawn toward them.

The young men in the chairs, one very blond, one dark and impressively profiled, did not stir. They lay in their swimming trunks, inert and sprawling, and when Mr. Hart asked, "Were you saving these other chairs?" they looked up indolently, two loafing demigods with mahogany hides. The blond one lifted his towel out of a chair, and Mr. Hart sat down with a sigh.

"What a place!" he said.

The blond one, Thomas, Mr. Hart remembered—turned his head. He seemed a pleasant sort of boy. "Like it?" he said.

Mr. Hart lifted his hands. "It's incredible. I had no idea—I've never been down before. Even the fishing boats coming in in the evening are a nice institution. Have you tried the fishing?"

"Once or twice," Thomas said. He slumped further down in his chair. Mr. Hart found a pack of cigarettes, stretched to pass them over Thomas' body. He got a shake of the head, no thanks, from the dark one, Tenney, but Thomas took one.

"I've been thinking I might hook up with a party," Mr. Hart said. "This water fascinates me. The water and these silly little mangrove islands. I've read about mangroves all my life—never saw one. Now I find they're not islands at all, not a spoonful of dirt in them, just clumps of ocean-going shrubs."

"Yeah," Thomas said. He lay with the cigarette between his lips, his eyes lidded like a lizard's against the sun. Tenney seemed to sleep.

"I guess I interrupted your siesta," Hart said. "I just can't get over this place. I'll keep quiet now."

"Not at all," Thomas said, but Mr. Hart leaned back and

watched the tennis. He had no desire to intrude on people. And it was good tennis to watch, he admitted. But Eastern tennis, the rhythmical and somehow mechanical tennis of people who learned the game as a social accomplishment. In an obscure way he felt superior to it. He had learned in a different school, municipal hard courts, worn balls. Still, he felt he could lick three out of four of these mechanical marvels.

His eye was caught by Tenney's feet, big naked feet, arched like the feet of a statued Mercury and brown as stained wood, the leather thongs of the sandals coming up between great and second toes. They struck him as arrogant feet. The boy had a lordly air, sure enough. There was something really admirable in the way he and his companion lolled. This was their birthright, and their arrogance was simply acceptance of something perfectly natural and right.

The blond youth turned, and Mr. Hart nodded toward the court. "The girl has nice shots."

"One of these tennis drunkards," Thomas said. "Lives tennis twenty-four hours a day."

"I like to see that," Mr. Hart said. "I like to see people simply dissolve themselves in the thing that interests them. I can remember when I was that way about tennis myself."

"Oh," Thomas said. "You're a tennis player."

Mr. Hart shrugged deprecatingly. "Used to be, in a way. Haven't done much with it since college, just a game now and then."

"What college?"

"I grew up in the West," Mr. Hart said. "Went to the local cow college."

Tenney leaned toward them. "I hate to interrupt," he said, "but look what's bearing down on us."

He jerked a thumb. The impossible little Englishman, in his pink polo shirt, was walking springily on the balls of his feet down the path from the cocktail garden. "Oh, my God," Hart said.

The two were both looking at him. "Has he got to you, too?" Tenney said. His look of distaste had dissolved into cynical amusement.

"For an hour at breakfast," Hart said. "Why can't people like that go to Miami, where they belong? Maybe we ought to run."

They smiled their relaxed, indolent smiles. "Lie and take it," Thomas said. "That's the least painful way."

Mr. Hart slid down in his chair and prepared his muscles for the relaxed indifference with which this interloper would have to be met. "But what a blowhard!" he said. "Did you know he was being bombarded from all sides to write a play for Cornell? My God."

He shut up abruptly. In a moment the British voice—vulgar British voice, Mr. Hart thought—was right above him. "Ah," it said. "Taking a little sun?"

"Hello," Thomas said, pleasantly enough. Tenney looked up and nodded. So did Mr. Hart. It was a cool reception, but it wasn't cool enough, Mr. Hart thought, for this rhinoceros to feel it.

"Topping day for it," the Englishman said. He sat down and took out his pipe, watching the tennis game while he filled and lighted. His fingers, holding the blown-out match, waved gently back and forth.

"She's not bad, you know," he said conversationally. "Pity she doesn't have a sounder backhand."

Mr. Hart regarded him coldly. "What's wrong with her backhand?" he said.

"Not enough follow-through," the Englishman said. "And she's hitting it too much on the rise."

Tenney said, grunting from his slumped chest. "She ought to be told."

The Englishman took his pipe from his mouth. "Eh?"

"You ought to put her right," said Mr. Hart.

All he got was a grin and wag of the head. "Not in front of these pros, you know. The beggars think they know it all."

Mr. Hart impatiently recrossed his neatly creased legs. "You sound as if you were an expert," he said, with just the suggestion of a slur. It was exactly the right tone, ambiguous without being insulting. Sooner or later anybody, confronted by that tone, would begin to wonder if he were wanted.

"Know a bit about it," the Englishman said. He waved his pipe at the court, talking too loud. "Watch her forehand, too. She's cocking her racket up too much at right angles with her wrist." His head moved back and forth, following a fast rally. "So's the pro," he cackled. "So's the pro, swelp me. Look at 'im!"

"The ball," said Mr. Hart, "seems to be going back and forth pretty fast."

"Ping-Pong," the Englishman said. "Anybody who hit it instead of slapping it that way would have put it away by now."

Tenney was lying back staring at the sky, where a man-o'-war hawk alternately soared and sped on dark, bent wings. Tenney was like a hawk himself, Mr. Hart thought. Dark and built for speed. The Mercury foot, and the arrogance to go with it. He was built to run down little webfooted gulls like this Englishman and take their fish away from them. But all he did was stare at the sky and wag one foot over the footrest. Thomas, ordinarily more talkative, now seemed to be asleep. Mr. Hart simmered. It had been very pleasant, very quiet, very friendly, till this terrier with the big yap butted in.

". . . thing I miss in America," the Englishman was saying. "Never can get up a good game. Any public-school boy in England plays a good game as a matter of course. Here nobody seems to."

The idea came gently to Mr. Hart's door, and he opened to it. It might boomerang, but he thought not. His mind went scornful. Pestered to write a play for Cornell. Like hell. Bothered to do articles for the *Britannica.* My Aunt Annica. Aldington wanting him to come in on an anthology. In a pig's physiology. British public school likewise. Tennis as well.

"It *is* hard to get a game, sometimes," he said. "If I wasn't afraid of getting out of my class I'd suggest we play."

"Yes," the Englishman said cordially. "Have to do that."

"How about this afternoon, now?"

Tenney started to whistle lightly. The whistle was encouraging to Mr. Hart. It said, Go ahead, pin his ears down.

"This weather might not last, even here," Hart said. "Little exercise'd do us good. That is, if you'd step down to my level."

"Oh, step down!" the Englishman said. "Not at all!"

"Let's have a set then. The court'll be empty in a minute."

The Englishman knocked out his pipe, looked back toward the empty cocktail garden, puckered his lips. He had a pulpy nose and prominent teeth. "I didn't bring a racket," he said. "Perhaps . . ."

"The pro'll have some."

The Englishman rose. "Very well," he said. "I'll go pop into my things." He went toward the hotel, walking springily, a preposterous, lumpy little blowhard, and Mr. Hart dropped a look of grim anticipation at the two lazy, amused youths.

"The International Matches," Tenney said. "Shall I cry 'Well struck, Cow College!' now and again?"

"Don't encourage me," said Mr. Hart. "I might start shooting for the little stinker's belt buckle."

The Englishman looked even more preposterous in shorts than he had in polo shirt and slacks. His muscles were knobbly; his bones stuck out like the elbows of characters in comic strips. Mr. Hart, leading the way onto the court, was aware of the young men watching from their somnolent chairs. It was as if he had made them a promise. Opening the can of balls he made another to himself. He was going to play every shot as if dollars depended on it.

"Here we go," he said cheerily, and wafted a warm-up ball across the net. From the very awkwardness of the Englishman's run he knew his plan was not going to boomerang. The goof looked as if he'd never been on a court before. This, he told himself happily, was murder.

It was a murder that he enjoyed thoroughly. For three quarters of an hour he ran the Englishman's tongue out, tricked him with soft chops that died in the clay, outran him with topped drives into the corners, aced him with flat services, left him going full steam in the wrong direction for an occasional Amer-

ican twist. He was playing carefully himself, not hitting anything too hard until he got a kill, and then plastering it with
everything he had. He blessed the high altitude and worn balls
of his youth which had made him learn to murder a high ball.
The Englishman's game, when there was any, gave him little
to hit except soft high bouncers, big as a basketball and begging to be swatted. As he went about his methodical mayhem
his amazement grew. The Englishman didn't have a thing. Then
why in the world would he have the consummate gall to talk
the way he had? Mr. Hart could not imagine; but he saw the
two watchers in their chairs, and his unspoken compact with
them kept him at the butchery. The Englishman got six points
the first set, and his face was a little strained as they changed
courts. You bloody upstart, Mr. Hart thought. This is where you
learn to be humble. He stepped up to the service line prepared
to skunk the Englishman—completely, never give him a point.

In the middle of the set the two young men rose and stretched
and picked up their towels. They lifted their hands and walked
off toward the bath-houses, and Mr. Hart, a little disappointed
at the loss of his audience, went on finishing the thing off. The
Englishman was feeling his shoulder between shots now. Obviously, thought Mr. Hart, he has pulled a muscle. Obviously.

At five-love the Englishman walked up to the net. "I say, do
you mind? I seem to have done something to my shoulder here.
Can't seem to take a decent swing."

Mr. Hart picked up the ball can and his sweater. Without really wanting to, he let the alibi establish itself. "No use to play
with a bad arm," he said. And looking at the grimace pretending to be pain on the little man's face, he said, almost kindly

and to his own astonishment, "it was spoiling your game. I could see you weren't up to scratch."

"Makes me damned mad," the Englishman said. "Here I've mucked up your whole afternoon. Couldn't hit a thing after the first game or two."

"Too bad," said Mr. Hart. And so, condoling one another, they went back to the hotel. It was funny. It was, Mr. Hart decided while he was dressing, so damned funny he ought to be rolling on the bed stuffing covers in his mouth. That he was not, he laid to the complete incorrigibility of that dreadful little man. People like that would never see themselves straight. No innuendo, no humiliation, would ever teach them anything. Hopelessly inadequate, they must constantly be butting into situations and places where they didn't belong. Mr. Hart shrugged. Let him live. The hell with him. If he couldn't be overlooked, he could be avoided.

He brushed off his white shoes, felt his tie, and looked in the mirror. Nose and forehead pretty red. For an instant of irritation he wished he wouldn't always burn and peel before he tanned. There was some system—tannic acid, was it?—but he always forgot till too late. The regulars around here, he was sure, never peeled.

In the dining room there were flowers bright against the stiff linen on every table, and the ladderlike shadow of a palm frond fell across the floor from the west windows. Mr. Hart answered the headwaiter's bow and stepped down into the cocktail lounge. There was no one there except two waiters, the bartender, and some stuffed fish. Outside, however, several tables were occupied. At one of them sat Thomas and Tenney, and as Mr. Hart started over he noticed that they still wore sandals and no socks. Their arrogant feet seemed at home and unembarrassed. He wondered if they wore socks to dinner, and it crossed his mind that he might be overdressing. White jacket might look like ostentation. He didn't want that.

"Well!" said Mr. Hart, and sat down. "What's a good drink here?"

Tenney shrugged. His amber, remote, hawklike eyes were away off down the garden, then briefly on Mr. Hart. "Rum Collins?"

Mr. Hart signaled a waiter. The three sat quietly while people came in twos and threes into the garden. The young men did not speak of the tennis match. Neither did Mr. Hart. And he did not remember, until a small party came pushing a blue wheelbarrow with a sailfish in it, that he had meant to go down and watch the boats come in.

There were a gray-haired man and a blonde older woman and a wind-blown, pretty girl in the party. They came through the garden in triumph, calling to people to witness. Everybody seemed to know them. Everyone got up and crowded around and admired. Thomas and Tenney went over with their glasses in their hands, and Mr. Hart rose, but did not want to push in. "Fifty-nine pounds," the girl said. "And I caught it. Little me." The tempo of the garden had picked up; the lazy afternoon was already accelerating into cocktail hour, dinner hour, the evening dance. Mr. Hart, standing at the edge of the crowd, thought what really pleasant fun it would be to spend a day that way. The fishing party seemed pleasant, agreeable people. And it would be fun to catch a thing like that sailfish. Lovely to see him break the peacock water.

"Come on," the girl said. "I'm buying the drinks on this one." She hooked arms with Tenney and Thomas, the gray-haired man picked up the handles of the wheelbarrow, and they went up the garden to a table under the hedge.

Mr. Hart stood a moment alone. Then he sat down. The chatter, the bright afternoon sounds, went over him, and he heard the fishing girl's brittle tinkle of laughter. The long light of evening lay over the palms and the flowering trees and the golf-green lawn. Waiters tipped the umbrellas sideways and lifted the steel butts from the holes and stacked the canvas against the hedge. Mr. Hart watched them; his eyes went beyond them to the party at the hedge table, Tenney and Thomas leaning forward, no languor about them now, their talk animated.

Beside his own table he saw his immaculate buck foot. It irritated him, somehow, and he put it out of sight. The bronze feet of Tenney and Thomas, he noticed, were in plain view as they tipped their chairs forward to talk to the fishermen. The dead fish's fin stuck up from the blue wheelbarrow like a black-violet lacquered fan. It was while he watched them that the cold finger touched Mr. Hart, and he knew what it was.

The garden was full of people now, brown-faced, casual. They were necessary, Mr. Hart thought, to complete the picture. The whole garden, tipped with light through the palms, was like a Seurat. And he sat alone, outside the picture. There were two rings of moisture on the enameled table, left by the

glasses of Tenney and Thomas. Very carefully Mr. Hart squee-
geed them off with his thumb and finger and wiped his hands
on his handkerchief. When he looked up he saw the Englishman, fantastically white and sluglike in this garden of brown
demigods, standing in the doorway of the lounge in white jacket
and ascot tie, looking around the tables.

For an instant Mr. Hart hesitated. He heard the brittle chatter and laughter from the other tables. His elbows felt the tug
of hands, heard the voices saying, "Come on, let's have a drink
on it," his bronze face felt the sun as he went with the others
across to a corner table....

His fingers went around the cold glass, raised it. With his
other hand he signaled the Englishman standing in the doorway.

The Tennis Court

PAUL THEROUX

Everyone hated Shimura; but no one really knew him: Shimura was Japanese. He was not a member of the Club. About every two weeks he would stop one night in Ayer Hitam on his way to Singapore. He spent the day in Singapore and stopped again on the way back. Using us—which was how Evans put it—he was avoiding two nights at an expensive hotel. I say he wasn't in our club; yet he had full use of the facilities, because he was a member of the Selangor Club in Kuala Lumpur and we had reciprocal privileges. Seeing his blue Toyota appear in the driveway, Evans always said, "Here comes the freeloader."

Squibb said, "I say, there's a nip in the air."

And Alec said, "Shoot him down."

I didn't join them in their bigoted litany. I liked Shimura. I was ashamed of myself for not actively defending him, but I was sure he didn't need my help.

That year there were hundreds of Japanese businessmen in Kuala Lumpur selling transistor radios to the Malays. It seemed a harmless enough activity, but the English resented them and saw them as poaching on what they considered an exclusively British preserve. Evans said, "I didn't fight the war so that those people could tell us how to run our club."

Shimura was a tennis player. On his fifth or sixth visit he had suggested, in a way his stuttering English had blunted into a tactless complaint, that the ball-boys moved around too much.

"They must stand quiet."

It was the only thing he had ever said, and it damned him. Typical Japanese attitude, people said, treating our ball-boys like prisoners of war. Tony Evans, chairman of the tennis committee, found it unforgivable. He said to Shimura, "There are courts in Singapore," but Shimura only laughed.

He seemed not to notice that he was hated. His composure was perfect. He was a small dark man, fairly young, with ropes of muscle knotted on his arms and legs, and his crouch on the court made him seem four-legged. He played a hard darting game with a towel wound around his neck like a scarf; he barked loudly when he hit the ball.

He always arrived late in the afternoon, and before dinner played several sets with anyone who happened to be around. Alec had played him, so had Eliot and Strang; he had won every match. Evans, the best player in the Club, refused to meet him on the tennis court. If there was no one to play, Shimura hit balls against the wooden backboard, barking at the hard ones, and he practiced with such determination you could hear his grunts as far as the reading room. He ate alone and went to bed early. He spoke to no one; he didn't drink. I sometimes used to think that if he had spent some time in the bar, like the other temporary members who passed through Ayer Hitam, Shimura would have no difficulty.

Alec said, "Not very clubbable."

"Ten to one he's fiddling his expenses," said Squibb.

Evans criticized his lob.

He could not have been hated more. His nationality, his size, his stinginess, his laugh, his choice of tennis partners (once he had played Eliot's sexually browsing wife)—everything told against him. He was aloof, one of the worst social crimes in Malaysia; he was identified as a parasite, and worst of all he seemed to hold everyone in contempt. Offenses were invented: he bullied the ball-boys, he parked his car the wrong way, he made noises when he ate.

It may be hard to be an American—I sometimes thought so when I remembered our beleaguered Peace Corps teachers—but I believe it was even harder to be a Japanese in that place. They had lost the war and gained the world; they were unreadable, impossible to know; more courtly than the Chinese, they used this courtliness to conceal. The Chinese were secretive bumblers and their silences could be hysterical; the Japanese gave nothing away; they never betrayed their frenzy. This contempt they were supposed to have: it wasn't contempt, it was a total absence of trust in anyone who was not Japanese. And what was perhaps more to the point, they were the opposite to the English in every way I could name.

The war did not destroy the English—it fixed them in fatal attitudes. The Japanese were destroyed and out of that destruction came different men; only the loyalties were old—the rest was new. Shimura, who could not have been much more than thirty, was one of these new men, a postwar instrument, the perfectly calibrated Japanese. In spite of what everyone said, Shimura was an excellent tennis player.

So was Evans, and it was he who organized the club game: How to get rid of Shimura?

Squibb had a sentimental tolerance for Malays and a grudging respect for the Chinese, but like the rest of the club members he had an absolute loathing for the Japanese. When Alec said, "I suppose we could always debag him," Squibb replied fiercely, "I'd like to stick a kukri in his guts."

"We could get him for an infraction," said Strang.

"That's the trouble with the obnoxious little sod," said Squibb. "He doesn't break the rules. We're lumbered with him for life."

The hatred was old. The word "Changi" was associated with Shimura. Changi was the jail in Singapore where the British were imprisoned during the war, after the fall of the city, and Shimura was held personally responsible for what had gone on there: the water torture, the rotan floggings, the bamboo rack, the starvation and casual violence the Japanese inflicted on people they despised because they had surrendered.

"I know what we ought to do," said Alec. "He wants his tennis. We won't give him his tennis. If we kept him off the courts we'd never see his face here again."

"That's a rather low trick," said Evans.

"Have you got a better one?" said Squibb.

"Yes," said Evans. "Play him."

"I wouldn't play him for anything," said Squibb.

"He'd beat you in any case," said Alec.

Squibb said, "But he wouldn't beat Tony."

"Not me—I'm not playing him. I suggest we get someone else to beat him," said Evans. "These Japs can't stand humiliation. If he was really beaten badly we'd be well rid of him."

I said, "This is despicable. You don't know Shimura—you have no reason to dislike that man. I want no part of this."

"Then bugger off!" shouted Squibb, turning his red face on me. "We don't need a bloody Yank to tell us—"

"Calm yourself," said Alec. "There's ladies in the bar."

"Listen," I said to Squibb, "I'm a member of this Club. I'm staying right here."

"What about Shimura?" said Alec.

"It's just as I say, if he was beaten badly he'd be humiliated," said Evans.

Squibb was looking at me as he said, "There are some little fuckers you can't humiliate."

But Evans was smiling.

The following week Shimura showed up late one afternoon, full of beans. He changed, had tea alone, and then appeared on the court with the towel around his neck and holding his racket like a sword. He chopped the air with it and looked around for a partner.

The court was still except for Shimura's busy shadow, and at the far end two ball-boys crouched with their sarongs folded between their knees. Shimura hit a few practice shots on the backboard.

We watched him from the rear verandah, sitting well back from the railing: Evans, Strang, Alec, Squibb, and myself. Shimura glanced up and bounced the racket against his palm. A ball-boy stood and yawned and drew out a battered racket. He walked toward Shimura, and though Shimura could not possibly have heard it there were four grunts of approval from the verandah.

Raziah, the ball-boy, was slender; his flapping blue sports shirt and faded wax-print sarong made him look careless and almost comic. He was taller than Shimura and, as Shimura turned and walked to the net to meet him, the contrast was marked—the loose-limbed gait of the Malay in his rubber flip-flops, the compact movements of the Japanese who made his prowl forward into a swift bow of salutation.

Raziah said, "You can play me."

Shimura hesitated and before he replied he looked around in disappointment and resignation, as if he suspected he might be accused of something shameful. Then he said, "Okay, let's go."

"Now watch him run," said Evans, raising his glass of beer.

Raziah went to the baseline and dropped his sarong. He was wearing a pair of tennis shorts. He kicked off his flip-flops and put on white sneakers—new ones that looked large and dazzling in the sunlight. Raziah laughed out loud; he knew he had been transformed.

Squibb said, "Tony, you're a bloody genius."

Raziah won the toss and served. Raziah was seventeen; for seven of those years he had been a ball-boy, and be had learned the game by watching members play. Later, with a cast-off racket, he began playing in the early morning, before anyone was up. Evans had seen him in one of these six o'clock matches and, impressed by Raziah's speed and backhand, taught him to serve and showed him the fine points of the game. He inspired in him the psychic alertness and confidence that makes tennis champions. Evans, unmarried, had used his bachelor's idleness as a charitable pledge and gave this energy and optimism to Raziah, who became his pet and student and finally his partner. And Evans promised that he would, one of these years, put Raziah up for membership if he proved himself; he had so far withheld club membership from the Malay, although the boy had beaten him a number of times.

Raziah played a deceptively awkward game; the length of his arms made him appear to swing wildly; he was fast, but he often stumbled trying to stop. After the first set it was clear that everyone had underestimated Shimura. Raziah smashed serves at him, Shimura returned them forcefully, without apparent effort, and Shimura won the first two sets six-love. Changing ends, Raziah shrugged at the verandah as if to say, "I'm doing the best I can."

Evans said, "Raziah's a slow starter. He needs to win a few games to get his confidence up."

But he lost the first three games of the third set. Then Shimura, eager to finish him off, rushed the net and saw two of Raziah's drop shots land out of reach. When Raziah won that game, and the next—breaking Shimura's serve—there was a triumphant howl from the verandah. Raziah waved, and Shimura, who had been smiling, turned to see four men at the rail, the Chinese waiters on the steps, and crouching just under the verandah, two Tamil gardeners—everyone gazing with the intensity of jurors.

Shimura must have guessed that something was up. He reacted by playing angrily, slicing vicious shots at Raziah, or else lifting slow balls just over the net to drop hardly without a bounce at Raziah's feet. The pretense of the casual match was abandoned; the kitchen staff gathered along the sidelines and others—mostly Malay—stood at the hedge, cheering. There was laughter when Shimura slipped, applause when the towel fell from his neck.

What a good story a victory would have made! But nothing in Ayer Hitam was ever so neat. It would have been perfect revenge, a kind of romantic battle—the lanky local boy with his old racket, making a stand against the intruder; the drama of vindicating not only his own reputation as a potentially great tennis-player, but indeed the dignity of the entire club. The match had its charms: Raziah had a way of chewing and swallowing and working his Adam's apple at Shimura when the Japanese lost a point; Raziah talked as he played, a muttering narration that was meant to unnerve his opponent; and he took his time serving, shrugging his shoulders and bouncing the ball. But it was a very short contest, for as Evans and the others watched with hopeful and judging solemnity, Raziah lost.

The astonishing thing was that none of the club staff, and none of Raziah's friends, seemed to realize that he had lost. They were still laughing and cheering and congratulating themselves long after Shimura had aced his last serve past Raziah's knees; and not for the longest time did the festive mood change.

Evans jumped to the court. Shimura was clamping his press to his racket, mopping his face. Seeing Evans he started to walk away.

"I'd like a word with you," said Evans.

Shimura looked downcast; sweat and effort had plastered his hair close to his head, and his fatigue was curiously like sadness, as if he had been beaten. He had missed the hatred before, hadn't noticed us; but the laughter, the sudden crowd, the charade of the challenge match had showed him how much he was hated and how much trouble we had gone to in order to prove it. He said, "So."

Evans was purple. "You come to the Club quite a bit, I see."

"Yes."

"I think you ought to be acquainted with the rules."

"I have not broken any rules."

Evans said curtly, "You didn't sign in your guest."

Shimura bowed and walked to the clubhouse. Evans glared at Raziah; Raziah shook his head, then went for his sarong, and putting it on he became again a Malay of the town, one of numerous idlers who'd never be members of the Ayer Hitam Club.

The following day Shimura left. We never saw him again. For a month Evans claimed it as a personal victory. But that was short-lived, for the next news was of Raziah's defection. Shimura had invited him to Kuala Lumpur and entered him in the Federation Championship, and the jersey Raziah wore when he won a respectable third prize had the name of Shimura's company on it, an electronics firm. And there was to be more. Shimura put him up for membership in the Selangor Club, and so we knew that it was only a matter of time before Raziah returned to Ayer Hitam to claim reciprocal privileges as a guest member. And even those who hated Shimura and criticized his lob were forced to admire the cleverness of his Oriental revenge.

The Phantom Drive

WILLIAM T. TILDEN

The departed shade of the Old Champion idly strummed with one hand on the golden strings of his celestial harp and arranged the folds of his celestial robes around him with the other.

It was nearly twenty years, as time is reckoned on earth, since he had left that sphere of strife and sorrow to join the heavenly chorus. Throughout all that time something seemed to be still calling from the world below. Heaven was not quite heaven to him. True, he had never succeeded in reasoning out the void in his existence. He only knew that on earth was something which he should never have left behind and which now day by day grew more insistent in his desires.

The harp was mute now as the shade of the Old Champion strove to recall the world and its details, while he sat, his hands folded in his lap. Out in space in the Celestial City or whatever it was, some lively shade newly arrived from earth, hurled a spectre clod of cloud toward him. "Look out," the spirit voice rang out distinctly. The Old Champion ducked and lifted the harp in protection.

"Twang," the cloud impinged against the golden strings. The sound stirred memories in the earthly consciousness of the departed spirit of the Old Champion.... Some time, some where on earth he had heard a sound like that and now it soothed the longing in his soul. What had it been and from whence had it come? Strings, but not golden, no, yellowish and inside a piece of wood.

Suddenly the shade of the Old Champion rose hastily from the golden chair, dropping the protesting harp at his feet. He remembered now—what was it called—oh yes, racquet; a tennis racquet, his old dearly loved tennis racquet, why had he not brought it with him twenty years before? Oh yes, he knew, he had given it away, to that delightful American whom he defeated only after the most bitter match of his whole life, given it as a memento of that match, and now his beloved racquet might be lost, gone forever. No, he would find it, he would go seek it.

He started off post haste for the Heavenly Office only to remember that but a year before he had applied for leave to visit the earth and had been informed that it would be two centuries before his turn would come. No, he could not get permission to go.

He turned the matter over carefully in his mind. Two centuries from now the racquet might be lost or destroyed beyond recall. Only that day the shade of King Tut had informed him that many treasures were lost before his grave had been discovered and that their loss weighed heavily on him. No, it was now or never for the Old Champion. Very well, he would take a chance. He would be A.W. O. L. from Heaven.

A short, stocky and very much flustered boy of eighteen stood at the referee's desk on the club-house porch at Westside

Club, Forest Hills, Long Island. His light brown hair waved in an unruly manner over his clear gray eyes while at the moment, a puzzled frown wrinkled not only his forehead but also the short nose below it. He addressed the impressive-looking gentleman seated at the table on which was spread out the big draw sheet of the tournament.

It was the opening day of the Lawn Tennis Championship of the United States, the presiding gentleman at the table was none other than Mr. Hyrock, former President of the Tennis Association and one of its foremost figures.

"Name?"

"Yes, sir; I'm Bobby Whitlock." The boy finally found his voice.

"Oh, you're Whitlock. Glad you're here. You play Richard Thomas on the Championship Court at three o'clock. You'll find your locker assigned upstairs. Thomas is here. Dress at once, please."

Mr. Hyrock dismissed the boy with a nod and turned back to his table.

Bobby Whitlock climbed the stairs to the locker-room in a daze.

He had to play Dick Thomas. This was Bobby's first tournament, while Dick Thomas had been a prominent figure in American tennis for twenty years. Thomas had been very young when he gained fame, a boy wonder when at sixteen he had carried the famous Old Champion, A. W. Smith, to that memorable five-set battle at Wimbledon just before the latter's lamentable death.

Thomas at thirty-six was still one of the greatest players in America, second only to Billy Jolson himself. Bobby could not believe he was really to play Thomas. There must be some mistake. Almost in a dream he located his locker and automatically began to undress. The clean-cut athletic man at the end of his corridor of lockers turned to watch him as the youngster drew out his only racquet from his tennis bag.

"Playing in the tournament?" The man spoke in a friendly quiet voice that stilled Bobby's nerves.

"Yes, at least I'm trying to." The boy's fingers were undoing the clasps on the racquet cover. "I'm not worrying much. I'll get licked first round."

"Oh, you'll do better than that," the man laughed, as he drew on his tennis shirt, his back to the boy. "Who do you play?"

"Nobody—I guess."

The man turned sharply at the note of the suffering boy's voice. The youngster stood staring at the racquet in his hand, three strings across the center dangling hopelessly and helplessly. The boy turned his head. "It's my only one."

"Never mind that racquet. We'll fix you up. Who did you draw?"

"Dick Thomas!"

"That's great. What's your name?"

"Whitlock, Bobby Whitlock."

"All right, Bobby, try one of my racquets. I'm Thomas!"

The boy flushed suddenly and drew back. "Oh, I couldn't, Mr. Thomas."

"Why not? Don't be foolish, try this one and see if it suits."

Thomas tossed over a Wright and Ditson which was the model he had used for years.

"Thank you." Bobby pitched it up and swung it gingerly. It felt a club in his hand, the handle many sizes too big. It seemed to weigh a ton.

Thomas anxiously watched the boy. "Too heavy. Sorry—mine are all alike, I'm afraid."

"That's quite all right, Mr. Thomas, I'll use my own anyway."

"You can't Bobby, it's impossible. Here, let me feel it."

Bobby tossed the bat to Thomas. Dick looked at it in momentary amusement. How old-fashioned it seemed in these days. It was an old Pim, cherished doubtless by Bobby's father for many years before it descended to Bobby. Where had he seen a racquet like that recently, Dick asked himself. Somewhere. He turned to the bell. The locker boy responded to the summons.

"Tell George the professional to send me my old racquet which he just strung up and has on exhibition in his office."

"Your own Wright and Ditson, Mr. Thomas?"

"No, the old English racquet; George will know."

The boy hurried off and Dick turned to Bobby.

"I have a racquet for you. It was given to me by the famous Old Champion, Smith, after he beat me at Wimbledon in 1903. Queer thing. It was my first big match, just as this is yours, and as it happened it was his last, poor old fellow. He died suddenly the following week. I've treasured the racquet, the frame is still good as new. Last week this club wanted me to allow the racquet to be placed on exhibition during the tournament so I had George string it up. I'm going to let you use it."

"Thanks a lot, Mr. Thomas, but I'd better not. Something might happen to it."

"I'll take a chance. Here it is, try it."

Bobby grasped the bat eagerly. It was almost a duplicate of his own.

"Gee, it's wonderful."

"Anyway it's a Pim, like yours and almost the same balance and weight. Come on, it's time to start," and grabbing his racquet in one hand and Bobby by the other, Dick Thomas hurried for the stairs.

The departed shade of the Old Champion was again on earth. He had slipped through the Golden Gate unobserved while St. Peter was assisting in the victims of a volcano eruption in the South Seas. His departure was not only unobserved but actually opportune, for his discarded harp found immediate use among the new arrivals.

The Old Champion was not completely happy. He enjoyed his invisibility on earth and made the most of it by indulging a spirit of mischief that had long been part of his nature, but full joy was not his. He could not recall the name of the young American to whom he had entrusted his beloved racquet. His twenty years' sojourn in Heaven, where music was the only language, had seriously interfered with his ability to read or to understand spoken words. Gradually these things came back from the hidden recesses of his memory and he finally succeeded in recalling enough to enjoy the papers over people's shoulders.

It was during a short stop in Boston that he finally recalled his friend's name. He was engrossed in the sporting news of a young lady's paper which was held enticingly in front of her in the lobby of the Copley Plaza while she flirted skillfully around the corner of it with a gentleman, seated near-by, when suddenly a headline caught the Old Champion's attention.

"AMERICAN TENNIS CHAMPIONSHIP STARTS TODAY."

"RICHARD THOMAS ACCORDED HONOR OF OPENING CLASSIC AGAINST YOUNG WHITLOCK."

Richard Thomas! That was the name he sought. In his excitement the Old Champion reached out and seized the paper.

The girl screamed and leaped to her feet. The gentleman dashed to her aid.

"What's the matter?"

The girl laughed self-consciously. "Nothing. Nothing at all. Only my paper shook suddenly and I—well, I just screamed. I couldn't help it."

The man smiled reassuringly. "Sit down, here with me. It's all right."

The Old Champion hovered in space over the settee. Where was Thomas playing? Oh, yes, there it was, Forest Hills, Long Island. Silently he floated out into space for New York.

The great stands were well filled for the opening match of the Championship when Dick Thomas and Bobby Whitlock entered the Championship enclosure. The famous veteran was tremendously popular and his marvelous comeback during the present season had aroused popular sentiment to fever heat.

Bobby Whitlock felt somewhat like the sacrificial lamb as

he heard the yell of welcome to his famous opponent rise from the multitude in the stands.

Into this colorful scene floated the departed shade of the Old Champion. This earthly existence seemed very real now and he yearned for the touch of the turf under his feet and the sound of the ball on his racquet and the feel of its impact on the strings.

The two players were warming up, rallying in preparation for the match. He hovered over the head of the boy, watching Thomas across the net, as he had done so many years before in his last match on earth.

It was the same graceful, dashing Dick, not much older in appearance. If only he, the Old Champion, were there in Bobby Whitlock's place! Suddenly the racquet in the boy's hand drew his attention. Could it be? Yes, there on the handle was the old scratch from a spike which he himself had made once when he had dropped the racquet and carelessly kicked it. It was his beloved old bat before his eyes. He must feel it once more in his hands. No! It was too late, already the umpire was calling play. Well, he would take one chance.

Invisibly he floated down and melted around the boy's body, his ghostly hand gripping the handle alongside Bobby's. Up flashed the racquet; a lightning service totally unlike anything Bobby had ever hit, sped through Thomas's court—

"15-love."

Bobby himself, to say nothing of Thomas and the expectant gallery, seemed stunned. Something unusual was about to take place.

The departed shade of the Old Champion was in the mood of a schoolboy playing "hookey," out for a good time. Never in all his years on earth had the Old Champion felt more like playing tennis. Never had he played better. He swept Bobby's willing, tireless young body around the court, making marvelous shots from all directions and places. Furiously Dick Thomas fought to stop the mad, capricious attack. The tremendous booming drive that raked his court held the veteran anchored to the base-line.

The Old Champion had been a confirmed base-line player. His marvelous driving had earned for him the nickname of the "Driving King" and the "Driving Demon." Back into his old style the departed shade automatically fell, once the racquet was between his fingers.

The gallery sat and marveled. Even the critics could not understand Bobby's game. There was one grizzled pen-wielder who sat spellbound among the press group. "Look," he said over and over again. "Watch! It is the reincarnation of Old Man Smith!"

"Gosh, what a wallop!" announced one youngster audibly to his father, as that tremendous forehand crashed its way past Thomas.

"That's nothing, Son. Wait till you see Ruth smash a baseball. This guy ain't so hot," and father chewed viciously on the end of an unlighted cigar.

Everywhere among the players the question was asked, where had Bobby learned the old style game? How well the youngster played it and how certain his racquet technique.

Billy Jolson finally arose from his seat in the committee box just as Bobby scored a sizzling placement to win the second set.

"It is wonderful," he said. "I have only once seen a game like it and that was old J. C. Parke, the Englishman. They say A. W. Smith was even better than Parke from the back court. How's the kid get that way?"

In the committee box sat three former Davis Cup men, stars of nearly twenty-five years before.

"I tell you that boy's game is a facsimile of old Al Smith's. I played him at Wimbledon back in '98 and if ever I saw a game reproduced it's out before you now."

"Maybe his soul is back in the boy's body," another cut in.

The Davis Cup veteran turned away in disgust. "Laugh all you want, but if I didn't know better I'd say Old Smith was out there today. It's marvelous!"

The match was short and sweet. Bobby Whitlock was announced winner, 6-4, 6-3, 7-5, while the multitude which had assembled to watch his annihilation stayed to cheer the new hero.

Bobby was the sensation of the moment. The press sang his praises long and loud. The departed shade of the Old Champion read all the stories over the shoulders of various unsuspecting men in the lobby of the Vanderbilt Hotel and chuckled in silent celestial glee. One story, that of the veteran reporter, a man of thirty years' experience in tennis, amused him particularly.

"Not since the days of the famous English star, A. W. Smith, has such a terrific forehand drive been seen on the courts. The style of young Whitlock is strangely reminiscent of the great Englishman. It almost seemed as if Smith's hand might have been directing the racquet. The believers in reincarnation may well claim Whitlock as proof of the return of Champion Smith.

"A curious angle to the case is the fact that Whitlock claims that his whole game yesterday was different from any he ever played before. His future performances will be closely watched by the Davis Cup Committee, as he seems destined for the heights of tennis fame."

The Old Champion hugged his celestial body in an ecstasy of joy. There was still one man on earth who remembered him at his best and rejoiced to see his game again. He decided to stay on and win for the lad if he could, and he believed it was possible.

The succeeding days certainly seemed to justify his faith. Bobby marched on in state to the semi-finals, where he, or rather the Old Champion, put a decisive and artistic finish to young Richard Vincey with so perfect a display of driving that the press again proclaimed the return of the Driving King.

Meanwhile Bobby, fondly as he clung to the Old Champion's racquet, had his own old one restrung in case of accident.

The day of the finals dawned bright and warm. The strings of cars poured out to Forest Hills early in the day. Long lines of eager fans formed at the gates by ten o'clock. By two o'clock every available inch of room was packed with an eager public, ready for the big tennis battle of all time, for Billy Jolson, the great defending champion from California, was to meet Bobby Whitlock, the Driving Demon, for the American title.

Around the court in the linesmen positions sat no less than

five former American champions, while Eddie Congdon, the doyen of umpires, graced the chair. Mr. Hyrock was net umpire, while even the ball-boys were of the chosen few.

Bobby stepped into the enclosure to be met by a yell of welcome that almost deafened him. Over his head the Old Champion grinned a celestial grin and dropped into position to play.

Billy Jolson, alert, wiry, nervous, eager, strode from the clubhouse and greeted Bobby cordially. The two men faced the battery of photographers, self-conscious and anxious to start.

"What will you have?" Jolson tossed his racquet in the air.

"Rough."

"It's smooth. I'll serve," Jolson cried.

"I'll start here."

The warm-up was short and snappy. Jolson seemed in unusually fine form, but Bobby had his customary speed and swapped drive for drive.

"Linesmen ready! Players ready! Play!" cried Congdon from the chair as Jolson stepped up to the line to serve.

The match was on.

The Old Champion quickly found he was up against a stiffer opponent than any he had ever met when he was playing in the flesh.

Modern tennis was a step beyond anything he had ever known, at least tennis as Billy Jolson played it. In the old days the Old Champion used to stand back and swap shots with his opponent until at last he found an opening through which to punch his terrific drive. In the old days his opponent rarely came in to the net for a kill or forced him seriously.

Jolson defied all the rules the Old Champion knew of how

the game should be played. In the first place there was no weakness to Jolson's game and, what was worse, in the second he never left openings for the other to hit through. One could never tell what Jolson would do. The old game of one great shot was done. The defending champion chopped, lobbed, cut and rushed the net in such a bewildering variety of tactics that the Old Champion felt all at sea.

Even his tremendous drive, played with all the power of Bobby's splendid young body, was unable to cope with Jolson's marvelous game. For a while he hung even. The first six games were divided to three all but only by the most tremendous efforts on the part of the celestial guide. Finally Jolson drove furiously to Bobby's forehand and came in. It gave the Old Champion his favorite opening down the sideline for his fast-passing drive.

Smash! Twang! The ball shot by Jolson so fast he hardly saw it. For a moment it shook even his iron nerve. His attack faltered slightly and the Old Champion jumped at his opening so ably that Bobby won the set, 6-4.

Jolson was annoyed. It was so ridiculous for an unheard-of youngster to spring from nowhere and walk away like this with the American Championship. Doggedly, silently, grimly, he set out to wear down the boy he faced.

Every point found Bobby chasing the ball from corner to corner as Jolson relentlessly pushed home his attack. The Old Champion was tired, disgusted and so hot that he began to wonder if he really had not made a mistake and missed the earth in his descent and gone all the way down. He could not find a chance to use his tremendous drive, for Bobby's legs never carried Bobby's body to the place where the Old Champion was anything more than an also-ran. Panting, puffing, protesting physically, Bobby dropped the second set, 6-3, and the third, 6-4.

The ten-minute rest gave him a meagre chance to recover his lost breath and the Old Champion a new lease on his grip of the racquet. The final struggle would be bitter.

"One all."

"Two all."

"Three all."

"Four all."

The games mounted with monotonous regularity. Both players held service against the most violent assaults of their opponent. It was a battering, all-powerful, awe-inspiring brand of tennis. The two greatest forehands in the world locked in a death grip, neither yielding an inch.

Jolson was cleverly offering up soft short shots at unexpected moments that disconcerted Bobby and nearly caused the Old Champion to pass away, if he had not already done that some years before. The gallery was tense, strung to the height of nervous excitement. All present realized that if Bobby pulled even by winning the set, his youth and daring might avail against Jolson.

The defending champion realized his position more acutely than anyone else. He knew it was now or never. Throughout the eight games which were divided, Jolson fought a growing weakness, by a dogged determination such as only he possessed.

In the ninth game, Bobby reached 30-40 on Jolson's delivery. Two wonderful drives, and a net by Jolson, had accounted for his points. It was now or never.

Jolson drove down the center line, figuring that an unexpected delivery to strength instead of the expected offering to weakness might catch Bobby napping. What a chance! The Old Champion saw his favorite opening, deep in Jolson's backhand corner, there awaiting his shot. Violently he pulled back Bobby's arm and viciously he smote the ball with that marvelous drive that had written tennis history twenty years before.

Crash! Crack! A splintering of wood and the ball fell short and soft in the net. Bobby stood staring at the broken frame in his hand. Then with a muttered cry he flung it under the umpire's chair and picked up his own old bat.

"Deuce," cried the umpire.

"I'm sorry." Jolson came in to the net. "Want to hit a few with that racquet?"

"No, that's all right. Go on."

The Old Champion was hovering over his beloved racquet. It was gone beyond repair. Never again could it respond to his wishes. If only he had never left Heaven for this!

The Old Champion floated back to the boy's side. His ghostly hand fell in position on the boy's racquet. Somehow it felt all wrong. He knew it was almost the same as his old one but it felt absolutely out of tune. Jolson served and he and Bobby swung.

The ball flashed far out over the base-line. The Old Champion almost wept as he flapped in Bobby's wake as the boy hopelessly chased Jolson's pitiless drives. He realized something which up to then he had not known. Material things were useless to him. Sentiment and love alone carried in the world of which he was now a part. It had been his deep affection for his old racquet which made it possible for him to play so well. That particular bit of gut and wood gone, he was helpless.

The press next day commented on the complete collapse of Whitlock's game after he broke his racquet. The final score of 4-6, 6-3, 6-4, 6-4, hardly told the whole story of the debacle.

Dick Thomas hurried up to Bobby before he left the court, after shaking hands with Jolson.

"Well played, Bobby!"

"Thank you, Mr. Thomas. I'm terribly sorry about the racquet. It was yours I broke."

"That's all right, Bobby, don't worry about it. I'm going to ask you to accept it from me as a souvenir of this tournament."

"Thank you, Mr. Thomas. I never played like this before. I may never again, but somehow I feel as if someone has taught me something I didn't know before. I feel I have learned that big drive so I can always make it. For a while it didn't seem as if it belonged to me, but now it does."

"That's fine, Bobby. Where's the racquet?"

"Under the umpire's chair."

"No it isn't."

"Why it must be. I threw it there!"

Bobby hurried over, pulling on his sweater as he came.

"It isn't though, Bobby."

The racquet had disappeared.

The wearied shade of the Old Champion wandered anxiously along the Golden Gate of Heaven. It was locked. He saw no chance of getting in and he needed rest. Even strumming on a harp would have appealed to him as undue exercise at the moment. Suddenly a hand fell on his shoulder. He turned to find the Guardian of the Gate, keys in hand, beside him.

"Where have you been?" chanted the Guardian.

The Old Champion spoke curtly.

"A. W. O. L."

"Splendid, so have I! What's that in your hand?"

The Old Champion gazed down at the twisted piece of wood and strings he clutched unconsciously in his right hand. Then, with a start, remembrance of his afternoon returned to him. He started back from the Guardian of the Gate.

"A tennis racquet, my old one I used on earth."

"Ah, tennis! Fine! You can teach me to play."

"No," cried the Old Champion fiercely. "No. On earth tennis may be Heaven, but if this modern game they call tennis gets into Heaven it may turn it into Hades. Let me in."

Wonderingly the Guardian of the Gate unlocked the golden lock with the golden key and the two shades A. W. O. L. from Heaven entered, one to resume his watch at the Gate, the other to search for the nearest harp.

The racquet lay unheeded by the Gate of Heaven.

Matilda's England
(I. The Tennis Court)

WILLIAM TREVOR

Old Mrs. Ashburton used to drive about the lanes in a governess cart drawn by a donkey she called Trot. We often met her as we cycled home from school, when my brother and my sister were at the Grammar School and I was still at the village school. Of the three of us I was Mrs. Ashburton's favourite, and I don't know why that was except that I was the youngest. "Hullo, my Matilda," Mrs. Ashburton would whisper in her throaty, crazy-sounding way. "Matilda," she'd repeat, lingering over the name I so disliked, drawing each syllable away from the next. "Dear Matilda." She was excessively thin, rather tall, and frail-looking. We made allowances for her because she was eighty-one.

Usually when we met her she was looking for wild flowers, or if it was winter or autumn just sitting in her governess cart in some farmer's gateway, letting the donkey graze the farmer's grass. In spring she used to root out plants from the hedges with a little trowel. Most of them were weeds, my brother said; and looking back on it now, I realize that it wasn't for wild flowers, or weeds, or grazing for her donkey that she drove about the lanes. It was in order to meet us cycling back from school.

"There's a tennis court at Challacombe Manor," she said one day in May, 1939. "Any time you ever wanted to play, Dick." She stared at my brother with piercing black eyes that were the colour of quality coal. She was eccentric, standing there in a long, very old and bald fur coat, stroking the ears of her donkey while he nibbled a hedge. Her hat was attached to her grey hair by a number of brass hat-pins. The hat was of faded green felt, the hat-pins had quite large knobs at the ends of them, inlaid with pieces of green glass. Green, Mrs. Ashburton often remarked, was her favourite colour, and she used to remove these hat-pins to show us the glass additions, emphasizing that they were valueless. Her bald fur coat was valueless also, she assured us, and not even in its heyday would it have fetched more than five pounds. In the same manner she remarked upon her summer hats and dresses, and her shoes, and the governess cart, and the donkey.

"I mean, Dick," she said that day in 1939, "it's not much of a tennis court, but it was once, of course. And there's a net stacked away in one of the outhouses. And a roller, and a marker. There's a lawn-mower, too, because naturally you'll need that."

"You mean, we could play on your court, Mrs. Ashburton?" my sister Betty said.

"Of course I mean that, my dear. That's just what I mean. You know, before the war we really did have marvellous tennis parties at Challacombe. Everyone came."

"Oh, how lovely!" Betty was fourteen and Dick was a year older, and I was nine. Betty was fair-haired like the rest of us, but much prettier than me. She had very blue eyes and a wide smiling mouth that boys at the Grammar School were always trying to kiss, and a small nose, and freckles. Her hair was smooth and long, the colour of hay. It looked quite startling sometimes, shining in the sunlight. I used to feel proud of Betty and Dick when they came to collect me every afternoon at Mrs. Pritchard's school. Dick was to leave the Grammar School in July, and on the afternoons of that warm May, as Betty and I cycled home with him, we felt sorry that he wouldn't be there next term. But Dick said he was glad. He was big, as tall as my father, and very shy. He'd begun to smoke, a habit not approved of by my father. On the way home from school we had to stop and go into a ruined cottage so that he could have a Woodbine. He was going to work on the farm; one day the farm would be his.

"It would be lovely to play tennis," Betty said.

"Then you must, my dear. But if you want to play this summer you'll have to get the court into trim." Mrs. Ashburton smiled at Betty in a way that made her thin, elderly face seem beautiful. Then she smiled at Dick. "I was passing the tennis court the other day, Dick, and I suddenly thought of it. Now why shouldn't those children get it into trim? I thought. Why shouldn't they come and play, and bring their friends?"

"Yes," Dick said.

"Why ever don't you come over to Challacombe on Saturday? Matilda, too, of course. Come for tea, all three of you."

Mrs. Ashburton smiled at each of us in turn. She nodded at us and climbed into the governess cart. "Saturday," she repeated.

"Honestly, Betty!" Dick glared crossly at my sister, as though she were responsible for the invitation. "I'm not going, you know."

He cycled off, along the narrow, dusty lane, big and red-faced and muttering. We followed him more slowly, talking about Mrs. Ashburton.

"Poor old thing!" Betty said, which was what people round about often said when Mrs. Ashburton was mentioned, or when she was seen in her governess cart.

The first thing I remember in all my life was my father breaking a fountain-pen. It was a large black-and-white pen, like tortoiseshell or marble. That was the fashion for fountain-pens then: two or three colours marbled together, green and black, blue and white, red and black-and-white. Conway Stewart, Waterman's, Blackbird. Propelling pencils were called Eversharp.

The day my father broke his pen I didn't know all that: I learnt it afterwards, when I went to school. I was three the day he broke the pen. "It's just a waste of blooming money!" he shouted. He smashed the pen across his knee while my mother anxiously watched. Waste of money or not, she said, it wouldn't help matters to break the thing. She fetched him the ink and a dip-pen from a drawer of the dresser. He was still angry, but after a minute or two he began to laugh. He kissed my mother, pulling her down on to the knee he'd broken the pen over. Dick, who must have been nine then, didn't even look up from his homework. Betty was there too, but I can't remember what she was doing.

The kitchen hasn't changed much. The old range has gone, but the big light-oak dresser is still there, with the same brass handles on its doors and drawers and the same Wedgwood-blue dinner-set on its shelves, and cups and jugs hanging on hooks. The ceiling is low, the kitchen itself large and rectangular, with the back stairs rising from the far end of it, and a door at the bottom of them. There are doors to the pantry and the scullery, and to the passage that leads to the rest of the house, and to the yard. There's a long narrow light-oak table, with brass handles on its drawers like the dresser ones, and oak chairs that aren't as light as all the other oak because chairs darken with use. But the table isn't scrubbed once a week any more, and the brass doesn't gleam. I know, because now and again I visit the farmhouse.

I remember the kitchen with oil-lamps, and the time, the day after my fifth birthday, when the men came to wire the house for electricity. My mother used to talk about an Aga, and often when she took us shopping with her she'd bring us to Archers', the builders' merchants, to look at big cream-coloured Agas. After a time, Mr. Gray of the Aga department didn't even bother to bustle up to her when he saw her coming. She'd stand there, lump and pink-cheeked, her reddish hair neat beneath the brim of her hat, touching the display models, opening the oven doors and lifting up the two big hot-plate covers. When we returned to the farmhouse my father would tease her, knowing she'd been to Archers' again. She'd blush, cutting ham at teatime or offering round salad. My father would then forget about it. "Well, I'm damned," he'd say, and he'd read out an item from the weekly paper, about some neighbouring farmer or new County Council plans. My mother would listen and then both of them would nod. They were very good friends, even though my father teased her. She blushed like a rose, he said: he teased her to see it.

Once, before the electricity came, I had a nightmare. It was probably only a few months before, because when I came crying down to the kitchen my father kept comforting me with the reminder that it would soon be my fifth birthday. "You'll never cry then, Matilda," he whispered to me, cuddling me to him. "Big girls of five don't cry." I fell asleep, but it's not that that I remember now, not the fear from the nightmare going away, or the tears stopping, or my father's caressing: it's the image of my parents in the kitchen as I stumbled down the back stairs. There were two oil-lamps lit and the fire in the range was glowing red-hot behind its curved bars, and the heavy black kettle wasn't quite singing. My father was asleep with last Saturday's weekly paper on his knees, my mother was reading one of the books from the bookcase in the dining-room we never used, probably *The Garden of Allah*, which was her favourite. The two sheepdogs were asleep under the table, and when I opened the door at the top of the stairs they both barked because they knew that at that particular time no one should be opening that door. "Oh, now, now," my mother said, coming to me, listening to me when I said that there were cows on my bedroom wall. I remember the image of the two of them because they looked so happy sitting there, even though my mother hadn't got her Aga, even though my father was sometimes worried about the farm.

Looking back on it now, there was a lot of happiness, although perhaps not more than many families experience. Everything seems either dismal or happy in retrospect, and the happiness in the farmhouse is what I think of first whenever I think now of that particular past. I remember my mother baking in the kitchen, flour all over her plump arms, and tiny beads of moisture on her forehead, because the kitchen was always hot. I remember my father's leathery skin and his smile, and the way he used to shout at the sheepdogs, and the men, Joe and Arthur, sitting on yellow stubble, drinking tea out of a bottle, on a day hay had been cut.

Our farm had once been the home-farm of Challacombe Manor, even though our farmhouse was two miles away from the manor house. There'd been servants and gardeners at Challacombe Manor then, and horses in the stables, and carriages coming and going. But the estate had fallen into rack and ruin after the First World War because Mr. Ashburton hadn't been able to keep it going and in the end, in 1924, he'd taken out various mortgages. When he died, in 1929, the extent of his debts was so great that Mrs. Ashburton had been obliged to let Lloyd's Bank foreclose on the mortgages, which is how it came about that my father bought Challacombe Farm. It was a tragedy, people round about used to say, and the real tragedy was that Mr. Ashburton had come back from the war in such a strange state that he hadn't minded about everywhere falling into rack and ruin. According to my father, Lloyd's Bank owned Challacombe Manor itself and had granted Mrs. Ashburton permission to live there in her lifetime. It wouldn't surprise him, my father said, if it turned out that Lloyd's Bank owned Mrs.

Ashburton as well. "He drank himself to death," people used to say about Mr. Ashburton. "She watched him and didn't have the heart to stop him." Yet before the First World War Mr. Ashburton had been a different kind of man, energetic and sharp. The Challacombe estate had been a showpiece.

To me in particular Mrs. Ashburton talked about her husband. She was lucky that he'd come back from the war, even if he hadn't been able to manage very well. His mind had been affected, she explained, but that was better than being dead. She told me about the men who'd died, gardeners at Challacombe Manor, and farm workers on the estate, and men she and her husband had known in the town. "I thanked God," Mrs. Ashburton said, "when he came safely back here all in one piece. Everything fell to bits around us, but it didn't matter because at least he was still alive. You understand, Matilda?"

I always nodded, although I didn't really understand. And then she'd go on about the estate as it had been, and then about her husband and the conversations they used to have. Sometimes she didn't address me directly. She smiled and just talked, always returning to the men who had been killed and how lucky she was that her husband had at least come back. She'd prayed, she said, that he'd come back, and every time another man from the estate or from the neighbourhood had been reported dead she'd felt that there was a better chance that her husband wouldn't die also. "By the law of averages," she explained, "some had to come back. Some men have always come back from wars, you convince yourself."

At this point I would always nod again, and Mrs. Ashburton would say that looking back on it now she felt ashamed that she had ever applied the law of averages to the survival or death of men. Doing so was as horrible as war itself: the women who were left at home became cruel in their fear and their self-ishness. Cruelty was natural in war, Mrs. Ashburton said.

At the time she'd hated the Germans and she was ashamed of that too, because the Germans were just people like other people. But when she talked about them the remains of the hatred were still in her voice, and I imagined the Germans from what she told me about them: people who ate black bread and didn't laugh much, who ate raw bacon, who were dour, grey and steely. She described the helmets they wore in wartime. She told me what a bayonet was, and I used to feel sick when I thought of one going into a man's stomach and being twisted in there to make sure the man would die. She told me about poison gas, and the trenches, and soldiers being buried alive. The way she spoke I knew she was repeating, word for word, the things her husband had told her, things that had maybe been the cause of his affected mind. Even her voice sounded unusual when she talked about the war, as though she was trying to imitate her husband's voice, and the terror that had been in it. He used to cry, she said, as he walked about the gardens, unable to stop the tears once they'd begun.

Dick didn't say anything while we rode the two miles over to Challacombe Manor that Saturday. He didn't even say anything when he suddenly dismounted and leaned his bicycle against a black gate, and climbed over the gate to have a smoke behind the hedge. If my father had come by he'd have known what was happening because he would have seen Betty and myself waiting in the lane, surrounded by the cloud of smoke that Dick always managed to make with his Woodbine. Our job was to warn him if we saw my father coming, but my father didn't come that afternoon and when Dick had finished we continued on our way.

We'd often been to tea at Challacombe Manor before. Mrs. Ashburton said we were the only visitors she had because most of her friends were dead, which was something that happened, she explained, if you were eighty-one. We always had tea in the kitchen, a huge room that smelt of oil, with armchairs in it and a wireless, and an oil-stove on which Mrs. Ashburton cooked, not wishing to have to keep the range going. There were oatcakes for tea, and buttered white and brown bread, and pots of jam that Mrs. Ashburton bought in the town, and a cake she bought also, usually a fruitcake. Afterwards we'd walk through the house with her, while she pointed out the places where the roof had given way, and the dry rot, and windows that were broken. She hadn't lived in most of the house since the war, and had lived in even less of it since her husband had died in 1929. We knew these details by heart because she'd told us so many times. In one of the outhouses there was an old motor-car with flat tyres, and the gardens were now all overgrown with grass and weeds. Rhododendrons were choked, and buddleia and kerria and hydrangeas.

The house was grey and square with two small wings, a stone Georgian house with wide stone steps leading to a front door that had pillars on either side of it and a fanlight above it. The gravel expanse in front of it was grassy now, and slippery in wet weather because of moss that had accumulated.

French windows opened on to it on either side of the hall door, from the rooms that had been the drawing-room and the dining-room. Lawns stretched around the house, with grass like a meadow on them now. The tennis court, which we'd never known about until Mrs. Ashburton mentioned it, was hidden away, beyond the jungle of shrubbery.

"You see?" she said. "You see, Dick?" She was wearing a long, old-fashioned dress and a wide-brimmed white hat, and sunglasses because the afternoon was fiercely bright.

The grass on the tennis court was a yard high, as high as the rusty iron posts that were there to support the net. "Look," Mrs. Ashburton said.

She led us to the stable-yard, past the outhouse where the motor-car was, and into a smaller outhouse. There was a lawn-mower there, as rusty as the tennis posts, and a marker in the same condition, and an iron roller. Tucked into the beams above our heads was a rolled-up tennis net. "He adored tennis," she said. "He really loved it."

She turned and we followed her across the stable-yard, into the kitchen by the back door. She talked about her husband while she made tea.

We ate the bought fruitcake, listening to her. We'd heard it all before, but we always considered it was worth it because of the cake and the biscuits and the buttered bread and the pots of jam. And always before we left she gave us ginger beer and pieces of chocolate broken up on a saucer. She told us about the child which might have been born to her husband and herself, six months after the old queen died, but which had miscarried. "Everything went wrong," she said. She told us about the parties there'd been at Challacombe Manor. Champagne and strawberries and cream, and parties with games that she described, and fancy dress.

"No reason at all," she said, "why we shouldn't have a tennis party." Dick made a sighing sound, a soft, slight noise that Mrs. Ashburton didn't hear.

"Tennis party?" Betty murmured.

"No reason, dear."

That morning Dick and Betty had had an argument. Betty had said that of course he must go to tea with Mrs. Ashburton, since he'd always gone in the past. And Dick had said that Mrs. Ashburton had been cunning: all these years, he said, she'd been inviting us to tea so that when the time was ripe she could get us to clean up her old tennis court. "Oh, don't be silly!" Betty had cried, and then had said that it would be the cruellest thing that Dick had ever done if he didn't go to tea with an old woman just because she'd mentioned her tennis court. I'd been cross with Dick myself, and none of us felt very happy because the matter of the tennis court had unattractively brought into the open the motive behind our putting up with Mrs. Ashburton. I didn't like it when she called me her Matilda and put her arms around me, and said she was sure her child would have been a little girl, and that she was almost as sure that she'd have called her Matilda. I didn't like it when she went on and on about the war and her husband coming back a wreck, or about the champagne and the strawberries and cream. "Poor Mrs. Ashburton!" we'd always said, but it wasn't because she was poor Mrs. Ashburton that we'd filled the emptiness of Saturday afternoons by cycling over to Challacombe Manor.

"Shall we go and have another look at it?" she said when we'd eaten all the food that was on the table. She smiled in her frail, almost beautiful way, and for a moment I wondered if Dick wasn't perhaps right about her cunning. She led the way back to the overgrown tennis court and we all four stood looking at it.

"It's quite all right to smoke, Dick," Mrs. Ashburton said, "if you want to."

Dick laughed because he didn't know how else to react. He'd gone as red as a sunset. He kicked at the rusty iron tennis post, and then as casually as he could he took a packet of squashed Woodbines from his pocket and began to fiddle with a box of matches. Betty poked him with her elbow, suggesting that he should offer Mrs. Ashburton a cigarette.

"Would you like one, Mrs. Ashburton?" Dick said, proffering the squashed packet.

"Well, you know, I think I would, Dick." She laughed and took the cigarette, saying she hadn't smoked a cigarette since 1915. Dick lit it for her. Some of the matches fell from the matchbox on to the long grass. He picked them up and replaced them, his own cigarette cocked out of the corner of his mouth. They looked rather funny, the two of them, Mrs. Ashburton in her big white hat and sunglasses.

"You'd need a scythe," Dick said.

That was the beginning of the tennis party. When Dick walked over the next Saturday with a scythe, Mrs. Ashburton had a packet of twenty Player's waiting for him. He scythed the grass and got the old hand-mower going. The stubble was coarse and by the time he'd cut it short there were quite large patches of naked earth, but Betty and Mrs. Ashburton said they didn't matter. The court would do as it was for this summer, but in the spring, Dick said, he'd put down fresh grass-seed. It rained heavily a fortnight later, which was fortunate, because Dick was able to even out some of the bumps with the roller. Betty helped him, and later on she helped him mark the court out. Mrs. Ashburton and I watched, Mrs. Ashburton holding my hand and often seeming to imagine that I was the child which hadn't been born to her.

We took to going to Challacombe Manor on Sunday mornings as well as Saturdays. There were always packets of Craven A, and ginger beer and pieces of chocolate. "Of course, it's not her property," my father said whenever anyone mentioned the tennis court, or the net that Mrs. Ashburton had found rolled up in an outhouse. At dinnertime on Sundays, when we all sat around the long table in the kitchen, my father would ask Dick how he'd got on with the court. He'd then point out that the tennis court and everything that went with it was the property of Lloyd's Bank. Every Sunday dinnertime we had the same: roast beef and roast potatoes and Yorkshire pudding, and carrots or brussels sprouts according to the seasonal variation, and apple pie and cream.

Dick didn't ever say much when my father asked him about the tennis court. "You want to be careful, lad," my father used to say, squashing roast potatoes into gravy. "Lloyd's is strict, you know." My father would go on for ages, talking about Lloyd's Bank or the Aga cooker my mother wanted, and you never quite knew whether he was being serious or not. He would sit there with his jacket on the back of his chair, not smiling as he ate and talked. Farmers were like that, my mother once told Betty when Betty was upset by him. Farmers were cautious and watchful and canny. He didn't at all disapprove of what Betty and Dick and Mrs. Ashburton were doing with the tennis court, my mother explained, rather the opposite; but he was right when he reminded them that everything, including the house itself, was the property of Lloyd's Bank.

Mrs. Ashburton found six tennis racquets in presses, which were doubtless the property of Lloyd's Bank also. Dick examined them and said they weren't too bad. They had an antiquated look, and the varnish had worn off the frames, but only two of them had broken strings. Even those two, so Dick said, could be played with. He and Mrs. Ashburton handed the racquets to one another, blowing at the dust that had accumulated on the presses and the strings. They lit up their cigarettes, and Mrs. Ashburton insisted on giving Dick ten shillings to buy tennis balls with.

I sat with Mrs. Ashburton watching Dick and Betty playing their first game on the court. The balls bounced in a peculiar way because in spite of all the rolling there were still hollows and bumps on the surface. The grass wasn't green. It was a brownish yellow, except for the bare patches, which were ochre-coloured. Mrs. Ashburton clapped every time there was a rally, and when Dick had beaten Betty 6-1, 6-4, he taught me how to hit the ball over the net, and how to volley it and keep it going. "Marvellous, Matilda!" Mrs. Ashburton cried, in her throaty voice, applauding again.

"Marvellous!"

We played all that summer, every Saturday and Sunday until the end of term, and almost every evening when the holidays came. We had to play in the evenings because at the end of term Dick began to work on the farm. "Smoke your cigarettes if you want to," my father said the first morning of the holidays, at breakfast. "No point in hiding it, boy." Friends of Dick's and Betty's used to come to Challacombe Manor to play also, because that was what Mrs. Ashburton wanted: Colin Gregg and Barbara Hosell and Peggy Goss and Simon Turner and Willie Beach.

Sometimes friends of mine came, and I'd show them how to do it, standing close to the net, holding the racquet handle in the middle of the shaft. Thursday, August 31st, was the day Mrs. Ashburton set for the tennis party: Thursday because it was half-day in the town.

Looking back on it now, it really does seem that for years and years she'd been working towards her tennis party. She'd hung about the lanes in her governess cart waiting for us because we were the children from the farm, the nearest children to Challacombe Manor. And when Dick looked big and strong enough and Betty of an age to be interested, she'd made her bid, easing matters along with fruitcake and cigarettes. I can imagine her now, on her own in that ruin of a house, watching the grass grow on her tennis court and watching Dick and Betty growing up and dreaming of one more tennis party at

Challacombe, a party like there used to be before her husband was affected in the head by the Kaiser's war.

"August the 31st," Betty reminded my parents one Sunday at dinnertime. "You'll both come," she said fiercely, blushing when they laughed at her.

"I hear Lloyd's is on the rampage," my father said laboriously. "Short of funds. Calling everything in."

Dick and Betty didn't say anything. They ate their roast beef, pretending to concentrate on it.

"Course they're not," my mother said.

"They'll sell Challacombe to some building fellow, now that it's all improved with tennis courts."

"Daddy, don't be silly," Betty said, blushing even more. All three of us used to blush. We got it from my mother. If my father blushed you wouldn't notice.

"True as I'm sitting here, my dear. Nothing like tennis courts for adding a bit of style to a place."

Neither my mother nor my father had ever seen the tennis court. My father wouldn't have considered it the thing, to go walking over to Challacombe Manor to examine a tennis court. My mother was always busy, cooking and polishing brass. Neither my father nor my mother knew the rules of tennis. When we first began to play Betty used to draw a tennis court on a piece of paper and explain.

"Of course we'll come to the tennis party," my mother said quietly. "Of course, Betty."

In the middle of the tennis party, my father persisted, a man in a hard black hat from Lloyd's Bank would walk on to the court and tell everyone to go home.

"Oh, Giles, don't be silly now," my mother said quite sharply, and added that there was such a thing as going on too much. My father laughed and winked at her.

Mrs. Ashburton asked everyone she could think of to the tennis party, people from the farms round about and shopkeepers from the town. Dick and Betty asked their friends and their friends' parents, and I asked Belle Frye and the Gorrys and the Seatons. My mother and Betty made meringues and brandy-snaps and fruitcakes and Victoria sponge cakes and scones and buns and shortbread. They made sardine sandwiches and tomato sandwiches and egg sandwiches and ham sandwiches. I buttered the bread and whipped up cream and wrapped the plates of sandwiches in damp teacloths. Dick cleared a place in the shrubbery beside the tennis court and built a fire to boil kettles on. Milk was poured into bottles and left to keep cool in the larder. August 31st was a fine, hot day.

At dinnertime my father pretended that the truck which was to convey the food, and us too, to the tennis court had a broken carburettor. He and Joe had been working on it all morning, he said, but utterly without success. No one took any notice of him.

I remember, most of all, what they looked like. Mrs. Ashburton thin as a rake in a long white dress and her wide-brimmed white hat and her sunglasses. My father in his Sunday clothes, a dark blue suit, his hair combed and his leathery brown face shining because he had shaved it and washed it specially. My mother had powder on her cheeks and her nose, and a touch of lipstick on her lips, although she didn't usually wear lipstick and must have borrowed Betty's. She was wearing a pale blue dress speckled with tiny white flowers. She'd spent a fortnight making it herself, for the occasion. Her reddish hair was soft and a little unruly, being freshly washed. My father was awkward in his Sunday suit, as he always was in it. His freckled hands lolled uneasily by his sides, or awkwardly held tea things, cup and saucer and plate. My mother blushed beneath her powder, and sometimes stammered, which she did when she was nervous.

Betty was beautiful that afternoon, in a white tennis dress that my mother had made her. Dick wore long white flannels that he'd been given by old Mr. Bowe, a solicitor in the town who'd been to other tennis parties at Challacombe Manor but had no further use for white flannel trousers, being seventy-two now and too large for the trousers he'd kept for more than fifty years. My mother had made me a tennis dress, too, but I felt shy that day and didn't want to do anything except hand round plates of meringues and cake. I certainly didn't want to play, for the tennis was serious: mixed doubles, Betty and Colin Gregg against Dick and Peggy Goss, and Simon Turner and Edie Turner against Barbara Hosell and Willie Beach.

People were there whom my father said he hadn't seen for years, people who had no intention of playing tennis, any more than he had. Between them, Dick and Betty and Mrs. Ashburton had cast a wide net, and my father's protests at the mounds of food that had been prepared met with their answer as car after car drew up, and dog-carts and pony and traps. Belle Frye and I passed around the plates of meringues, and people broke off in their conversations to ask us who we were. Mrs.

Ashburton had spread rugs on the grass around the court, and four white ornamental seats had been repainted by Dick the week before. "Just like the old days," a man called Mr. Race said, a corn merchant from the town. My mother nervously fidgeted, and I could feel her thinking that perhaps my father's laborious joke would come true, that any moment now the man from Lloyd's Bank would arrive and ask people what on earth they thought they were doing, playing tennis without the Bank's permission.

But that didn't happen. The balls zipped to and fro across the net, pinging off the strings, throwing up dust towards the end of the afternoon. Voices called out in exasperation at missed shots, laughter came and went. The sun continued to shine warmly, the tennis players wiped their foreheads with increasing regularity, the rugs on the grass were in the shade. Belle Frye and I collected the balls and threw them back to the servers. Mr. Bowe said that Dick had the makings of a fine player.

Mrs. Ashburton walked among the guests with a packet of Player's in her hand, talking to everyone. She kept going up to my mother and thanking her for everything she'd done. Whenever she saw me she kissed me on the hair. Mr. Race said she shook hands like a duchess. The rector, Mr. Throataway, laughed jollily.

At six o'clock, just as people were thinking of going, my father surprised everyone by announcing that he had a barrel of beer and a barrel of cider in the truck. I went with him and there they were, two barrels keeping cool beneath a tarpaulin, and two wooden butter-boxes full of glasses that he'd borrowed from the Heart of Oak. He drove the truck out from beneath the shade of the trees and backed it close to the tennis court. He and Dick set the barrels up and other men handed round the beer and cider, whichever anyone wanted. "Just like him," I heard a woman called Mrs. Garland saying. "Now, that's just like him."

It was a quarter to ten that evening before they stopped playing tennis. You could hardly see the ball as it swayed about from racquet to racquet, looping over the net, driven out of court. My father and Mr. Race went on drinking beer, and Joe and Arthur, who'd arrived after milking, stood some distance away from them, drinking beer also. Mrs. Garland and my mother and Miss Sweet and Mrs. Tissard made more tea, and the remains of the sandwiches and cakes were passed around by Belle Frye and myself. Joe said he reckoned it was the greatest day in Mrs. Ashburton's life. "Don't go drinking that cider now," Joe said to Belle Frye and myself.

We all sat around in the end, smacking at midges and finishing the sandwiches and cakes. Betty and Colin Gregg had cider, and you could see from the way Colin Gregg kept looking at Betty that he was in love with her. He was holding her left hand as they sat there, thinking that no one could see because of the gloom, but Belle Frye and I saw, all right. Just before we went home, Belle Frye and I were playing at being ghosts round at the front of the house and we came across Betty and Colin Gregg kissing behind a rhododendron bush. They were lying on the grass with their arms tightly encircling one another, kissing and kissing as though they were never going to stop. They didn't even know Belle Frye and I were there. "Oh, Colin!" Betty kept saying. "Oh, Colin, Colin!"

We wanted to say goodbye to Mrs. Ashburton, but we couldn't find her. We ran around looking everywhere, and then Belle Frye suggested that she was probably in the house.

"Mrs. Ashburton!" I called, opening the door that led from the stableyard to the kitchen. "Mrs. Ashburton!"

It was darker in the kitchen than it was outside, almost pitch-dark because the windows were so dirty that even in daytime it was gloomy.

"Matilda," Mrs. Ashburton said. She was sitting in an armchair by the oil-stove. I knew she was because that was where her voice came from. We couldn't see her.

"We came to say goodbye, Mrs. Ashburton."

She told us to wait. She had a saucer of chocolate for us, she said, and we heard her rooting about on the table beside her. We heard the glass being removed from a lamp and then she struck a match. She lit the wick and put the glass back. In the glow of lamplight she looked exhausted. Her eyes seemed to have receded, the thinness of her face was almost sinister.

We ate our chocolate in the kitchen that smelt of oil, and Mrs. Ashburton didn't speak. We said goodbye again, but she didn't say anything. She didn't even nod or shake her head. She didn't kiss me like she usually did, so I went and kissed her instead. The skin of her face felt like crinkled paper.

"I've had a very happy day," she said when Belle Frye and I had reached the kitchen door. "I've had a lovely day," she said, not seeming to be talking to us but to herself. She was crying, and she smiled in the lamplight, looking straight ahead of her. "It's all over," she said. "Yet again."

We didn't know what she was talking about and presumed she meant the tennis party. "Yet again," Belle Frye repeated as we crossed the stable-yard. She spoke in a soppy voice because she was given to soppiness. "Poor Mrs. Ashburton!" she said, beginning to cry herself, or pretending to. "Imagine being eighty-one," she said. "Imagine sitting in a kitchen and re-membering all the other tennis parties, knowing you'd have to die soon. Race you," Belle Frye said, forgetting to be soppy any more.

Going home, Joe and Arthur sat in the back of the truck with Dick and Betty. Colin Gregg had ridden off on his bicy-cle, and Mr. Bowe had driven away with Mrs. Tissard beside him and Mr. Tissard and Miss Sweet in the dickey of his Mor-ris Cowley. My mother, my father and myself were all squashed into the front of the truck, and there was so little room that my father couldn't change gear and had to drive all the way to the farm in first. In the back of the truck Joe and Arthur and Dick were singing, but Betty wasn't, and I could imagine Betty just sitting there, staring, thinking about Colin Gregg. In Betty's bedroom there were photographs of Clark Gable and Ronald Colman, and Claudette Colbert and the little Princesses. Betty was going to marry Colin, I kept saying to myself in the truck. There'd be other tennis parties and Betty would be older and would know her own mind, and Colin Gregg would ask her and she'd say yes. It was very beautiful, I thought, as the truck shuddered over the uneven back avenue of Challacombe Manor. It was as beautiful as the tennis party itself, the white dresses and Betty's long hair, and everyone sitting and watching in the sunshine, and evening slowly descending. "Well, that's the end of that," my father said, and he didn't seem to be talking about the tennis party because his voice was too serious for that. He repeated a conversation he'd had with Mr. Bowe and one he'd had with Mr. Race, but I didn't listen because his voice was so lugubrious, not at all like it had been at the tennis party. I was huddled on my mother's knees, falling asleep. I imagined my father was talking about Lloyd's Bank again, and I could hear my mother agreeing with him.

I woke up when my mother was taking off my dress in my bedroom.

"What is it?" I said. "Is it because the tennis party's over? Why's everyone so sad?"

My mother shook her head, but I kept asking her because she was looking sorrowful herself and I wasn't sleepy any more. In the end she sat on the edge of my bed and said that people thought there was going to be another war against the Germans.

"Germans?" I said, thinking of the grey, steely people that Mrs. Ashburton had so often told me about, the people who ate black bread.

It would be all right, my mother said, trying to smile. She told me that we'd have to make special curtains for the windows so that the German aeroplanes wouldn't see the lights at night. She told me there'd probably be sugar rationing.

I lay there listening to her, knowing now why Mrs. Ashburton had said that yet again it was all over, and knowing what would happen next. I didn't want to think about it, but I couldn't help thinking about it: my father would go away, and

Dick would go also, and Joe and Arthur and Betty's Colin Gregg. I would continue to attend Miss Pritchard's School and then I'd go on to the Grammar, and my father would be killed. A soldier would rush at my father with a bayonet and twist the bayonet in my father's stomach, and Dick would do the same to another soldier, and Joe and Arthur would be missing in the trenches, and Colin Gregg would be shot.

My mother kissed me and told me to say my prayers before I went to sleep. She told me to pray for the peace to continue, as she intended to do herself. There was just a chance, she said, that it might.

She went away and I lay awake, beginning to hate the Germans and not feeling ashamed of it, like Mrs. Ashburton was. No German would ever have played tennis that day, I thought, no German would have stood around having tea and sandwiches and meringues, smacking away the midges when night came. No German would ever have tried to recapture the past, or would have helped an old woman to do so, like my mother and my father had done, and Mr. Race and Mr. Bowe and Mr. Throataway and Mrs. Garland, and Betty and Dick and Colin Gregg. The Germans weren't like that. The Germans wouldn't see the joke when my father said that for all he knew Lloyd's Bank owned Mrs. Ashburton.

I didn't pray for the peace to continue, but prayed instead that my father and Dick might come back when the war was over. I didn't pray that Joe and Arthur and Colin Gregg should come back since that would be asking too much, because some men had to be killed, according to Mrs. Ashburton's law of averages. I hadn't understood her when Mrs. Ashburton had said that cruelty was natural in wartime, but I understood now. I understood her law of averages and her sitting alone in her dark kitchen, crying over the past. I cried myself, thinking of the grass growing on her tennis court, and the cruelty that was natural.

Poems

A Lawn-Tennisonian Idyll

ANONYMOUS

I, who a decade past had lived recluse,
Left for a while the dust of books and town
To share the pastimes of a country-house;
And thus it chanced that I beheld a scene
That steeped my rusted soul in wonderment.
The morn was passing fair; no vagrant cloud
Obscured the summer sun, as from the porch
I sallied forth to saunter at my will
Adown the garden path. Anon I came
To where a lawn outspread its verdant robe,
Whose decoration filled me with amaze.
Lawns many I had seen in days gone by,
But never lawn before the like of this;
For o'er its grassy plain a strange device
Of parallelograms rectangular
Was limned in lines of exceeding whiteness;
Athwart the centre of this strange device
A threaden net was stretched a full yard high,
And clasped in its reticulated arms,

As ivy clasps the oak, two sturdy staves
Upreared on either side. At either end,
Holding opposing corners of the field,
A youth and a damsel did disport themselves
In costume airy, mystic, and wonderful;
The while in dexter hand each held a quaint
and spoon-shaped instrument of chequered strings,—
Modelled, perchance, upon the ancient lute,—
Whereby they nimbly urged the bounding sphere
Across the meshy bar.

                  No space had I
To ponder, ere they spied me and did call
A welcome. "Hast thou come to see us play?"
"What is the game?" I asked. They answered, "Love."
"A pretty game," quoth I, "for a man and a maid,
But one wherein a third is out of place.
Fain would I, therefore, go."

                       "Nay, nay," they cried;
"Prithee remain, and thou shalt stand as umpire."
And so I stayed, and presently besought
To know their prospects. Then the maiden said,
"I'm fifteen now." The gallant, he replied,
"And thirty I." Whereupon methought at first
That he did somewhat overstate his case,
Though she seemed rather underneath the mark.
But when they said that she was thirty, too,
And next, that he was forty, I perceived
They told of other things than length of years;

Since mortals ages, e'en at census time,
Could scarce be subject to such fluctuations.
Thus did they wage the contest, hither thither,
Running and striking, till, triumphantly,
The damsel shouted, "Deuce!" Alas! mused I,
That lips so fair should utter word so base!
Yet would have held my peace, had not the youth
Turned unto me—"How's that? Was that a fault?"
"A fault!" I answered; "aye, and worse than that:
Indeed, 'tis nigh a sin." "Go to, " he said
"Thou makest merry." So the sport went on.
And then she cried, "Advantage, and I win!"
And then, "'Tis deuce again!" And then, "Advantage
To thee!" And then she strove to reach the ball,
And failed; and in despair exclaimed, "Oh, dear,
I'm beaten!" and fell back upon the sward.
"And this," quoth I, "is your game of love?
Well, I have heard men say that oftentimes
True love, once smooth, is scattered to the deuce!
And she that first advantage hath obtained
Doth lose at last, and suffer sad reverse.
Sweet maid, when thou art wed, the deuce avoid
And thou shalt ne'er at least deserve a beating!"
She laughed, he frowned; I turned and went my way.

Tennis

MARGARET AVISON

Service is joy, to see or swing. Allow
All tumult to subside. Then tensest winds
Buffet, brace, viol, and sweeping bow.

Courts are for love and volley. No one minds
The cruel ellipse of serve and return,
Dancing white galliardes at tape or net
Till point, on the wire's tip, or the long burn-
ing arc to nethercourt marks game and set.
Purpose apart, perched like an umpire, dozes,
Dreams golden balls whirring through indigo.
Clay blurs the whitewash but day still encloses
The albinos, bonded in their flick and flow.
Playing in musicked gravity, the pair
Score liquid Euclids in foolscaps of air.

A Subaltern's Love-song

JOHN BETJEMAN

Miss J. Hunter Dunn, Miss J. Hunter Dunn,
Furnish'd and burnish'd by Aldershot sun,
What strenuous singles we played after tea,
We in the tournament—you against me!

Love-thirty, love-forty, oh! weakness of joy,
The speed of a swallow, the grace of a boy,
With carefullest carelessness, gaily you won,
I am weak from your loveliness, Joan Hunter Dunn.

Miss Joan Hunter Dunn, Miss Joan Hunter Dunn,
How mad I am, sad I am, glad that you won.
The warm-handled racket is back in its press,
But my shock-headed victor, she loves me no less.

Her father's euonymus shines as we walk,
And swing past the summer house, buried in talk,
And cool the verandah that welcomes us in
To the six o'clock news and a lime-juice and gin.

The scent of the conifers, sound of the bath,
The view from my bedroom of moss-dappled path,
As I struggle with double-end evening tie,
For we dance at the Golf Club, my victor and I.

On the floor of her bedroom lie blazer and shorts
And the cream-coloured walls are betrophied with sports,
And westering, questioning settles the sun
On your low-leaded window, Miss Joan Hunter Dunn.

The Hillman is waiting, the light's in the hall,
The pictures of Egypt are bright on the wall,
My sweet, I am standing beside the oak stair
And there on the landing's the light on your hair.

By roads "not adopted," by woodland ways,
She drove to the club in the late-summer haze,
Into nine-o'clock Camberley, heavy with bells
And mushroomy, pine-woody, evergreen smells.

Miss Joan Hunter Dunn, Miss Joan Hunter Dunn,
I can hear from the car-park the dance has begun.
Oh! full Surrey twilight! importunate band!
Oh! strongly adorable tennis-girl's hand!

Around us are Rovers and Austins afar,
Above us, the intimate roof of the car,
And here on my right is the girl of my choice,
With the tilt of her nose and the chime of her voice,

And the scent of her wrap, and the words never said,
And the ominous, ominous dancing ahead.
We sat in the car park till twenty to one
And now I'm engaged to Miss Joan Hunter Dunn.

The Olympic Girl

SIR JOHN BETJEMAN

The sort of girl I like to see
Smiles down from her great height at me.
She stands in strong, athletic pose
And wrinkles her *retroussé* nose.
Is it distaste that makes her frown,
So furious and freckled, down
On an unhealthy worm like me?
Or am I what she likes to see?
I do not know, though much I care.
εἰθε γενιομην ...Would I were
(Forgive me, shade of Rupert Brooke)
An object fit to claim her look.
Oh! would I were her racket press'd
With hard excitement to her breast
And swished into the sunlit air
Arm-high above her tousled hair,
And banged against the bounding ball
"Oh! Plung!" my tauten'd strings would call,
"Oh, Plung! my darling, break my strings

For you I will do brilliant things."
And when the match is over, I
Would flop beside you, hear you sigh;
And then, with what supreme caress,
You'ld tuck me up into my press.
Fair tigress of the tennis courts,
So short in sleeve and strong in shorts,
Little, alas, to you I mean,
For I am bald and old and green.

On Watching a Young Man Play Tennis

KELLY CHERRY

The male poets run, lifting their feet like pros.
Others fish, and then there are those
Whose driving force
Sends them to the sandtraps of an eighteen-hole course

In search of metaphor. I have no yen
For sun and sky and earth, no kin-
Ship for the sea.
The element of mind is quite enough for me,

And dreaming in the damp of poolside shade,
I let imagination wade
Through the shallow
Stretch of time beyond a bend of tanning elbow,

And burning thigh, to where the poet plays
A love game with my yesterdays.
I have no zest
For exercise, no yearning after limberness

For the sake of limb alone, but enjoy,
Girlishly, this energy of Boy
That seeks to know
The meaning of *mens sana in corpore sano.*

Turning on my side, I see the shadow
Of his racket on the court grow
Long and widen
Till its very silence trespasses on the Haydn

Which carries from the house, and I put down
My drink and move inside where sound
And light and drift
Of dinner's smells serve, albeit fleetingly, to lift

My spirits to a plane of praise upon
Which I can stand and frankly own
That I am tired,
And lazy, and will leave to others more inspired

The satisfaction of the outdoor sports.
A young man in his tennis shorts
Suffices to
Realign the balance of my mind and body so

That I am paralyzed with memory
Of verse and versifier. (Yet I
Remember when
I volleyed more than words with the artfullest of men.)

Tennis in San Juan

REUEL DENNEY

Thin under the arc lights,
Pin legs in their chalk whites;
The bug of the slammed ball
Trying in vain to get out;
All done in a slow dance
To night tune of the tree frog,
An inch long, glass, *co-kí,*
co-kí he says, *co-kí,*
Never seen but heard now,
Heard then, heard and heard
After the sundown, all night.

When the ball goes *co-kí*,
The tree frog says: *co-kí*,
Much Sabby, good stroke,
Señor Spalding, strong gut,
Like a firework, long lob,
With muscle guitar, good slam,
On C sharp, a good ping,
High the way the girls sing
Dancing the momba in Bay View
With tales told to just you.

Down at the dock they work ship,
Off the shore they see shark,
Under the reef they pull shell,
Into the boat they haul eel;
Up at the tennis, same way,

Professors work with white ball
Very hard, bang, bang
Lecturing night with hard work,
Possessing dark with bard play,
Under the arcs, with *co-kí*
Who also works with much breath.
So many ways they say love
So many ways they say death,
Up in the tennis tree, *co-kí*.

My Tennis Pro Is Shot

GARY FINCKE

In January, I wake up
with backhand anxiety.
I am fifteen, nearly
too old to change, and
winter is when I think
about the deadlines
for success, how others
meet them. With topspin.
With kick serves. I see
on an inside page
of the *Press,* a picture
of Stahovic, my foreign
pro, and learn he has
four bullets in him.
A column describes
his wounds, and I wonder,
at once, whether
conditioning will save him,
think of drugs and thieves

and outraged lovers,
list them like rankings:
I am #7 in Pittsburgh,
16 and under. No one
goes pro from there.

Doc Stavic Coaches

GARY FINCKE

Tennis is chess; tennis is war,
Doc Stavic explained to us.
Know this battlefield and where
That army is weakest. You lay
Siege on that man; you break
His will like a famine and
He'll go belly up and die.
Doc Stavic said stamina, patience;
He ran us side to side, baseline
To net. You be Russians, he said.
You endure no matter what country
Wants your land. When winter comes,
You'll be ready. Wait for
That cold snap, the first real snow.
That man will understand war;
He'll shake his head and slump
Like you've shot him. Napoleon,
He said. Hitler. Whoever
The next invader might be

You have the time and the endurance
Doc Stavic said he was making sure
We lived; he said "I'm telling you 'Yes.'"

Tennis Elbow

JIM HALL

From having fun
one way only,
doing the same thing,
the same way exactly,
grinding membranes
that once oiled
every movement,
that once made
the fluid glide
of bone on bone
the thud absorbed,
again absorbed,
until the thin pad
cushioning the heavy
parts of me from
the heavy parts of me
crumbles, disintegrates.
From years of grooving
the stroke: bounce-hit

bounce-hit, rehearse,
rehearse, racket back,
stroke, strike, follow
through. I know no
other way. The one trick
I know has worn thin
the cartilage,
has ground it down,
until it absorbs no more,
until I am in touch
with myself. Parts
never meant to touch
are touching. They touch
again, crush and grind,
until I am bright with ache.
And every winner I ever hit,
every exquisite triumph
has made me tender,
put a twinge in my step,
a shine in every act I do.

Watching Tennis

JOHN HEATH-STUBBS

Light, in light breezes and a favoring sun,
You moved, like a dancer, to the glancing ball,
And the dance and the game seemed one
To me, unmarked spectator by the wall—

Always spectator, nor apt at any sport—
And you free burgess of the summer air;
Embraced with the iron maiden, Thought,
I of my body's poverty am aware.

How could I guess that all-consoling night,
Confider and concealer of secrets, should conduct
You to lie easy in my fumbling arms?

Yet, by the chances of the game betrayed,
Your mouth on mine found out its silent need,
And my discordant nerves peace in your limbs.

A Dialogue Concerning the Question
Whether a Tennis Ball May Be Said
to Hanker for the Other Side of the Net

CONRAD HILBERRY

A. Now, for example, when the ball lays its ear
to the strings of the racket, the moment comes whole.
Satisfied in the round completion of muscle,
sun, and rubber, it wishes itself gone
so that the woman across the net may
run back, watch the lob float down,
and drop her brown shoulder for the slam.

B. Let's keep things straight. *You* foresee the tan
arch of muscles in the far court. The moment
doesn't care. Feeling is a weed sending runners
through the roots of the grass. Seized
at the center, it may be pulled in one stroke,
leaving the facts: the net, the wood, the woman
whose footwork you admire are particles in motion.

————

A. The grain of the wood is desire. If you begin extracting,
an instant flattens to splotches of color
on cardboard. Never longing for the stretch
of a body or a ball singing as the strings
taught it, the dead present could create
nothing. Uncaused, uncausing, it would have
no reason to perish into a new time.

On the Tennis Court at Night

GALWAY KINNELL

We step out on the green rectangle
in moonlight; the titles glow,
which for many have been the only lines
of justice. We remember
the thousand trajectories the air has erased
of that close-contested last set—
blur of volleys, soft arcs of drop shots,
huge ingrown loops of lobs with topspin
which went running away, crosscourts recrossing
down to each sweet (and in exact proportion, bitter)
✪ in Talbert and Olds' *The Game of Doubles in Tennis*
The breeze has carried them off but we still hear
the mutters, the doublefaulter's groans,
cries of "Deuce!" or "Love two!",
squeak of tennis shoes, grunt of overreaching,
all dozen extant tennis quips—"Just out!"
or, "About right for you?" or, "Want to change partners?"
and *baaah* of sheep translated very occasionally
into *thonk* of well-hit ball, among the pure

· 363 ·

right angles and unhesitating lines
of this arena where every man grows old
pursuing that repertoire of perfect shots,
darkness already in his strokes,
even in death cramps waving an arm back and forth
to the disgust of the night nurse
(to whom the wife whispers, "Well,
at least I always knew where he was!");
and smiling; and a few hours later found dead—
the smile still in place but the ice bag
left on the brow now inexplicably
Scotchtaped to the right elbow—causing
all those bright trophies to slip permanently,
though not in fact much farther, out of reach,
all except the thick-bottomed young man
about to doublefault in soft metal on the windowsill:
"Runner-Up Men's Class B Consolation Doubles
St. Johnsbury Kiwanis Tennis Tournament 1969"...
Clouds come over the moon;
all the lines go out. November last year
in Lyndonville: it is getting dark,
snow starts falling, Zander Rubin wobble-twists
his worst serve out of the black woods behind him,
Stan Albro lobs into a gust of snow,
Don Bredes smashes at where the ball theoretically
could be coming down, the snow blows down
and swirls about our legs, darkness flows
across a disappearing patch of green-painted asphalt

in the north country, where four men,
half-volleying, poaching, musing, grunting,
begging mercy of their bones, hold the ground,
as winter comes on, all the winters to come.

Autumn: Evening Tennis

MARK KIRBY

Taken pulling flowers,
Persephone,
her arms full of color,
Hades carried like a torch
into the underworld.

Now that sunset has settled
into evening, our play,
its mute, gesticulating arcs,
slashes holes in the dark
where green is grey and yellow
is too

Dark swoons through a
fence of trees into
our school of motion
where character learns
the stubbornness of boundaries.

———————

The racket is
an intransigent elbow
with which to make our designs;
and we are slowed by dark
and caution and punchy with misses,
and our time is short.

The fragrance of burning wood
is everywhere. Our playing ground
is cracked beneath us; random
grass spills out, smoke
from Persephone's torch.

Prothalamion

MAXINE KUMIN

The far court opens for us all July.
Your arm, flung up like an easy sail bellying,
comes down on the serve in a blue piece of sky
barely within reach, and you, following,
tip forward on the smash. The sun sits still
on the hard white canvas lip of the net. Five-love.
Salt runs behind my ears at thirty-all.
At game, I see the sweat that you're made of.
We improve each other, quickening so by noon
that the white game moves itself, the universe
contracted to the edge of the dividing line
you toe against—limbering for your service,
arm up, swiping the sun time after time—
and the square I live in, measured out with lime.

Clobber the Lobber

FELICIA LAMPORT

<pre>
                        slobs
            tennis   who
        with   have
        play   the
        to   urge
        need   to
        the   lengthen
        from   points
        us   with
        spare   lofty
        O   lobs!
</pre>

Tennis Instructor, 1971
(from "Two Summer Jobs")

BRAD LEITHAUSER

Transformed: the high school graduate, now
himself a teacher for the city.
Not sure who my students are, or how
exactly a tennis class is run,
I show up an hour ahead of time.
Odd; nobody here. But one by one
they appear and—and they're all women!
Maddeningly shy, the truth is I'm
more alarmed than pleased at this, although
a number of them are pretty,
and one, Mrs. Shores, extremely so.

———————

Mine's a small but adequate domain.
Three mornings a week I hold court
on two courts beside the railroad track—
giving, to those I can, assistance,
and verbally patting on the back
the irretrievably maladroit
whose shots are always rocketing
the fence. Occasionally a train hurtling to or from Detroit
rumbles through, erasing everything
before it fades into the distance.

Distant but surreally vast,
exclusive, quick to take offense,
the "Big H," Harvard, which only last
April accepted me, now conspires
(my latest crazy daydream runs)
to bar me from settling in a dorm
because I typed "No class presidents,
please" on my roommate selection form.
Just as I'm lunging for the ball,
a sniping voice within inquires,
"What will happen in the fall?"

———————

The days are changeless, but the weeks pass,
edging me closer to fall, and school.
Mrs. Shores, the day of our last class,
gives a party on her patio,
where I'm handed a glass-bottom mug
—surprise!—engraved with my name.
Beer's offered; I'm too proud to confess
I hate the stuff. It's hot as a blow-
torch now, and not yet noon. The first slug
of Stroh's goes down in a cool
wash of cleansing bitterness.

The party warms up, visibly. Ice
crackles in the drinks. I'm nonplussed
when Mrs. Binstock unfolds a tale
which—though nothing you shouldn't say
among men—is not exactly nice.
My face, which lets me down without fail
at such times, blushes. They laugh at me.
Then, and this is odd, I am discussed
in a fond and distant-seeming way,
as if I were no longer here.
The ghost accepts another beer.

———————

Mrs. Dow speaks of a friend's friend's son
who committed suicide after
his first Harvard exam. A lighter
flares beside me, and cigarette smoke
crowds the air. "Teacher don't allow
any smoking." Freshened laughter
greets sad Mrs. Klein's unlikely quip.
Then, from Mrs. Shores: "What kind of writer
do you want to be?" How, how, how
did she ever draw from me my one
most private wish? I'm tempted to joke,

but a stilled politeness in the air
and the depths of her dark handsome eyes
forbid it. Yet when I stumblingly
begin a pained, self-conscious reply
she is mercifully there
to cut me off; conversation drifts
lightly away, as once more I
find myself taking shelter in
something that soothes as it puzzles me—
a solicitude that's graceful, wise,
and impenetrably feminine.

———————

I drain my mug. A white film adheres
to the glass bottom, and then bursts:
disclosing these my students seated
around me in the Michigan sun,
the last of our lessons completed.
Wobbly I rise, drunk with success
(successfully having drunk four beers!),
and wave good-bye—but forget the press
to my racket. I'm called back amid
much laughter. Once more I gravely bid
them all farewell: So long. It's been fun.

... And what a day this is! The air
humming in my ears, the sun stroking
overhead in the treetops! Now
a second film breaks, revealing how
the light-drinking trees, the houses, cars,
power lines, a peeling wooden fence
and the pavement's constellated stars
are a network, supple and immense,
and all linked to distance Mrs. Shores,
who calls—but surely she is joking—
"Never forget: the world is yours."

Tennis

OSIP MANDELSTAM

Summer cabins with rough log walls
Where a hand organ's quavers rise;
Flying high on its own, a ball
Magically lures as it flies.

Who is this, his coarse passion cooled
Under garments of Alpine snow,
Who begins an Olympic duel
With a sportive maid as his foe?

The lyre strings were worn and split;
The Englishman cannot grow old:
He put strings on a golden racket
And tossed it into the world.

He performs the rites of the game
With his fragile weaponry—
Attic warriors were just the same,
Each in love with his enemy.

It is May. Scraps of black cloud
Cast a blight upon everything green.
Motors everywhere, horns too loud,
Lilacs reeking of gasoline.

Now the jolly sportsman drains
A dipper filled at the spring;
Then the battle is joined again,
A bare arm flashing.

The Old Pro's Lament

PAUL PETRIE

Each year the court expands,
the net moves back, the ball
hums by—with more spin.

I use my second serve,
lob deeper, slice more,
stay away from the net, and fail
to win.

As any fool can tell,
it is time
to play the game purely
for the game's sake—to applaud
the puff of white chalk,
shake hands
and grin.

———————

Others retire
into the warm corners of memory,
invent new rules, new games
and win.

Under the hot lances
of the shower, I play each point over,
and over,
and over,
again.

Wisdom is the natural business
of old men—
to let the body go,
the rafters, moth-eaten and decayed,
cave in.

But nightly in dreams I see
an old man
playing in an empty court
under the dim floodlights
of the moon
with a racket gone in the strings—
no net, no ball, no game—
and still playing to win.

Tennis

ROBERT PINSKY

(To Howard Wilcox)

I. The Service

The nerve to make a high toss and the sense
Of when the ball is there; and then the nerve
To cock your arm back all the way, not rigid

But loose and ready all the way behind
So that the racket nearly or really touches
Your back far down; and all the time to see

The ball, the seams and letters on the ball
As it seems briefly at its highest point
To stop and hover—keeping these in mind,

The swing itself is easy, forgetting cancer,
Or panic learning how to swim or walk,
Forgetting what the score is, names of plants,

———————

And your first piece of ass, you throw the racket
Easily through Brazil, coins, mathematics
And *haute cuisine* to press the ball from over

And a slight slice at two o'clock or less,
Enough to make it loop in accurately
As, like a fish in water flicking itself

Away, your mind takes up the next concern
With the arm, ball, racket still pressing down
And forward and across your obedient body.

     II. Forehand
Straightforwardness can be a cruel test
A kind of stagefright threatening on the cold
And level dais, a time of no excuses.

But think about the word *"stroke,"* how it means
What one does to a cat's back, what a brush
Does through a woman's hair. Think about

The racket pressing, wiping, guiding the ball
As you stay on it, dragging say seven strings
Across the ball, the top edge leading off

To give it topspin. Think about the ball
As a loaf of bread, you hitting every slice.
Pull back the racket well behind you, drop it

And lift it, meeting the ball well out in front
At a point even with your left hip, stroking
To follow through cross-court. The tarnished coin

Of "follow through," the cat, the loaf of bread,
"Keep your eye on the ball," the dull alloy
Of homily, simile and coach's lore

As maddening, and as helpful, as the Fool
Or Aesop's *Fables,* the coinage of advice:
This is the metal that is never spent.

III. Backhand

Here, panic may be a problem; in the clench
From back to jaw in manic you may come
Too close and struggling strike out with your arm,

Trying to make the arm do everything,
And failing as the legs and trunk resist.
All of your coinages, and your nerve, may fail . . .

What you need is the Uroborus, the serpent
Of energy and equilibrium,
Its tail between its jaw, the female circle

Which makes it easy: all is all, the left
Reflects the right, and if you change the grip
To keep your hand and wrist behind the racket

You suddenly find the swing is just the same
As forehand, except you hit it more in front
Because your arm now hangs in front of you

And not behind. You simply change the grip
And with a circular motion from the shoulder,
Hips, ankles, and knees, you sweep the inverted swing.

IV. Strategy

Hit to the weakness. All things being equal
Hit crosscourt rather than down the line, because
If you hit crosscourt back to him, then he

Can only hit back either towards you (crosscourt)
Or parallel to you (down the line), but never
Away from you, the way that you can hit

Away from him if he hits down the line.
Besides, the net is lowest in the middle,
The court itself is longest corner-to-corner,

So that a crosscourt stroke is the most secure,
And that should be your plan, the plan you need
For winning—though only when hitting from the baseline:

From closer up, hit straight ahead, to follow
The ball to net; and from the net hit shrewdly,
To get him into trouble so he will hit

An error, or a cripple you can kill.
If he gets you in trouble, hit a lob,
And make it towering to make it hard

For him to smash from overhead and easy
For you to have the time to range the backcourt,
Bouncing in rhythm like a dog or seal

Ready to catch an object in mid-air
And rocking its head—as with your plan in mind
You arrange yourself to lob it back, and win.

V. Winning

Call questionable balls his way, not yours;
You lose the point but you have your concentration,
The grail of self-respect. Wear white. Mind losing.

Walk, never run, between points: it will save
Your breath, and hypnotize him, and he may think
That you are tired, until your terrible

Swift sword amazes him. By understanding
Your body, you will conquer your fatigue.
By understanding your desire to win

And all your other desires, you will conquer
Discouragement. And you will conquer distraction
By understanding the world, and all its parts.

Bjorn Borg

WILLIAM SCAMMELL

Eyes criminally close together,
fastest feet in the business,
Borg's groundstrokes would have landed
in Kensington but for
one small consideration: topspin.

He struck them as stepmothers
once brushed their daughters' hair.

Nobody knew what went on
behind that block of stone,
whether chess against a breaking wave
or just a corny Abba tune.

At the end of the end
he'd sink to his knees
in a parody of prayer
as the lightning went through him
eyes fists hair

The Pregnant Lady Playing Tennis

KAREN VOLKMAN

The pregnant lady playing tennis
bobs on her toes at the court's left side,
raises the green ball high, and sets it

spinning. Then moving in circles
of deliberate size, she returns the lob
with the same giddy grace. In the quiet glide

of the lady playing tennis,
there's a knowledge of speeds and angles,
arcs and aims. From the other courts,

the players watch, dismayed, half-fearing
for the safety of the lady playing tennis,
half-wishing this odd distraction shut away.

Tennis, they notice, is a dangerous game.
But the ovals close
on the lady playing tennis, as if

the tight-knit mesh of her racket
were a magnet, with the ball
a perfect pole veering home. Watching

each hard-shot lob clear the net,
the pregnant lady playing tennis
braces in the pure sensation of her game,

in her body's stretch and haul, and plants
a crazy slam past the net: past the lines,
past the out zone, past the court's steel network wall.

A Snapshot for Miss Bricka Who Lost in the Semi-Final Round of the Pennsylvania Lawn Tennis Tournament at Haverford, July, 1960

ROBERT WALLACE

Applause flutters onto the open air
like starlings bursting from a frightened elm,
and swings away across the lawns
in the sun's green continuous calm

of far July. Coming off the court,
you drop your racket by the judge's tower
and towel your face, alone, looking off,
while someone whispers to the giggling winner,

and the crowd rustles, awning'd in tiers
or under umbrellas at court-end tables,
glittering like a carnival
against the mute distance of maples

along their strumming street beyond
the walls of afternoon. Bluely, loss
hurts in your eyes—not loss merely,
but seeing how everything is less

that seemed so much, how life moves on
past either defeat or victory,
how, too old to cry, you shall find steps
to turn away. Now others volley

behind you in the steady glare;
the crowd waits in its lazy revel,
holding whiskey sours, talking, pointing,
whose lives (like yours) will not unravel

to a backhand, a poem, or a sunrise,
though they may wish for it. The sun
brandishes softly his swords of light
on faces, grass, and sky. You'll win

hereafter, other days, when time
is kinder than this worn July
that keeps you like a snapshot: losing,
your eyes, once, made you beautiful.

The Tennis

E.B. WHITE

Circled by trees, ringed with the faded folding chairs,
The court awaits the finalists on this September day,
A peaceful level patch, a small precise green pool
In a chrysanthemum wood, where the air smells of grapes.
Someone has brought a table for the silver cup.
Someone has swept the tapes. The net is low;
Racket is placed on racket for the stretch.
Dogs are the first arrivals, loving society,
To roll and wrestle on the sidelines through the match.
Children arrive on bicycles. Cars drift and die, murmuring.
Doors crunch. The languorous happy people stroll and wave,
Slowly arrange themselves and greet the players.
Here, in this unpretentious glade, everyone knows everyone.
And now the play. The ball utters its pugging sound:
Pug pug, pug pug—commas in the long sentence
Of the summer's end, slowing the syntax of the dying year.
Love-thirty. Fifteen-thirty. Fault.
The umpire sits his highchair like a solemn babe.
Voices are low—the children have been briefed on etiquette;
They do not call and shout. Even the dogs know where to stop,

And all is mannerly and well behaved, a sweet, still day.
What is the power of this bland American scene
To claim, as it does, the heart? What is this sudden
Access of love for the rich overcast of fall?
Is it the remembered Saturdays of "no school"—
All those old Saturdays of freedom and reprieve?
It strikes as quickly at my heart as when the contemptuous jay
Slashes the silence with his jagged cry.

Permissions

Author Biographies

Fiction

ROGER ANGELL is an editor at the *New Yorker* and is best known for his baseball writing in such books as *The Summer Game, Five Seasons,* and *Late Innings.* The stepson of the late E. B. White, he is one of the players in the match described in White's poem "The Tennis," which ends this collection.

BERYL BAINBRIDGE is a prolific English novelist known for her black humor. Her works include *The Dressmaker, The Bottle Factory Outing, Sweet William, A Quiet Life,* and *Richard Soleway.*

JONATHAN BAUMBACH is a novelist whose works include *A Man to Conjure With, Chez Charlotte and Emily,* and *My Father More or Less.* "The Return of Service" appeared in *The Best American Short Stories, 1978.*

J. P. DONLEAVY is a playwright and novelist whose works include *The Ginger Man, The Beastly Beatitudes of Balthazar B,* and *De Alphonce Tennis: The Superlative Game of Eccentric Champions.*

DOUGLAS DUNN is a Scottish writer, best known for his poetry, including *Elegies,* which won the Whitbread Literary Award for book of the year in 1985. "The Tennis Court" is from his short story collection *Secret Villages.*

ELLEN GILCHRIST is the author of many short story collections and novels, including *Starcarbon, Victory Over Japan,* which won the National Book Award for fiction in 1984, and *In the Land of Dreamy Dreams,* the title story of which appears here.

BRENDAN GILL, for many years an editor at the *New Yorker* magazine, is the author of the bestselling book about his career there, *Here at The New Yorker.*

BARRY HANNAH is the author of the novels *Geronimo Rex, Ray,* and *Airships,* the collection of short stories from which "Return to Return" was taken. That story appears in slightly altered form as a part of his novel *The Tennis Handsome.*

JAMES JONES gained immediate fame with his first novel, *From Here to Eternity,* which won the National Book Award in 1952. His other works include *The Thin Red Line, The Merry Month of May,* and *The Ice Cream Headache and Other Stories,* from which "The Tennis Game" was taken.

RING LARDNER was a newspaper reporter and short story writer known for his ability to capture the colorful language of the common man. His book of stories about baseball player Jack Keefe, *You Know Me Al,* was a critical and literary success when it first appeared in 1916.

PETER LASALLE is the author of *The Graves of Famous Writers and Other Stories,* in which "An FBI Story" appears.

W. SOMERSET MAUGHAM was a British playwright and novelist whose best-known work includes the autobiographical novel *Of Human Bondage, Cakes and Ale,* and *The Razor's Edge.*

A. A. MILNE was a prolific playwright, novelist, and poet but is most famous as the creator of the Winnie-the-Pooh books and other works for children.

VLADIMIR NABOKOV, a Russian novelist and poet, was one of the most original writers of the twentieth century and gained fame particularly for his novel *Lolita,* which created a scandal when it was published in 1958 because of its depiction of an aging professor's obsession with an adolescent girl.

KENT NELSON is the author of, among other works, the novel *All Around Me Peaceful* and the short story collection *The Tennis Player and Other Stories,* the title story of which appears here.

FREDERIC RAPHAEL's work includes novels, short stories, translations, and screenplays. Among his books are *California Times, Sleeps Six,* and *Oxbridge Blues.*

IRWIN SHAW wrote novels, short stories, plays, and screenplays during a career that spanned nearly five decades. Among his best-known works are *The Young Lions, Rich Man, Poor Man,* and *Nightwork.*

ROBERT T. SORRELLS's short stories have appeared in numerous literary magazines. "The Blacktop Champion of Ickey Honey" was included in *The Best American Short Stories, 1978.*

WALLACE STEGNER was an influential teacher of writing, as well as a novelist, whose works include *Angle of Repose,* which won the Pulitzer Prize in 1971, and *The Spectator Bird,* which won the National Book Award in 1977.

PAUL THEROUX is the author of numerous books of travel writing and novels, including *The Mosquito Coast, Half Moon Street,* and most recently,

Millroy the Magician. "The Tennis Court" is from his short story collection *The Consul's File.*

WILLIAM T. TILDEN was one of the greatest tennis players who ever lived, winning seven U.S. national singles titles and three Wimbledon titles. In addition to the book of short stories, *The Phantom Drive and Other Tennis Stories,* from which the title story is included here, Tilden published some of the best instructional writing on the game in his books *The Art of Lawn Tennis* and *Match Play and the Spin of the Ball.*

WILLIAM TREVOR was born in Ireland and is one of the most respected writers of English prose today. His novels include *The Children of Dynmouth* and *Fools of Fortune,* both of which won the Whitbread award. His short fiction has been compiled in *The Collected Stories,* in which "Matilda's England: I. The Tennis Court" appears.

Poetry

MARGARET AVISON is a Canadian poet whose books include *Winter Sun, The Dumbfounding,* and *Sunblue.*

JOHN BETJEMAN was a poet laureate of England. The light tone and urbane posture of his work gained him a wide following, particularly with his *Collected Poems,* published in 1958.

KELLY CHERRY is a poet, novelist, and essayist whose works include *Sick and Full of Burning, The Exiled Heart,* and *Writing the World.*

REUEL DENNEY was a scholar, author, teacher, journalist, and poet, whose first poetry collection, *The Connecticut River and Other Poems,* won the Yale Younger Poets Award in 1939. He is better known for a study of twentieth-century American society called *The Lonely Crowd.*

GARY FINCKE's most recent book of poetry is *Inventing Angels*. He is also the author of a book of short stories, *For Keepsies*, and is an English instructor and tennis coach at Susquehanna University.

JIM HALL is the author of the novels *Gone Wild, Bones of Coral*, and *Hard Aground* and the book of poems *The Lady from the Dark Green Hills*.

JOHN HEATH-STUBBS is an English poet and critic whose books of poetry include *Beauty and the Beast, The Divided Ways*, and *Naming the Beasts*, among others.

CONRAD HILBERRY's poems have appeared in *The Virginia Quarterly Review* and *The Oxford Book of Creatures*.

GALWAY KINNELL is one of America's most prominent poets. His *Collected Poems* won the Pulitzer Prize in 1983, and his most recent book is *Imperfect Thirst*.

MARK KIRBY has published several poems in *Commonweal*.

MAXINE KUMIN is a novelist, poet, and essayist whose work includes *Up Country, Our Ground Time Here Will Be Brief: New and Selected Poems*, and *Nurture*.

FELICIA LAMPORT, for many years a teacher at Harvard University, is the author of *Mink on Weekdays, Ermine on Sunday, Scrap Irony*, and *Light Metres*.

BRAD LEITHAUSER is a poet, novelist, and critic, whose books include the novels *Hence* and *Equal Distance* and two collections of poetry, *Hundreds of Fireflies* and *Cats of the Temple*.

OSIP MANDELSTAM, regarded as one of the major poets of the twentieth century, was a Russian writer whose first collection, *Stone*, was published in 1913 and whose second, *Tristia,* appeared in 1922. He was later imprisoned for reciting a poem against Stalin and died in the late 1930s on his way to a hard-labor camp.

PAUL PETRIE is the author of *Light from the Furnace Rising* and *Not Seeing Is Believing,* both collections of poetry.

ROBERT PINSKY is the author of the book-length poem *An Explanation of America,* among other works, and most recently has drawn wide praise for his translation of Dante's *Inferno.*

WILLIAM SCAMMELL is a British poet who is the author of the collections *Yes and No, A Second Life, Time Past,* and *The Game: Tennis Poems,* from which the poem "Bjorn Borg" is taken.

KAREN VOLKMAN's poetry has appeared in numerous literary journals, including *The Paris Review,* the *Partisan Review, Prairie Schooner,* and the *American Poetry Review.*

ROBERT WALLACE edits a journal of light verse called *Light Year* and is the author of the poetry collections *Common Summer* and *Ungainly Things.*

E. B. WHITE was known primarily as an essayist and author of books for children such as *Charlotte's Web* and *Stuart Little.* He was awarded the Gold Medal for Essays and Criticism from the American Academy of Arts and Letters, in addition to the National Medal for Literature and the Presidential Medal of Freedom.